Sarah gregory
SP15 O'Neil
   Thick and Thin

DIGNITY IN ADVERSITY

To the Memories of John E. Smith
and David E. Apter

DIGNITY IN ADVERSITY

Human Rights in Troubled Times

Seyla Benhabib

polity

First published in 2011 by Polity Press

Reprinted 2013, 2014 (twice)

Polity Press
65 Bridge Street
Cambridge CB2 1UR, UK

Polity Press
350 Main Street
Malden, MA 02148, USA

ISBN-13: 978-0-7456-5442-3
ISBN-13: 978-0-7456-5443-0(pb)

A catalogue record for this book is available from the British Library.

Typeset in 10.5 on 12 pt Sabon
by Toppan Best-set Premedia Limited
Printed and bound in the USA by Edwards Brothers, Inc.

The publisher has used its best endeavours to ensure that the URLs for external websites referred to in this book are correct and active at the time of going to press. However, the publisher has no responsibility for the websites and can make no guarantee that a site will remain live or that the content is or will remain appropriate.

Every effort has been made to trace all copyright holders, but if any have been inadvertently overlooked the publisher will be pleased to include any necessary credits in any subsequent reprint or edition.

For further information on Polity, visit our website: www.politybooks.com

CONTENTS

CONTENTS

PREFACE

Around September 18, 2001, almost a decade ago, I crossed Whitney Avenue in New Haven, Connecticut, with my 14-year-old daughter, traveling from our house to a Red Cross center to give blood for the victims and rescuers of the Twin World Towers 90 miles away. As I gave my name, Seyla Benhabib, to the nurse in attendance, she froze for a moment: "Ben-Habib" – wasn't Habib an Arabic name? "Who was this lady with a foreign accent," she seemed to be thinking, "coming in to give blood?"

My daughter, who noted the nurse's hesitation, immediately under-stood that I was being assessed as an Arab or a Muslim, and she squeezed my hand in solidarity. I could not help feeling, that early evening in Connecticut, that my gesture of solidarity with the victims of 9/11 and the fire-fighters and policemen of New York City was not wanted and, as it turned out, not needed: students of Yale University and other schools had already rushed to the Red Cross banks across New Haven, and actually, the blood banks were well stocked.

Nevertheless, something in me ached. The moral of this story is not about discrimination against Middle Easterners, Muslims, or Arab Americans, real though it is. Rather, it is about the complexity and multiplicity of identities to which my name testifies, but which bureaucratic administration shorthands in an increasingly securitized world political environment reduced to unequivocal signals of danger during the so-called "war on terror." The lady at the Red Cross station could not have known that I was a Sephardic Jew born in Istanbul, whose earliest known ancestor was called "Jacob Ibn-Habib," from the city of Zamora in Spain, and whose descendants were Rabbis and prominent members of a Jewish community first in

Spain and then in Salonica and Galipoli. According to some historical records, when my ancestors tried but failed to persuade Christian authorities to permit the Jews to stay in Spain, they, like thousands in that period, left to seek refuge in the Ottoman Empire.[1]

Islam for them was not a religion of war and *jihad* but a religion of tolerance that respected the Jews and granted them the "right of hospitality," in Kant's sense, and not only because they were "people of the book," namely, the Torah, which Islam, along with the New Testament, acknowledged as being holy. Certainly, the history of the Jews of the Ottoman Empire has its experiences of discrimination, prejudice, oppression, and exclusion. Yet when I read about *l'affair du foulard* – the scarf affair – that erupted in France when French authorities banned Muslim girls from attending public schools with their heads covered, and about the "turban or basörtü meselesi" in Turkey, I think of my own grandmothers and aunts. They covered and uncovered their hair in much the same way as their Muslim neighbors did. I also think of Orthodox Jewish women who wear wigs in public places in Brooklyn, Queens, Jerusalem, as well as Paris and London. And I ask, "a Turkish-Jew?" "A Jewish Turk?" "A Sephardic Jew growing up in a Muslim-majority country"? "A child of Ataturk's Republic?" What does it all mean?

The eruption of political Islam into world politics after September 11, 2001, has thrust these aspects of my biography, which I had considered of private import only, into theoretical and political debates concerning the "dialectic of Enlightenment" and the Jewish experience, international law and the Holocaust, Islam in contemporary Europe, and the meaning of contemporary cosmopolitanism.

The essays collected in this volume, which were written in the period from 2006 to 2010, document this trajectory. They continue the projects of discourse ethics and communicative rationality and freedom, which I have outlined in various works since the early 1990s, by extending them into the terrain of legal cosmopolitanism and recent world political events.

At the center of much contemporary political discourse is the concept of "human rights": their justification; their scope; the relationship of philosophical accounts of rights to international declarations and to international human rights law, and their diversity across constitutions and legal traditions.

The following chapters discuss the philosophy and politics of human rights by offering a systematic account of their place within the project of discourse ethics and communicative rationality. They also examine rights against the background of changing conceptions of citizenship in Europe, in particular, as a consequence of Muslim migration, and they look at contentious debates since September 11, 2001, some of which dismiss demands for human rights as hypocritical justifications for "humanitarian" interventions, at best, and neo-imperialist ventures of global capitalism, at worst. But considerations of rights cannot be entertained independently of transformations of state sovereignty. Today, the tensions between the changing status of state sovereignty in international law and the normative ideal of a democratically self-governing people are the source of much acrimony. For some, international law undermines democratic sovereignty; for others – and I count myself among them – it enhances it. My aim in this book is to explore this complex landscape and to situate human rights discourse within a vision of democratic iterative politics.

ACKNOWLEDGMENTS

A sabbatical from Yale University from January to July 2009, also generously supplemented by the *Wissenschafstkolleg zu Berlin*, first enabled me to conceptualize this collection. A subsequent stay from mid-June to mid-July 2010, in the *Forschungskolleg Humanwissenschaften* in Bad-Homburg, permitted me to develop it further. My thanks go to Dieter Grimm, Andrea Büchler, and Dipesh Chakrabarty, who shared their time at the *Wissenschaftskolleg* with me, and to Rainer Forst and Stefan Gosepath, from the University of Frankfurt, who enabled and funded my stay in Bad-Homburg through the "Exzellenzcluster Initiative." Many thanks also to Peter Niesen and David Owen for their sharp observations during my stay in Bad-Homburg.

Conversations with Benjamin Barber, Ken Baynes, Richard Bernstein, Hauke Brunkhorst, Maeve Cooke, Nancy Fraser, Alessandro Ferrara, Jürgen Habermas, Regina Kreide, Thomas McCarthy, David Rasmussen, Bill Scheuerman, and Christian Volk have enriched my life as well as my thinking. Among my Yale colleagues, I am grateful to criticisms and observations by Bruce Ackerman, Alec Stone Sweet, Anthony Kronman, Karuna Mantena, and Andrew March. David Garcia Alvarez, a Spanish Fulbright Scholar at Yale, has been a most stimulating conversation partner on issues of cosmopolitanism in the last several years and has generously provided me with multiple references to literature I would have otherwise missed.

My collaboration with the RESET Foundation on *Dialogue of Civilizations,* and the seminars we have conducted since 2007 in Istanbul, called "Philosophers Cross the Bosphorus. Encounters Across all Divides," have enabled me to return to Turkey on a regular basis and therefore to relive and rethink the meaning of human rights in these turbulent times. I am grateful to Giancarlo Bosetti and Nina von Fürstenberg for making the Istanbul seminars possible.

A special word of thanks is due to Judith Resnik, my tireless friend and colleague from the Yale Law School, whose interests in gender, federalism, migration, and human rights have inspired my thinking in the last decade. To Robert Post, current Dean of the Yale Law School, I am grateful for co-teaching a course on "Human Rights and Sovereignty," during which many of the themes discussed in this book first gained sharper focus. In the summer of 2010, Leora Bilsky of the Tel-Aviv Law School and I co-taught a mini version of the Human Rights and Sovereignty seminar at the Zvi Meitar Center for Advanced Legal Studies, by situating these topics within the context of the Holocaust and twentieth-century Jewish history. The interaction between normative theory and legal thinking, which these three scholars exemplify in their work, has inspired many of the essays in this collection.

My students Anna Jurkevics, Peter Verovsek, and Axel Wodrich have provided much bibliographic help and commentary. Anna Jurkevics, in particular, has been a tireless and meticulous assistant in helping with various drafts of these essays.

Turkuler Isiksel, who completed her excellent dissertation on "Europe's Functional Constitution: A Theory of Constitutionalism Beyond the State" in the fall of 2010, has inspired me for many years with her observations and writing on the European Union.

To my husband, Jim Sleeper, I owe not only suggestions for the title of this book, but gratitude for editorial and logistical assistance across continents. I am heartened as well as proud that my daughter Laura Schaefer has made fighting for human rights her life's goal.

This book is dedicated to the memory of two teachers whom I lost in 2009–10. John E. Smith, the Clarke Professor of Moral Philosophy at Yale University, was my dissertation advisor and moral guide after 1972. From him, I learned to enter into and extend the conversation between German Philosophy and American Pragmatism.

David E. Apter, the Heinz Professor of Political Science and Sociology at Yale, was my cosmopolitan mentor, whose commitment to social change and high theory in the social sciences set a shining example for me throughout the years. I miss John and David as I write these words.

Seyla Benhabib
Alford, Massachusetts, and NY City
December 2010

— 1 —

INTRODUCTION
Cosmopolitanism without Illusions

Cosmopolitans and Dead Souls

In the spring of 2004, the far-seeing even if irritating political scientist Samuel P. Huntington published "Dead Souls. The Denationalization of the American Elite."[1] Huntington, who only a decade earlier had created the famous phrase, "the clash of civilizations," resorted in this 2004 essay to attaching another memorable image to an argument. He quotes from Walter Scott's "The Lay of the Last Minstrel": "Breathes there the man with soul so dead/Who never to himself hath said:/ 'This is my own, my native Land?'/Whose heart hath ne'er within him burned/As home his footsteps he hath turned . . . /From wandering on a foreign strand?"[2]

Yes, answers Huntington; the number of "dead souls" is growing "among America's business, professional, intellectual and academic elites." Some of these elites are *universalists*, who take American nationalism and exceptionalism to the extreme and who want to spread democracy across the world because America is the "universal nation" (6). Others are *economic* elites who see globalization as a transcendent force that is breaking down national boundaries and giving rise to a new *civitas maxima* in the shape of the global market. Still a third group of dead souls, in Huntington's view, are *moralists* who deride patriotism and nationalism and argue that "international law, institutions, regimes and norms are morally superior to those of individual nations" (6). In contrast, for most ordinary citizens of most states, he argues, nationalism is a potent force that still lights fire in their hearts and makes them feel happy to return home, from "wandering on a foreign strand."

1

Are cosmopolitans dead souls, then? Is cosmopolitanism the privileged attitude of globe-trotting and world-hugging elites, removed from the concerns of ordinary citizens?

The essays collected in this volume contend that "cosmopolitanism" denotes no such privileged attitude but rather, a field of unresolved contrasts: between particularistic attachments and universalist aspirations; between the multiplicity of human laws and the ideal of a rational order that would be common to all human cities; and between belief in the unity of humankind and the healthy agonisms and antagonisms generated by human diversity.

Cosmopolitans become dead souls only if they forget these tensions and contrasts and embrace instead a Polyannaish, ceaseless affirmation of global oneness and unity. As David J. Depew wisely observes, "Cosmopolitanism, then, *considered as a positive ideal*, whether formally or materially, generates antinomies that undermine its internal coherence . . . Considered, however, as a critical ideal, these difficulties largely disappear. The resulting conception of cosmopolitanism [is] a negative ideal aimed at blocking false totalization."[3]

Pursuing this conception of cosmopolitanism as a critical and, in some ways, "a negative ideal aimed at blocking false totalization," the following essays explore the tensions at the heart of this project. I focus on the unity and diversity of human rights; on the conflicts between democracy and cosmopolitanism; on the vision of a world with porous borders and the closure required by democratic sovereignty. That I choose the term *cosmopolitanism* to carry out such a project may surprise some. Until recently, the term lay buried in the study of ideas of the eighteenth century; by the nineteenth-century, historians were already struggling with the rise of nationalism. Cosmopolitanism seemed a forgotten expression of a discredited European and North American Enlightenment.[4]

The last two decades have seen a remarkable revival of interest in cosmopolitanism across a wide variety of fields, ranging from law to cultural studies, from philosophy to international politics, and even to city planning and urban studies.[5] Undoubtedly, the most important reason for this shift in our sensibilities and cognitions is the confluence of epoch-making transformations, referred to as "globalization" and the end of the "Westphalian-Keynesian-Fordist" paradigm by many;[6] as the spread of neo-liberal capitalism by some; and as the rise of multiculturalism and the displacement of the West by still others. Cosmopolitanism has become a place-holder for thinking beyond the confusing present towards a possible and viable future. Pheng Cheah characterizes this present in the following words:

2

What is distinctively new about the revival of cosmopolitanism that began in the 1990's is the attempt to ground the normative critique of nationalism in analyses of contemporary globalization and its effects. Hence, studies of various global phenomena such as transcultural encounters, mass migration and population transfers between East and West, First and Third Worlds, North and South, the rise of global financial and business networks, the formation of transnational advocacy networks, and the proliferation of transnational human rights instruments have been used to corroborate the general argument that globalizing processes, both past and present, objectively embody different forms of normative, non-ethnocentric cosmopolitanism because they rearticulate, radically transform, and even explode the boundaries of regional and national consciousness and local ethnic identities.[7]

In view of these contradictory tensions, the term "cosmopolitanism" when it suggests a positive normativity, becomes at once seductive and deeply problematic.[8] It may seem as if merely invoking the forces which "explode the boundaries of regional and national consciousness and local ethnic identities" (Cheah) is sufficient to transcend them toward a cosmopolitan ideal whose own content is indeterminate. It clearly is not.

Nevertheless, I wish to argue that, as misleading as the project of cosmopolitanism may be in some of its formulations, it needs to be saved both from its nationalist-communitarian critics on the right and its cynical detractors on the left,[9] no less than from its postmodernist and deconstructionist skeptics. Caught between the nostalgia for communities unriven by difference and the cynicism that reduces cosmopolitanism to a bid for imperial domination, much contemporary thought misses what is new in the development of a cosmopolitan human rights discourse.[10]

To appreciate the depth and tenacity of these tensions it is important to explore briefly some themes which have been historically associated with cosmopolitanism.

A Brief History

The term *cosmopolites* is composed of *kosmos* (the universe) and *polites* (citizen). And the tension between these perspectives is significant.[11] Montaigne recalls that Socrates was asked:

where he came from. He replied not "Athens," but "the world." He, whose imagination was fuller and more extensive, embraced the universe as his city, and distributed his knowledge, his company, and his affections to all mankind, unlike us who look only at what is underfoot.[12]

Whether or not Socrates said anything of this kind is in dispute, but the story is repeated by Cicero in *Tusculum Disputationes*, by Epictetus in his *Discourses*, and by Plutarch in *De Exilio*, where he praises Socrates for saying that "he was no Athenian or Greek, but a Cosmian."[13]

What does it mean to be a Cosmian? To live outside the boundaries of the city, according to Aristotle, one needed to be either a beast or a god, but since men were neither and since the *kosmos* was not the *polis*, the *kosmopolites* was not really a citizen at all but some other kind of being.

To Cynics such as Diogenes Laertius this conclusion was not particularly disturbing, since he claimed that rather than being at home in *the* city, the cosmopolitan was *indifferent* to them *all*. The *kosmopolites* was a nomad without a home, at peace with nature and the universe but not with the human city, from whose follies he distanced himself. Some of the negative connotations of the term which we have become familiar with in modern history, such as "rootless cosmopolitanism," also alluded to by Huntington, have their roots in this early period of the history of cosmopolitanism, during which the ancient Cynics' opposition to and contempt for the practices of various human cities originates.

The negative vision of cosmopolitanism as a form of nomadism without attachments to a particular human city, as espoused by the Cynics, is transformed by the Stoics. By drawing attention to the absurd and incompatible plurality of human *nomoi* – the laws of their individual cities – Stoics argue that what humans share is not in the first place their *nomoi*, but *logos*, that in virtue of which they are capable of reason. In his *Meditations*, Marcus Aurelius writes:

> If we have intelligence in common, so we have reason (logos) . . . If so, then the law is also common to us and, if so, we are citizens. If so we share a common government. And if so, the universe is, as it were, a city.[14]

In the centuries that follow, the idea of an order that transcends differences among the laws of various cities, and is rooted instead in the rationally comprehensible structure of nature, converges with the Christian doctrine of universal equality.[15] The Stoic doctrine of

4

natural law inspires the Christian ideal of *the city of God versus the city of men*, and eventually finds its way into the modern natural law theories of Thomas Hobbes, John Locke, Jean-Jacques Rousseau, and Immanuel Kant.

The negative and positive dimensions of *kosmopolites*, which we first encounter in Greek and Roman thought, accompany the term across the centuries: a *kosmopolites* is one who distances himself either in thought or in practice from the habits and laws of his city and judges them from the standpoint of a higher order, often considered to be identical with reason, with nature or with some other transcendent source of validity. And because the cosmopolitan entertains a perspective that transcends the city and its ordinary human attachments, s/he is the object of suspicion and resentment by those who love their cities.

These tensions between citizenship in a bounded community and cosmopolitanism are transformed when Kant, at the end of the eighteenth century, resuscitates the Stoic meaning of cosmopolitanism by giving the term a new turn that places it at the heart of the Enlightenment project. It is also with Kant that the term "cosmopolitan" is transformed from a denial of citizenship into that of "citizenship of the world," and is linked to a new conception of human rights as cosmopolitan rights. Hence, to understand why, even under current world conditions, cosmopolitanism offers itself as a positive but potentially false normativity – or, in my preferred terminology, "as a negative ideal aimed at blocking false totalization" – we have to turn briefly to Kant but also to move beyond Kant. Let me explain this double move of going back to Kant and yet moving away from him.

Despite its ambiguous links to Western imperialist expansion, Kant's vision of cosmopolitanism is valuable for the space it creates for conceptualizing international law beyond the state as a juridical order that would encompass non-state actors, as well as individuals. Kant's conceptual initiative culminates later in international human rights law, developed particularly after 1948. These transformations do not resolve or dissolve the normative ambiguities of cosmopolitanism, but they enable the emergence of a space of "jurisgenerativity" for thinking through the unity and diversity of human rights across borders.

Kant's Transformation of Cosmopolitanism

In his famous 1795 essay on "Perpetual Peace," Kant formulated three "definitive articles." These read: "The Civil Constitution of

5

Every State shall be Republican"; "International Right shall be based on the Federalism of Free States"; and "The Law of World Citizenship Shall be Limited to Conditions of Universal Hospitality."[16]

Kant himself designates the Third Article of perpetual peace with the term of "Weltbürgerrecht." "Das Weltbürgerrecht soll auf Bedingungen der allgemeinen Hospitalität eingeschränkt sein"; "Cosmopolitan Right shall be limited to the conditions of universal hospitality" (Kant [1795] 1923: 443, 2006: 82). As I have argued elsewhere, Kant himself notes the oddity of the locution "hospitality" in this context, and remarks that "it is not a question of philanthropy but of right."[17] In other words, hospitality is not to be understood as a virtue of sociability, as the kindness and generosity one may show to strangers who come to one's land or who become dependent upon one's act of kindness through circumstances of nature or history; rather, hospitality is a right which belongs to all human beings insofar as we view them as potential participants in a world republic.

Kant writes:

> Hospitality (Wirtbarkeit) means the right of a stranger not to be treated as an enemy when he arrives in the land of another. One may refuse to receive him when this can be done without causing his destruction; but, so long as he peacefully occupies his place, one may not treat him with hostility. It is not the right to be a permanent visitor (Gastrecht) that one may demand. A special beneficent agreement (ein . . . wohltätiger Vertrag) would be needed in order to give an outsider a right to become a fellow inhabitant for a certain length of time. It is only a right of temporary sojourn (ein Besuchsrecht), a right to associate, which all men have. They have it by virtue of their common possession of the surface of the earth, where, as a globe, they cannot infinitely disperse and hence must finally tolerate the presence of each other. (Kant 1923: 443, 2006: 82; my translation)

Kant's claim that, first, entry cannot be denied to those who seek it if this would result in their "destruction" (*Untergang*) has become incorporated into the Geneva Convention on the Status of Refugees of 1951 as the principle of *non-refoulement*. This principle obliges signatory states not to forcibly return refugees and asylum seekers to their countries of origin if doing so would pose a clear danger to their lives and freedom. Of course, just as sovereign states manipulate this Article to define life and freedom more or less narrowly when it fits their purposes, it is also possible to circumvent the *non-refoulement* clause by depositing refugees and asylees in so-called "safe third countries." Many European countries resorted to this practice throughout the 1990s during the refugee crisis generated by the Yugoslav Civil War (see chapter 6 of this volume).

In Kant's formulations, as in subsequent state practice, there remains an element of unchecked sovereign power. As Jacques Derrida has argued, hospitality always entails a moment of dangerous indeterminacy. Does the host know that the intentions of the guest are not hostile? How does one establish these intentions across vast communicational divides? Doesn't hospitality often begin with mutual suspicion that needs to be overcome? Doesn't this indeterminacy account for the linguistic proximity of the terms *hostis* and "hospice" – hostility and hospitality? This indeterminacy prompted Derrida to coin the term "hostipitality,"[18] in order to capture that dangerous moment when the cosmopolitan project can get mired in hostility rather than hospitality.

Kant's legacy is ambiguous: on the one hand, he wanted to justify the expansion of commercial and maritime capitalism in his time insofar as these developments brought the human race into closer contact; on the other hand, he did not support or encourage European imperialism. The cosmopolitan right of hospitality gives one the right of peaceful temporary sojourn, but as Kant's comments on European attempts to penetrate into Japan and China make clear,[19] it does not entitle one to plunder and exploit, to conquer and overwhelm by superior force those peoples and nations among whom one is seeking sojourn.

We owe Kant the following distinctions: *Staatsrecht*, which concerns relations of Right between persons within a state – in the dual German sense of law and rights as entitlements of persons; *Völkerrecht*, which pertains to relations of Right between states; and "the Right for all nations" or "cosmopolitan Right" – *jus cosmopoliticum* – which concerns relations of Right between persons viewed not as citizens of determinate human communities but as members of a world civil society.[20] In claiming that relevant actors in the international domain are not only states and heads of states but also civilians and their various associations, which themselves could be subject to a new sphere of law, Kant gave the term *kosmopolites* a new meaning as the designation of a world citizen. *World citizenship* involves a utopian anticipation of world peace to be attained as a consequence of increased communication between human beings, including *le doux commerce* (sweet trade). Through increased human contact, too, "the injustices done in one part of the world would be felt by all." Cosmopolitan citizenship means first and foremost the creation of a new world legal order and of a public sphere, in which the human being would be entitled to rights in virtue of her humanity alone.[21]

The Cosmopolitan Legacy and Human Rights

Kantian cosmopolitanism has come under attack not only from philosophers of deconstructive critique such as Derrida and Cheah, but also from liberals in the Rawlsian tradition, beginning with John Rawls himself in *The Law of Peoples* (1999).[22] This critique will be at the center of my discussion in the following chapters (see, in particular, chapters 3 and 4).

Rawls made amply clear his rationale for choosing a state-centric perspective in reasoning about international justice, rather than a cosmopolitan one:

> An important role of a people's government, however arbitrary a society's boundaries may appear from a historical point of view, is to be the representative and effective agent of a people as they take responsibility for their territory and its environmental integrity, as well as for the size of their population. (Rawls, *The Law of Peoples*: 38–9)

Rawls adds in the footnote to this passage that "a people has at least a qualified right to limit immigration. I leave aside here what these qualifications might be" (ibid.: 39 n.48). In choosing bounded political communities as the relevant units for developing a conception of domestic and international justice, Rawls was departing significantly from Kant and his teaching of cosmopolitan law. If Kant's major advance was to articulate a domain of relations of justice which could be binding for all individuals as moral persons in the international arena, in *The Law of Peoples* individuals are not the principal agents of justice but are instead submerged in unities which Rawls names "peoples." For Kant, the essence of *ius cosmopoliticum* was the thesis that all moral persons were members of a world society in which they could potentially interact with one another. Rawls, by contrast, sees individuals as members of peoples and not as cosmopolitan citizens.

There has been considerable debate as to why Rawls would choose to develop a view of international justice from the standpoint of peoples rather than of individuals.[23] His methodological starting point led him to articulate principles of international justice not for individuals, considered as units of equal moral respect and concern in a world society, but for peoples and their representatives.

Rawls not only rejected the cosmopolitan alternative, but he also restricted the list of human rights that would be acceptable from the perspective of a law of peoples to just a fraction of what the 1948 Universal Declaration of Human Rights enumerates. This discrepancy between recent philosophical discussions of human rights – their justification and extent – and the internationally acknowledged human rights documents is taken up in chapters 3 and 5.

There is a dizzying variety of contemporary positions concerning the place of human rights in moral and political philosophy. Some argue that human rights constitute the "core of a universal thin morality" (Michael Walzer), while others claim that they form "reasonable conditions of a world-political consensus" (Martha Nussbaum). Still others narrow the concept of human rights "to a minimum standard of well-ordered political institutions for all peoples"[24] (Rawls) and caution that a distinction needs to be made between the list of human rights included in the Law of Peoples (which are thus defensible from the standpoint of a global public reason) and the human rights listed in the Universal Declaration of Human Rights of 1948.

In "Another Universalism" (chapter 4), I argue that it is necessary to shift both the *justification* strategy and the *content* of human rights away from minimalist concerns toward a more robust understanding of human rights in terms of the "right to have rights." While I owe the phrase "the right to have rights" to Hannah Arendt, I maintain that in her work, this right is viewed principally as a *political* right and is narrowly identified with the "right to membership in a political community." I propose that the "right to have rights" needs to be understood more broadly as the claim of each human person to be recognized and to be protected as a legal personality by the world community. This reconceptualization of the "right to have rights" in non-state-centric terms is crucial in the period since the 1948 Declaration of Human Rights, in which we have moved away from strictly international toward thicker cosmopolitan norms of justice.

For me, cosmopolitanism involves the recognition that human beings are moral persons equally entitled to legal protection in virtue of rights that accrue to them not as nationals, or members of an ethnic group, but as human beings as such. But how can such a strong claim be justified? What compelling reasons can we give to defend such moral recognition? And can the reasons we adduce be part of an overlapping consensus around public reason in a world whose many religions, cultures, and worldviews clash, mix, jostle, and compete with one another? Isn't minimalism in the justification of human rights both desirable and necessary as an alternative strategy?[25] Chapter 5 addresses Joshua Cohen's distinction between "substantive" and "justificatory minimalism." *Substantive* minimalism concerns the content of human rights, and is "more broadly, about norms of global justice." "Justificatory minimalism," by contrast, is about how to present "a conception of human rights, as an essential element of a conception of global justice for an ethically pluralistic world – as a basic feature of . . . 'global public reason'."[26]

I argue that neither substantive nor justificatory minimalism are persuasive: substantive minimalism about the content of human rights fails to take seriously the *political-institutional* developments in the international law of human rights in the last half a century. There is a sociological remoteness in some of these debates which comes from ignoring the transformations that have been initiated by the various human rights declarations and treaties since 1948.

Justificatory minimalism is attractive to many thinkers not only because it seems to offer a plausible vision of human rights in an ethically pluralistic world, but also because the stronger cosmopolitan project that would be an alternative to it appears so hopelessly mired in an indefensible philosophical universalism. It is the burden of chapter 4, "Another Universalism," to address varieties of universalism. I begin by distinguishing among essentialist universalism, justificatory universalism, moral universalism, and juridical universalism. *Essentialist universalism* is the belief that there is a fundamental human nature or human essence which defines who we are as humans. Some say, as did most philosophers of the eighteenth century, that human nature consists of stable and predictable passions and dispositions, instincts and emotions, all of which can be rationally discovered and analyzed. Still others repudiate empirical psychology, philosophical anthropology, and rationalist ethics, and maintain that what is universal about the human condition is that we are doomed to choose for ourselves and to create meaning through our actions in a universe devoid of such standards and values.

Universalism in contemporary philosophical debates has come to mean, most prominently, a *justification strategy*. Hermeneuticists, strong contextualists, postmodern skeptics, and power/knowledge theorists all question whether there can be an impartial, objective, and neutral philosophical reason (cf. Michel Foucault, Jean-François Lyotard, and the early Jacques Derrida).

Opposed to these contextualist critics are *justificatory universalists*, most of whom are not essentialists at all. Some entertain very few

10

rock-bottom beliefs about human nature and psychology; but they all share and defend strong beliefs in the normative content of human reason, that is, in the validity of procedures of inquiry, evidence, and questioning that have been the cognitive legacy of Western philosophy since the Enlightenment. (Karl Otto-Apel, Jürgen Habermas, Hilary Putnam, Robert Brandom, and John Rawls, and many others, are in this sense justificatory universalists.)

Universalism, still others argue, is not primarily a term of cognitive inquiry; equally significantly, it has a *moral meaning*. It is often defined as the principle that all human beings, regardless of race, gender, sexual orientation, bodily or physical ability, ethnic, cultural, linguistic, and religious background are entitled to equal moral respect.

Finally, universalism can be understood in *juridical* terms. Many who are skeptical about providing definitive accounts of human nature and rationality may nonetheless urge that the following norms and principles *ought* to be respected by all legal and political systems claiming legitimacy: all human beings are entitled to certain basic human rights, including, minimally, the rights to life, liberty, security and bodily integrity, some form of property and personal ownership, due process before the law and freedom of speech and association, including freedom of religion and conscience (see chapter 7, below).

I will argue that any political justification of human rights – that is, *juridical universalism* – presupposes recourse to *justificatory universalism*. The task of justification, in turn, cannot proceed without the acknowledgment of the communicative freedom of the other, that is, of the right of the other to accept as legitimate only those norms as rules of action of whose validity she has been convinced with reasons. Justificatory universalism then rests on *moral universalism*, that is, equal respect for the other as a being capable of communicative freedom. But this "resting upon" is not a relationship of moral entailment. Moral universalism does not *entail or dictate* a specific *list of human rights* beyond the protection of the communicative freedom of the person; nor does justificatory universalism do so. As I will clarify below, I am *not* following a foundationalist justification strategy here, but engaging in presuppositional analysis.

This defense of justificatory universalism as central to the cosmopolitan project will strike some as too strong and others as not strong enough. Together with the concepts of the "generalized" and "concrete other," which I had first developed in 1992 in *Situating the Self: Gender, Community and Postmodernism in Contemporary Ethics,*[27] I defend justificatory universalism as crucial to a vision of human rights that is non-essentialist, non-reductionist, and deeply imbricated in the democratic project. Do justificatory universalism and the communicative vision of the person imply or compel us to accept a definitive list of human rights? If so, which list? And what is the relationship between such an account of human rights and the variety of human rights codified in various legal documents across political regimes which we would be ready to consider legitimate? These are questions that run like a red thread through the following chapters.

Human Rights: Moral Claims and Legal Entitlements

Modern constitutions incorporate cosmopolitan ideals in the form of a list of basic rights, formulated either as a Bill of Rights, as in the USA Constitution, or as a *Déclaration des droits de l'homme et du citoyen*, as in the French tradition. This cosmopolitan legacy can also be honored, as in the German Constitution, through an enumeration of "basic rights" in Articles 1 through 19; the Charter of Fundamental Rights of the European Union, which is now part of the Lisbon Treaty, follows this format.[28] Yet there can often exist tensions between the moral and legal principles articulated through these basic rights and other Articles of the same Constitution, and between the interpretation of these basic rights by judicial bodies and their concretization by democratic legislatures in the form of specific laws. A great deal of constitutional debate concerns this legal-hermeneutic task. The interpretation of basic rights is a political project, in the sense that such interpretations concern how a people that wishes to live by certain principles in the light of its own changing self-understanding rearticulates the binding principles under which it has constituted itself as a polity. It is a fundamental mistake to assume that rights, which are principles, can be concretized without the continuous interpretation and articulation of self-governing polities (see chapters 6 and 7). Central to my understanding of the cosmopolitan project – and this differentiates my own from that of others – is my belief that cosmopolitanism need not posit a human being as a legal subject who is not a member of a specific polity. Cosmopolitan rights cannot be realized without contextualization and articulation through self-governing entities.

In addition to the tensions that may exist between the interpretation of basic rights and other aspects of democratic constitutions both in theory and practice, today most states operate in an increasingly transformed international legal environment, surrounded by many

12

intergovernmental organizations, non-governmental organizations, and new post-national reconfigurations of sovereignty such as the European Union. Cosmopolitan norms also structure this international environment through many international treaties, as is the case with the Universal Declaration of Human Rights (UDHR). In this respect as well, the democratic will of the people has to bind itself in accordance with these international covenants.

As I observe in "Claiming Rights Across Borders: International Human Rights and Democratic Sovereignty," it is now widely accepted that since the UDHR of 1948, the evolution of global civil society is moving from international to cosmopolitan norms of justice. The Universal Declaration's Preamble states that the "peoples" of the United Nations' Charter affirm their faith in "the dignity and worth of the human person and in the equal rights of men and women."[29] All persons "without distinction of any kind, such as race, color, sex, language, religion, political or other opinion, national or social origin, property, birth or other status" are entitled to dignified treatment regardless of "the political, jurisdictional or international status of the country or territory to which a person belongs."[30]

These public law documents have introduced crucial transformations into international law. While it may be too utopian to name them as steps toward a "world constitution," they are certainly more than mere treaties among states. They are constituent elements of a global civil society. In this global civil society, *individuals are rights-bearing not only in virtue of their citizenship within states, but in the first place in virtue of their humanity.* Although states remain the most powerful actors, the range of their legitimate and lawful activity is increasingly limited.

The spread of a cosmopolitan legal order brings its own problems: what sense does it really make to defend a cosmopolitan position when to be a rights-bearing person means first and foremost to be a member of a sovereign polity that can protect one's "right to have rights" (Hannah Arendt)? In chapter 6, "Twilight of Sovereignty or the Emergence of Cosmopolitan Norms," I ask: is the post-Westphalian dispensation towards which we seem to be moving, predicated on the decline of the nation-state and the twilight of sovereignty, a progressive development from the standpoint of human rights and the practice of citizenship? Or are we facing the spread of a neo-liberal empire in which the human rights discourse acts merely as a shield or Trojan horse to introduce neo-liberal commodification and monetarization into all corners of the world? What about the "contaminated normativity of human rights in global capitalism," in

13

Pheng Cheah's terms?[31] Doesn't legal cosmopolitanism amount to a justification of moral interventionism and moral imperialism? Without a doubt, some of the recent reticence in contemporary thought about justifying human rights in universalistic terms can be traced back to the fear that they would be instrumentalized for political ends and that a robust language of human rights would be used to justify moral imperialism (see chapter 5, "Is There a Human Right to Democracy?").

This ambiguous legacy, which is at the heart of cosmopolitanism, makes many ask if cosmopolitanism is only a thinly veiled version of the imperialism of yesterday, now parading as the neo-liberal globalization of our own times. Is the spread of human rights norms actually an achievement of humankind that we ought to celebrate and defend, or is it rather a cynical maneuver undertaken by the victorious nations of World War II to entrench their own narrow visions of the human person through a so-called Universal Declaration of Human Rights?[32] As is well known, the first vociferous objections to the UDHR came from the American Anthropological Association, which saw in this document the illegitimate universalizing of Western visions of order to the rest of humanity.[33]

Thus we face a conundrum: in the last 50 years legal cosmopolitanism has proceeded apace and nation-states, like Gulliver's giant, have been pinned down by hundreds of threads of covenants, treaties, and declarations; and, unexpectedly, skepticism toward the validity of these declarations and the spread of universal human rights norms has also grown. Particularly in the light of recent world political events, faith in international law and human rights has been shaken to its core: an illegal war was carried out against Iraq by the United States and its Allies; the US Patriot Act of 2001 gave the President unlimited and quasi-emergency powers to conduct the so-called "global war on terror"; the war on al-Qaeda in the territories of Pakistan and Afghanistan, originally justifiable according the UN Security Council Resolutions and NATO agreements, has morphed into a kind of nation-building with no clear goals or end in sight. And, adding insult to injury, the Guantanamo Camp in Cuba, Baghram Airbase in Afghanistan, and Abu Ghraib in Iraq have become new sites of the deepest violations of human rights law through the use of torture, illegal interrogation techniques, and the general flouting of the Geneva Conventions. The cosmopolitan project appears in tatters.

I will argue in these pages, however, that this would be the wrong conclusion to draw; and that we need rather a *cosmopolitanism* _without illusions._ We need, that is, to use the public law documents of our world and the legal advances in human rights covenants soberly, without too much utopian fanfare, to enable the growth of counter-hegemonic transnational movements, claiming rights across borders in a series of interlocking democratic iterations, and reinventions and reappropriations of valuable norms that have often been misunderstood and abused as they have been advanced.

For a Cosmopolitanism Without Illusions

A central argument of this book is that much interpretation of developments in contemporary human rights law and cosmopolitan norms misunderstands their _jurisgenerative effect._ By "jurisgenerativity," a term originally suggested by Robert Cover,[34] I understand the law's capacity to create a normative universe of meaning that can often escape the "provenance of formal lawmaking" to expand the meaning and reach of law itself. "The uncontrolled character of meaning exercises a destabilizing influence upon power," writes Cover.[35] My claim is that the "jurisgenerative" effects of human rights declarations and treaties enable new actors – such as women and ethnic, linguistic, and religious minorities – to enter the public sphere, to develop new vocabularies of public claim-making, and to anticipate new forms of justice to come in processes of cascading democratic iterations.

Democratic iterations is a term I use to describe how the unity and diversity of human rights is enacted and re-enacted in strong and weak public spheres, not only in legislatures and courts, but often more effectively by social movements, civil society actors, and transnational organizations working across borders. Herein lies the distinctiveness of an approach like mine, based on communicative freedom: it understands freedom of expression and association not merely as citizens' political rights, the content of which simply varies from polity to polity; rather, they are crucial conditions for the recognition of individuals as beings who live in a political order of whose legitimacy they have been convinced with good reasons. Rights of expression and association that are exercised in democratic iterations undergird the communicative exercise of freedom itself, and, therefore, they are basic human rights as well. Only if the "people" are viewed and indeed encountered not merely as subject to the law but also as authors of the law, can the contextualization and interpretation of human rights be said credibly to have emerged from public and free processes of democratic opinion and will-formation. Such contextualization, in addition to being subject to the various legal traditions of different countries, attains democratic legitimacy insofar as it is carried out through the interaction of legal and political institutions within the free public spaces of civil society. When such rights principles are appropriated by people as their own, these rights lose their parochialism as well as the suspicion of Western paternalism often associated with them.

I have suggested elsewhere, and argue in these pages, that _democratic iterations_ involve complex processes of public argument, deliberation, and exchange through which universalist rights claims are contested and contextualized, invoked and revoked, posited and positioned throughout legal and political institutions, as well as in the associations of civil society.[36] But is this concept an empirical or a normative one? Furthermore, what is the relationship of democratic iterations to discourses of normative justification? Most importantly, what guarantee is there that democratic iterations will result in "jurisgenerativity" rather than in "jurispathos'"? These are the questions which chapter 8 on "Democratic Exclusions and Democratic Iterations" addresses by revisiting the discourse-theoretic approach to political membership in liberal democracies that I developed in _The Rights of Others_ (2004). Exploring here the interconnections of practical discourses and democratic iterations, I argue that democratic iterations is a normative concept with empirical import. It enables us to judge macro-processes of contentious discourses according to certain normative criteria that derive their justification from the program of communicative ethics.

At the center of chapter 9, entitled "The Return of Political Theology: The Scarf Affair in Comparative Constitutional Perspective in France, Germany, and Turkey," is a consideration of processes of contemporary democratic iterations as they bear on the rights of Muslim girls and women to wear the _hijab_ in the public spaces of secular liberal democracies. I examine the complex transnational legal and political dialogue, as well as political controversies and legislation concerning the wearing of "the hijab," in its various forms. This issue has become a focal point for balancing the rights of freedom of religion and association that belong among human as well as legally guaranteed civil rights, on the one hand, and supposed state interests in defending _laïcité_ and public security, on the other. At bottom, the scarf affair is about accommodating Islamic forms of cultural difference in secular democracies – be they in majority Muslim countries, such as Turkey, or in societies of immigration, such

16

as contemporary France and Germany, in which large numbers of Muslims reside. These processes of democratic iterations are not always successful: in many cases, they result in exclusions and marginalizations rather than in the expansion of the public sphere through the entry of new public actors and the emergence of new vocabularies of claim-making.

Here we face some real challenges to contemporary cosmopolitanism. Yet haven't we heard before such concerns about preserving an authentic or "core" Europe that is/ought to be supposedly white, enlightened, and predominantly Christian? Are we not facing another "dialectic of Enlightenment," not vis-à-vis Judaism this time, but with regards to Islam? Is not this discourse of inclusion and exclusion about Islam, which is manifesting itself in the European – and now increasingly the North American – public sphere, repeating some well-known tropes of a dogmatic Enlightenment that could only tolerate otherness by forcing it to become like itself?

Prompted by these developments and questions, this volume opens with two chapters on European anti-Semitism as discussed by Horkheimer and Adorno, on the one hand, and Arendt and Lemkin, on the other. In their time, the European Enlightenment confronted its "others" first in the Jews of Europe, from the wealthy banking families of England and France to the huddled masses of Poland and Silesia. In Horkheimer and Adorno's view, this encounter proved disastrous, not only because it culminated in the Holocaust but also because it revealed a deep rot in the Western understanding of reason as *ratio*, *as the search for abstract equivalence*. In revisiting these theses from the *Dialectic of Enlightenment*, I contrast their diagnoses of the sources of European anti-Semitism with that of Hannah Arendt's, whose focus on the failed promises of the modern nation-state system permits us to face its resistance to accommodating the give and take of rights and identities through democratic iterations. In nation-states, Arendt showed, the cosmopolitan promise of human rights threatens always to be sacrificed, for the end of consolidating a homogeneous nation. The collapse of the European interwar state system was the political and human disaster out of which has emerged a renewed twentieth-century cosmopolitanism, one that insists on the principles of the *right to have rights* and *crimes against humanity*. To understand the tragic origins of contemporary cosmopolitanism is to understand cosmopolitanism itself more fully, as "a negative ideal aimed at blocking false totalizations."

"International Law and Human Plurality in the Shadow of Totalitarianism: Hannah Arendt and Raphael Lemkin" (chapter 3) reconstructs a missed encounter between the world-famous author of *The Origins of Totalitarianism*, and, until recently, the little-noted Polish jurist, the father of the Genocide Convention, Ralph Lemkin. Arendt and Lemkin passionately believed that the crime of genocide constituted the greatest crime against humanity – albeit for different reasons. Lemkin wanted the Genocide Convention to identify and prosecute the crime of the elimination of entire human groups, which in the twentieth century assumed unimaginable proportions. By coining a new word out of Greek and Latin roots – *genos* and *cide* – through the instrument of law, he attempted to capture crimes which appeared and were monstrous. For Lemkin, the human group possesses an ontological primacy which, for Arendt, it does not. Although Arendt, too, believes that no matter how monstrous the crime, a system of laws must address it, she insists that the crime of genocide destroys not only the group but the human capacity for plurality, that is, human beings' capacity to form unions and associations on the basis of their affinities and choices. For Lemkin, groups are primordial and given; for Arendt, they are not given but created. Arendtian associations emerge out of the experience of forming unions with like-minded individuals.

When I write of cosmopolitanism "as a negative ideal aimed at blocking false totalizations," I am thinking along with one of the most important utopian thinkers of the last century, Ernst Bloch. Bloch saved the concept of utopia from the dustbin of history and science fiction, and restored its centrality as a principle of hope. Every present moment, he believed, contains within itself an openness toward future otherness: as creatures capable of action and association, we open ourselves toward this future with our deeds and words. Bloch spoke of "concrete utopia" or "reflective utopia."[37] Social utopias did not exhaust themselves in the social engineering dreams of early bourgeois thinkers, but aimed at the *noch-nicht*, the not-yet. When and how does the "not-yet" manifest itself? Bloch's great achievement is to have retained utopian hopes even after the demise of the Hegelian-Marxist philosophy of history, which relied heavily on the "cunning of reason."

In a radio lecture of 1961, with the title "Naturrecht und menschliche Würde" ("Natural Right and Human Dignity"), intended to introduce the book of the same title to a larger audience, Bloch writes:

> Granted that human dignity (which is the fundamental intention of all natural right theories) is not at all possible without economic emancipation, economic emancipation, however, cannot take place without

18

human rights being realized in it either . . . No real establishment of human rights without an end to exploitation, but neither a true end to economic exploitation without the establishment of human rights. (My translation)[38]

Confronted with the greatest world-economic meltdown since the Great Depression of the 1930s, we still don't know how to achieve human dignity precisely because we have not attained economic emancipation. Yet neither have the utopian schemes of really-existing socialisms, which have lacked full respect for full human rights and democratic liberties, proven viable. Bloch understood that while no human rights can be attained without an end to socio-economic exploitation, neither can exploitation be ended without the establishment of human rights. In September 2009, I was honored with the Ernst Bloch Prize of the City of Ludwigshafen. This book concludes with the revised and expanded address delivered on that occasion.

FROM *THE DIALECTIC OF ENLIGHTENMENT* TO *THE ORIGINS OF TOTALITARIANISM*

Theodor Adorno and Max Horkheimer in the Company of Hannah Arendt

Confronting Anti-Semitism: Adorno, Horkheimer, and Arendt

At the center of the Critical Theory of the Frankfurt School is the reckoning with the European catastrophe of the past century – the rise of National Socialism, Soviet Communism and the Holocaust.[1] One of the earliest undertakings of the Institut für Sozialforschung was the study on "Authority and the Family," investigating why the German working and salaried classes shifted their support away from left parties generally and toward more authoritarian political solutions.[2] The undermining of the authority of the father through the loss of his economic independence in the marketplace and his increasing subjection to the impersonal forces of the growing economic and state conglomerates, they argued, drained the sources of revolt against patriarchy, and led to the emergence of weakened personality types, incapable of resisting the established status quo.

Already in this study a strong presupposition was visible which would guide the work of the Frankfurt School in later years as well, namely, the assumption that the rise of European anti-Semitism,

This chapter originally appeared as "From 'The Dialectic of Enlightenment' to 'The Origins of Totalitarianism' and the Genocide Convention: Adorno and Horkheimer in the Company of Arendt and Lemkin," in *The Modernist Imagination: Intellectual History and Critical Theory*. Festschrift for Martin Jay on his 65th Birthday, edited by Warren Breckman, Peter E. Gordon, A. Dirk Moses, Samuel Moyn, and Elliot Neaman (New York: Berghan Books, 2009), pp. 299–330. It has been revised and abridged for inclusion in this volume.

and eventually the Holocaust, needed to be explained within a *universalistic* framework, within which anti-Semitism was *one* among many other kinds of prejudice that still dominated European society in the wake of the Enlightenment. This universalist orientation continued in the major study with which Adorno collaborated during his stay in New York in the 1940s, and for which Max Horkheimer acted as Director of the Department of Scientific Research of the American Jewish Committee. It was named *The Authoritarian Personality* and appeared in the series *Studies in Prejudice*, edited by Horkheimer and Samuel H. Flowerman.[3] As Martin Jay notes, when questioned about the absence of a separate study of anti-Semitism in relation to authoritarianism in the earlier studies on authority and the family, Friedrich Pollock replied, " 'one didn't want to advertise that.' It perhaps also corresponded to the Institut's unwillingness to draw unnecessary (sic!) attention to the overwhelmingly Jewish origins of its members"[4] (my emphasis). Even the more psychoanalytically oriented passages on "Elements of Anti-Semitism" in the *Dialectic of Enlightenment* do not abandon this universalistic perspective.

By contrast, for many Jewish thinkers and historians of this period such as Gershom Scholem, Leo Strauss, Jacob Taubes, Martin Buber, Leo Baeck, and Kurt Blumenfeld, among others,[5] the European catastrophe was first and foremost a *Jewish* catastrophe that only manifested the transmutation of traditional Christian–Jewish hatred or "Jew hatred" (Leo Strauss) into the modern project of mass extermination, supported now by all the means at the disposal of a technologically advanced state. According to this view, only the technology and mechanism of Jewish extermination were different, but neither the logic nor the structure of centuries-old hatred toward the Jews changed. Still, what remained unintelligible to many thinkers, as well as to many functionaries and officials of Jewish organizations inside and outside the Reich – what in fact was almost beyond comprehension for them – was the *totalizing* logic of the Nazi program of Jewish genocide.[6] Settling itself beyond instrumental logic, Nazi anti-Semitism aimed at the elimination of the Jewish race as such. This defied categories of Christian "Jew hatred" or even modern German anti-Semitism, which had still permitted salvation to individual Jews through conversion, intermarriage, societal passing and other kinds of compromise and subterfuge, while denying a distinct Jewish collective existence. Nazi anti-Semitism, which was based on pseudo-scientific race thinking, defied particularistic Jewish logics of explanation. In the more than

21

half-century since the end of World War II, these differences in theoretical orientation between the *universalistic* and *particularistic* modes of considering anti-Semitism and the events of the Holocaust have continued, and even intensified, as the scope and magnitude of the destruction of European Jewry has continued to defy our moral imagination.[7]

In this chapter, I examine Adorno and Horkheimer's views on anti-Semitism in relation to Hannah Arendt's theses in *The Origins of Totalitarianism* and elsewhere.[8] Adorno and Horkheimer, as well as Arendt, are universalists in their methodological as well as normative orientations to the "Jewish question," and their explanations of anti-Semitism. What divides them in their approach to these matters is the theoretical utilization of political economy and psychoanalysis, in the case of Adorno and Horkheimer, versus ideographic[9] historical narrative and culturally more holistic sociology in the case of Arendt. By exploring this topic, I hope to contribute to a long-overdue conversation among these thinkers, each of whom have marked many on both sides of the Atlantic very deeply. With the collapse of "really existing socialism" and the eclipse of Marxism, Hannah Arendt's star has risen in recent decades, while that of the Frankfurt School has dimmed. Nevertheless, there is still much to be gained from a careful comparative analysis of their work, because, however deep their differences, their reaction to the catastrophe of the twentieth century was a *political* as opposed to a *theological* or a merely *philosophical* one. They never lost faith in human beings' capacity to "start anew" and change their collective conditions of existence (Arendt), or to anticipate the "wholly other" (*das ganz Andere*) and imagine a better future (Horkheimer). Arendt tried to retrieve the project of political freedom, in the sense of building republics in which freedom could be housed, from the mystificatory clutches of Heideggerian philosophy. Members of the Frankfurt School repeatedly evoked the hope that human emancipation would not only herald an empty but a concrete utopia. Hannah Arendt and members of the Frankfurt School are fundamentally united in their insistence upon the power of human beings to change their world, even in the face of developments where despair was more tempting. Yet these subterranean bonds have not always been visible, and competition among these "émigré intellectuals," their personal dislikes, and ancient grievances, have dominated our understanding of their legacy.

To initiate this dialogue between Arendt and the Frankfurt School, I will focus on their approaches to anti-Semitism. The question of anti-Semitism is a particularly sharp lens through which to observe Arendt's and Adorno and Horkheimer's theoretical differences. Arendt's universalistic approach to explaining the origins of European anti-Semitism, and the solutions she offers to go beyond it, are strongly inflected by her commitments to an autonomous Jewish politics in the inter-war period that is neither simply Zionist nor anti-Zionist. She urges the Jews to defend themselves *politically as* Jews against the assault upon them. In highlighting this aspect of Arendt's thought, I also wish to argue that Martin Jay's 1978 description of Arendt as a "political existentialist," who believes in the "primacy of the political," indebted to Carl Schmitt and Alfred Baeumler, is implausible.[10] For Arendt, "the primacy of the political" is grounded in her own historical attempt to explain the rise of European anti-Semitism in the light of the political paradoxes and eventual failures of modern nation-states in the inter-war period and beyond. Arendt discovered politics as a young student at the Universities of Marburg and Freiburg, not in the lectures or arms of Martin Heidegger, but through her interest in the Jewish question and through her friend and guide, Kurt Blumenfeld, the Zionist leader, whom she met at Heidelberg in 1926.

In conclusion, I briefly contrast Adorno and Horkheimer's as well as Arendt's considerable skepticism toward the "force of law" (Derrida), with Raphael Lemkin's response to the destruction of European Jewry by developing, from within the law of nations, a conception of genocide which is comparative and historical in scope. Lemkin's "legal universalism," which I examine at greater length in chapter 3, much like Arendt's and that of Adorno and Horkheimer's, also attempts to mediate the universal and the particular. The Holocaust, for him as well, becomes *an example* rather than the *unique paradigm* of that chief crime against humanity – the crime of genocide.

The "Jews and Europe" (1939) and "Elements of Anti-Semitism" (1941)

Max Horkheimer's 1939 essay, "The Jews and Europe," is a terse piece, written in apodictic style, containing many memorable phrases such as "He who does not wish to speak of capitalism should also be silent about fascism."[11] The essay is dominated by the contention that fascism and/or National Socialism – which are not clearly distinguished from one another – "is the truth of modern society."[12]

Horkheimer argues that in the general transition from liberal society to the authoritarian state (an ambiguous formula which refers to National Socialism as well as to Stalinist communism), the decline in relevance of the sphere of circulation has rendered the Jews also "superfluous," that is, dispensable from the standpoint of state power. The Jews represented individualism and the principle of exchange, and thus embodied the ideals and illusions of liberal capitalism in the nineteenth century. With the rise of "state capitalism,"[13] which imposed direct political controls on the economy and suspended, without wholly eliminating, the laws of the market, the function and usefulness of the Jews came to an end.

Not only in its reductionist explication of the complexity of Jewish experience in modern society since the Enlightenment in political economic terms, but also in its insistence on the primacy of the economic, this early essay displays a "functionalist" account of anti-Semitism that is extremely short-sighted. Would any other group besides the Jews occupy a similar position in the economy and society and be subject to the same kinds of prejudice? Was anti-Semitism merely a function of economic positionality? Was not the presence of the Jews in the sphere of circulation as bankers, money lenders, itself only explicable in the light of the anti-Semitic measures which, in much of Europe, and throughout the Middle Ages, prohibited the Jews from owning land, joining the military, and holding public office until and even after the French Revolution? How could the position of the Jews in modern European society be abstracted from the long history of reprisals, exclusions, and eliminations to which they had been subject? Horkheimer's formulae fall very short here.

The only topic around which Horkheimer shows some cultural sensitivity to the particular fate of European Jews, rather than viewing them only as place-holders within a general theory of capitalist class society, is their condition as refugees and asylum seekers. He finds it understandable that the Jews as "emigrants" are unlikely to hold a mirror to capitalism, in which it may see its own fascist core, precisely in those countries where they are granted asylum.[14] Yet Horkheimer's empathy has its limits: the Jewish lamentations about the lost past, about the failure of liberalism, and so on, he argues, are short-sighted as well as hypocritical, since:

> Even the French Revolution, which helped bourgeois economics gain a political victory and which gave Jews equality, was more ambivalent than many Jews today can even imagine. Not their ideas but usefulness

defines the bourgeoisie . . . The order which started as progressive in 1789 carried from its inception the tendency towards National Socialism within it.[15]

As Jay has documented,[16] Horkheimer and Adorno's position on anti-Semitism was changing throughout the 1940s. In a letter to Herbert Marcuse of 1943 Horkheimer argued that:

> the problem of anti-Semitism is much more complicated than I thought in the beginning. On the one hand we have to differentiate radically between the economic-political factors which cause and use it, and the anthropological elements in the present type of man which respond to anti-Semitic propaganda as they would to other oppressive incentives; on the other hand we must show these factors in their consistent interconnection and describe how they permeate each other.[17]

Anson Rabinbach has noted that in this period, while the economic dimension continues to be very significant in Adorno and Horkheimer's explication of anti-Semitism, "the emphasis here is no longer on the *presence* of the Jews in the sphere of circulation, but on the Jews in the mental 'imagery' of Nazism, which metaphorically substitutes the Jews as the 'hated mirror image of capitalism.'"[18] This new analysis of anti-Semitism is announced in the "Elements of Anti-Semitism," in the *Dialectic of Enlightenment*.

In the *Dialectic of Enlightenment*, Adorno and Horkheimer maintain that the two moments which constitute the legacy of Western modernity and the Enlightenment – namely, the value of the autonomous personality and the emergence of a value-free and technologically based science of nature – are mutually incompatible. The promise of the Enlightenment to free humans from their self-incurred tutelage cannot be attained via a reason that functions as a mere instrument of self-preservation. "The worldwide domination of nature turns against the thinking subject himself; nothing remains of him but this eternally self-identical 'I think' that should accompany all my representations."[19]

The critique of the domination of nature, which is one of the central themes of this work, holds that the Marxist view of history, as enabling human emancipation through the increasing control of nature via the technological organization of social labor, is wrong. Man's emancipation from nature is not progress; rather it carries within itself the seeds of regression, and ultimately, of the oppression of inner as well as outer nature. The Marxian philosophy of history

Marx vs Nietzsche

is now replaced by a Nietzschean vision of progress as the increasing sublimation of life instincts, self-repression, and the growth of resentment. Laboring activity, the act through which man uses nature for his own ends by acting as a force of nature himself, is indeed an instance of human cunning. Nevertheless, as the interpretation of Odysseus reveals, the effort to master nature by becoming like it (*mimesis*) is paid for by the internalization of sacrifice. Labor is indeed the sublimation of desire; but the act of objectification in which desire is transformed into a product is not an act of self-actualization, but an act of fear which leads to controlling the nature within oneself. The Marxian view of the humanization of the species through social labor must be rejected.

One of the Notes appended to the text, "The Interest in the Body," announces this new orientation:

> Beneath the familiar history of Europe runs another, subterranean one. It consists of the fate of those human instincts and passions repressed and displaced by civilization. From the perspective of the fascist present, in which what was hidden emerged to light, manifest history appears along with its darker side, omitted by the legends of the national state no less than by their progressive criticisms.[20]

The story of Odysseus and the Holocaust act almost as bookends to this self-destructive dynamic of the Enlightenment: the myth which is Enlightenment and the Enlightenment which becomes myth through Nazi propaganda. We witness the birth of Western civilization and its transformation into barbarism. The Jews are caught in the wild currents of this civilizational dynamic and become its privileged objects of sacrifice.

Myth, which relates how the hero constitutes his identity by repressing the forces of nature which threaten to engulf him, also expresses its obverse. Humanity pays for overcoming the fear of the other by internalizing the victim in an act of *mimesis*.[21] Yet, as the regression from culture to barbarism brought about by National Socialism shows, Odysseus's cunning (*List*), the origin of Western *ratio*, has not been able to overcome humanity's original fear of the "other." The Jew remains the other, the stranger: the one who is human and subhuman at once. Whereas Odysseus's cunning consists in the attempt to appease otherness by becoming like it – Odysseus offers the Cyclops human blood to drink; sleeps with Circe, and listens to the Sirens – fascism, through false projection, makes the other like itself:

26

If mimesis makes itself like the surrounding world, so false projection makes the surrounding world like itself. If for the former the exterior is the model which the interior has to approximate, if for it the stranger becomes familiar, the latter transforms the tense inside ready to snap into exteriority and stamps even the familiar as the enemy. (*Dialektik der Aufklärung*: 167)

Fascism is a special case of organized paranoid delusion. Under the pressure of the super-ego, claim Adorno and Horkheimer, the ego projects its aggressive wishes as "evil intentions onto the outside world . . . either in fantasy by identification with the supposed evil, or in reality by supposed self-defense" (ibid.: 192). What makes the Jews specially suitable to be the object of such paranoid fantasies, however, is not clearly identified. In their analysis, the choice of the Jews as the privileged object of paranoid delusions is related less to the condition of the Jews in modern society and more to the history of Christian anti-Judaism. The God of Judaism is distant, forbidding, and "entangles his creatures in the net of guilt and merit" (ibid.: 177). Christianity, by contrast, tries to "lessen the horror of the absolute" by imagining God in the image of man. The Jewish God, who forbids representation in "graven images," is the originator of Enlightenment, and also of the distinction between religion and magic, of word and object, of concept and referent. Monotheistic Judaism heralds the beginning of the *Entzauberung* (the loss of magic) in the world. God is not in nature, but the Lord of Nature and its Creator. Through the covenant with their God, the Jews oblige themselves not to be tempted by natural instincts alone but to follow a moral code. The Ten Commandments are moral instruments of repression, contributing no less than the "wily" Odysseus himself to the eventual emergence of the subject of Western civilization, namely, the individual characterized by rational self-mastery and self-repression.

In these reflections, Adorno and Horkheimer are obliquely refer-ring to the treasure trove of anti-Judaistic imagery, amply present in German philosophy from Hegel to Nietzsche.[22] What is noteworthy is that the metaphoric significations associated with the Jews are multiple, unstable, and equivocal: the Jews are viewed not only as the *originators* of the Enlightenment but also as a nomadic people *resisting* Enlightenment; they are not only *enemies* of magic but were suspected, throughout the Middle Ages, of *engaging* in magic; they are not only the source of *repressive morality* but also the source of *immorality and of licentiousness*. The Jews are the "floating

27

signifiers" of the National Social imagination. But if the sources of anti-Semitism lie in the deep entanglements of mimesis and false projection, of self-identity and domination of the other in the phylo-genetic development of the human species, then, as Anson Rabinbach points out, "It is ultimately not clear whether this version of primal anti-Semitism can usefully distinguish modern racism, Christian Jew-hatred (ancient or primordial), anti-Judaism, or whether – in the end – it has anything to do with the Jews at all."[23] By locating the sources of anti-Semitism in what has been called "the primordial history of subjectivity,"[24] Adorno and Horkheimer go so deep that they come dangerously close to dehistoricizing anti-Semitism and making it an eternal aspect of Western and Christian thought. As Jay also notes, "For Horkheimer and Adorno, then, perhaps the ultimate source of anti-Semitism and its functional equivalent is the rage against the nonidentical that characterizes the totalistic dominating impulse of Western civilization."[25] But at this level of generality, concrete Jewish historical experiences across different centuries and countries become mere "ciphers" of forces that lie much deeper. This is a conclusion with which Adorno and Horkheimer could have been satisfied, but which, bereft of specification, seems to repeat the thesis of "eternal anti-Semitism."

In Adorno's and Horkheimer's various attempts to explain anti-Semitism, we witness a dilemma that is conceptual in nature: not only in the case of anti-Semitism, but with prejudice and racism generally, if one's explanatory scheme is too general it will miss the specific constellation of experiences, images, and metaphors which define others as "the Other;" if, on the other hand, one attempts to account for the "othering" of human groups in terms of the specific qualities of these groups themselves, one will be accused of blaming the victim. Attaining the right balance between the standpoint of the victim and that of the victimizer, between the agent of racism and its object, is a difficult task. This is not only the situation for Adorno and Hork-heimer – Arendt too has been accused of blaming the victim.[26]

Hannah Arendt and the "Jewish Question"

Arendt met the Zionist leader Kurt Blumenfeld in 1926, at a student event in Heidelberg. The two formed a lifelong friendship, only to be interrupted by the publication of Arendt's book, *Eichmann in Jeru-salem* (1963).[27] When Arendt was arrested by the Gestapo in the spring of 1933, and forced to flee to Paris through Prague with her mother, she had been carrying out research in the Prussian State Library, at the request of Blumenfeld, on the extent of anti-Semitic measures undertaken by non-governmental organizations, business associations and professional clubs. Blumenfeld, in turn, was preparing to present this material at the 18th Zionist Congress.

Arendt's interest in Jewish matters has been amply documented, but what remains unexplained is why this interest was so acute on the part of the daughter of a middle-class assimilated Jewish family. Undoubtedly, as Elisabeth Young-Brühl has argued, part of the answer lies in the familial background:[28] Arendt's paternal grandfather, Max Arendt, was a staunch leader of the Jewish Community in Königsberg and, although an anti-Zionist, was clearly a man who explicitly identified himself as a Jew. Her mother, an early sympathizer of Rosa Luxemburg, was a fiercely proud woman, who instructed her daughter to report to her immediately every word or gesture of anti-Semitism in school. Also not incidental is Arendt's deep awareness of the contrast between the experience of German Jewry, to whom she belonged, and that of the East European Jewish refugees and permanent and temporary workers who flocked to the city of Königsberg (Kaliningrad), where Arendt grew up. This contrast between the affluent and emancipated German Jewry, who enjoyed civil and political rights, and their Eastern brethren, affected Arendt deeply and gave her a sense for the contrast among the experiences of various Jewish communities, which was quite unusual for its time.[29]

After completing her dissertation on St Augustine's concept of love, Arendt turned to the biography of Rahel Levin Varnhagen, a Jewish *salonnière* born in Berlin in 1771, and whose *salon* enjoyed considerable prestige until Napoleon's invasion of Germany in 1806. Intended as her *Habilitationsschrift*, this study was completed in 1933, except for the last two chapters which were finished during her exile in 1938 in France. It appeared in English first in 1957 and in German in 1959.[30]

There are manifold layers of reading, which must be disentangled in approaching Arendt's attempt to tell Rahel Levin Varnhagen's story as she herself "might have told it."[31] In the early 1930s, Arendt's own understanding of Judaism and her relationship to her own Jewish identity were undergoing profound transformations, which were taking her away increasingly from the egalitarian, humanistic ideals of Kant, Lessing, and Goethe toward a recognition of the ineliminable fact of Jewish difference within German culture. The Rahel book documents the paradoxes of Jewish emancipation between the

29

breakdown of the ghetto and the emergence of the nineteenth-century bourgeois Christian nation-state. It is in this small intermezzo between 1790 and 1806, at which point Napoleon enters Berlin, that Rahel Levin's *salon*, in her "Berliner Dachstube," flourishes.

From the standpoint of Arendt's political philosophy as a whole and her subsequent analysis of anti-Semitism, the book on Varnhagen puts forth a category toward which Arendt remains deeply ambivalent – namely, "society" and "the social." Varhagen presided over an ephemeral social phenomenon, the *salons*, which were often the drawing rooms of well-to-do bourgeois houses, in which the public and the private, the personal and collective mixed and mingled, in unpredictable and flowing ways. Intimacy was encouraged, although one pretended not to notice; one had to take care not to violate the unwritten rules of good manners – what is now called *salonfähiges Verhalten*.

Almost in every respect, the *salons*, as models of public space, contradict the *agonal* model of the public sphere that predominates in Arendt's *The Human Condition*. Whereas the Greek *polis* and the public sphere characteristic of it exclude women (and children and servants generally), the *salons* are spaces dominated by female presence. Whereas, in the public spaces of the *polis*, speech is "serious," guided by the concern for "the good of all," speech in *salons* is playful, amorphous, and freely mixes the good of all with the advantage of each. Whereas the public sphere of the *polis* suppresses *eros*, the *salons* cultivate it.

Yet Arendt does not use the *salons* as an alternative model of the public sphere; rather, she sees in them the shortcomings of the "social" in general. The social tends toward conformity and the ennobling of private pursuits at the expense of collective goals. I believe Arendt believed in this not because she was under the spell of Martin Heidegger, with whom she had already concluded her affair when she began writing the Varnhagen book, but because she became an increasingly political person who was critical of the illusions of the German-Jewish assimilated bourgeoisie. As the years proceeded and Arendt experienced the collapse of the political order upon her own flesh, her schemata for understanding anti-Semitism shifted from "the social" to the "political."[32] Much later, in *The Origins of Totalitarianism*, and with respect to Jewish acceptance into society, she was to remark: "This perversion of equality from a political into a social concept is all the more dangerous when a society leaves but little space for special groups and individuals, for then their differences become all the more conspicuous."[33]

In her reflections on anti-Semitism in the aftermath of the Holocaust and after the fate of German-Jewry had become sealed, Arendt put forth a radical contention: modern anti-Semitism, she argued, far from being an "eternal" dimension of the relationship between Jews and gentiles, represented, rather, a thoroughly modern phenomenon.[34] As such, it reflected the disintegration of traditional political structures in Europe, and, in particular, the decline of the nation-state in the aftermath of European imperialism. According to Arendt, anti-Semitism had to be understood not in isolation, but in the context of a crisis of Western civilization that far exceeded the importance of the "Jewish Question."

In thus framing the "Jewish Question" against a much broader political background, Arendt challenged a number of traditional views on anti-Semitism. Foremost among them was the idea that modern anti-Semitism simply represented a new form of religiously motivated "Jew-hatred." Against this view, Arendt argued that, in effect, "even the extent to which the former derives its arguments and emotional appeal from the latter is open to question." As she wrote in a crucial and characteristically controversial passage from the *Origins of Totalitarianism*:

> The notion of an unbroken continuity of persecutions, expulsions and massacres from the end of the Roman Empire to the Middle Ages, the modern era, and down to our own time, frequently embellished by the idea that modern antisemitism is no more than a secularized version of popular medieval superstitions, is no less fallacious (though of course less mischievous) than the corresponding antisemitic notion of a Jewish secret society that has ruled, or aspired to rule, the world since antiquity. (*OT*: xi)

Arendt's strong language in this passage is meant to drive home her point unambiguously: to understand the new in light of the old was, she suggests, to fundamentally misunderstand it. No amount of historical detail about the persecution of Jews could explain what she considered an unprecedented phenomenon. An adequate analysis of modern anti-Semitism therefore required new categories of thought. And to forge these categories, Arendt believed, it was necessary to reassess not only Jewish history, but European history as a whole.[35]

Arendt's understanding of anti-Semitism challenged established views that anti-Semitism was a constant in history in several important ways. First, it suggested that it was possible, and, indeed, necessary to construct a *theory* of anti-Semitism. Second, Arendt insisted that, in contrast to the religiously motivated anti-Semitism of the Middle Ages, modern anti-Semitism was a *political* phenomenon. And, third, she argued that, as a political phenomenon, it was situated at the nexus of three fundamental developments: the rise of European imperialism; the decline of the nation-state; and the failure of liberal emancipation. Underpinning all these contentions, and thus Arendt's theory of anti-Semitism as a whole, was a fundamental paradox: modern anti-Semitism rose as the modern nation-state declined; therefore, the suggestion that anti-Semitism was a by-product of nationalism was simply mistaken. As she explained, "unfortunately, the fact is that modern anti-Semitism grew in proportion as traditional nationalism declined, and reached its climax at the exact moment when the European system of nation-states and its precarious balance of power crashed" (*OT*: 3). It was only in light of these events, unfolding on a European and indeed a global scale, that it was possible to understand what would have been an otherwise deeply perplexing development: the enormous significance that the Jewish problem acquired for the Nazis.

In Arendt's view, which is reflected in her careful historical reconstruction of the Jewish Question in Part I of *The Origins of Totalitarianism*, at least part of the explanation is to be found in the convergence of political, economic, and psychological factors that both tied the Jews to the nation-state and undermined their ability to adapt to its transformations. The nation-state needed the Jews, since, from its very emergence, it relied both on their financial resources and on their political loyalty for its consolidation. In return, it rewarded wealthy Jews with a host of social privileges that made them dependent upon state power and prevented their integration into society. The Jews didn't much object, as this privileged status coincided with their own aspiration to maintain a separate identity. The interests of the state and the interests of the Jews therefore seemed perfectly well matched (*OT*: 13).

It is precisely because the nation-state, unlike its absolutist predecessor, was not allied with any specific class in society that it allied itself with the Jews (OT: 17). The class of Jews that had inherited their wealth from the Court-Jews of absolutist times seemed ideally suited for this purpose since they formed the only group in society that "did not form a class of [its] own and [. . .] did not belong to any of the classes in their countries" (OT: 13). As a result, they could offer the emergent state both the financial backing and the political loyalty it so desperately needed. The distance from Court Jew to

European banker seemed but a short step away. And indeed, the European banker continued to be of use to the state even as it subsequently achieved a higher degree of consolidation. Even as their political role diminished as the result of subsequent political developments, Jewish bankers nevertheless remained useful as international mediators *among* nation-states.

As the fortunes of the nation-state waned, so did those of the Jews. The extraordinary capitalist development of the nineteenth century pushed the expansion of national economies eventually beyond the borders of the nation-state and came to rely increasingly on the exploitation of external resources. Unluckily for the Jews, in the ensuing imperial scramble, the bourgeoisie, which constituted the driving force behind economic expansion, came to rely on a very different kind of ally, "the mob" (*les déclassés*), in its quest for power.[36]

For their greed, then, Arendt argues, the bourgeoisie paid a high price indeed. Even though they had been initial allies, bourgeoisie and mob soon found themselves at mortal odds, as the imperial scramble for Africa[37] turned out to be less a display of imperial power and more of a dress rehearsal for the bourgeoisie's own destruction at home – in the heart of Europe.[38] Indeed, there was little reason why the violence, greed, and lawlessness unleashed by imperialism should stop at the boundaries of Europe. "The bourgeoisie succeeded in destroying the nation state but won a Pyrrhic victory; the mob proved quite capable of taking care of politics by itself and liquidated the bourgeoisie along with all other classes and institutions" (*OT*: 124).

First and foremost among the mob's victims were the Jews, who had failed to make the transition from nation-state to imperialism, thus becoming the most vulnerable group in European society and an easy target for the murderous impulses of the mob. What made the Jews particularly vulnerable to the mob, according to Arendt, was their status as both political and social outsiders. On this latter point, Arendt points to the fact that Jewish political emancipation coincided with the rise of imperialism in the late nineteenth century (in Germany, Jews achieved full political emancipation in 1879). As a result, Jews were cast into society en masse, that is, wealthy bankers and impoverished Jewish masses alike. Society, however, was no more inclined to accept the newly emancipated Jewish masses as equals than the new imperialist regimes were to maintain the formerly privileged status of wealthy Jews under the nation-state. In contrast to the nation-state, imperialism had little use for either.

Politically obsolete and socially vulnerable, they were rendered "superfluous" in the context of the general disintegration of traditional political and social structures in the aftermath of the imperial collapse during World War I. "Anti-Semitism reached its climax when the Jews had [. . .] lost their public functions and their influence, and were left with nothing but their wealth" (*OT*: 4) – a turning point in European history that coincided with "the exact moment when the European system of nation states and its precarious balance of power crashed" (*OT*: 3).

It is instructive to compare Arendt's with Horkheimer's views here: they agree that the peculiar economic position occupied by the Jews as lenders and bankers, bailing out and supporting first the absolutist regimes of Europe and subsequently national governments, gave them a unique and problematical profile. Jews were "within the nation" but never really "of the nation." Both touch upon the resentment that the economic condition of the Jews gave rise to: for Horkheimer, given their prominence in the circulation sphere, Jews became like a lightning rod toward which all sorts of anti-capitalist resentment on the part of the masses would be channeled. For Arendt, the economic position of the Jews gave them a "supra-national" and "proto-cosmopolitan" existence, which at one and the same time called forth and belied the universal belief in "the rights of man." The Jews seemed to represent "human rights as such." Yet, at the same time, their problematic position within the nation also evidenced the vulnerability to which they were subject in virtue of not clearly belonging to a collectivity which would stand up for them. This is why, for Arendt, as well as for Theodor Herzl, the Dreyfus case was so significant. Even after the legacy of the French Revolution, and within the "civic nation" of France, the Jews remained outsiders. After the Franco-Prussian War (1870–1), Dreyfus, an Alsatian Jew, officer in the French army, was accused of being a spy for the Germans! Jewish existence thus revealed the fragile balance between the universalistic aspirations of the modern nation-state and the principle of national sovereignty. Such sovereignty would repeatedly be defined not in terms of a community of citizens and equals, but in terms of an ethos of blood and belonging.[39]

Arendt's attempt to locate the sources of anti-Semitism not in the economic sphere alone, which she certainly did not ignore, but in the unresolved paradoxes of the modern state after the French Revolution would have seemed to members of the Frankfurt School as a case of naive idealism or, even worse, liberalism. They never accepted the autonomy of the state from the economy and never really developed a theory of the modern liberal state, even when they speculated, as in Marcuse's case, on the terrible consequences of its demise.[40] Arendt, who saw the fate of the Jews as bound up with the frailty of the ideals of human rights, the rule of law for all, and popular sovereignty, was on firmer ground here. Her analysis of anti-Semitism led her to unearth much deeper tensions in the modern state system as such.

Undoubtedly, however, Arendt's antagonism toward psychological and psychoanalytical explanations in accounting for anti-Semitism, and their plausibility in helping understand political phenomena in general are exaggerated as well. Every citizen was once a child; the public persona hides the private individual. By emphatically focusing on the "dignity of the public sphere," Arendt accomplished a much-needed correction against the reduction of political phenomena to economic behavior and motivations, as practiced by orthodox Marxists and liberals alike, but in decidedly pushing away the socio-psychological and cultural context which also shaped the sphere of the political and the psyche of the individual citizen, she may have undercut some of the prescience of her own vision of the political.

What has increasingly gained prominence in our times, during which the nation-state system of the post-World War II period is caught in the throes of deep and unpredictable transformations, at times referred to as "post-nationalism" or "post-sovereignty," are Arendt's reflections on minorities, statelessness, and the plight of refugees. It is also at this point that we see revealed the threads connecting the experiences of the failed liberal emancipation of the German Jews to the collective experiences of the majority of Eastern European Jews, as articulated for us most poignantly through Raphael Lemkin's category of genocide.

Arendt on Statelessness and The "Right to Have Rights"

Arendt was one of the few political theorists of the past century who focused on the significance of the nationalities' and minorities' question which emerged in the wake of World War I as a harbinger of totalitarianism. The dissolution of the multinational and multiethnic empires such as the Russian, the Ottoman, the Austro-Hungarian, and the defeat of the Kaiserreich, led to the emergence of nation-states, particularly in Eastern-Central Europe that enjoyed little religious, linguistic, or cultural homogeneity. These successor states – Poland, Austria, Hungary, Czechoslovakia, Yugoslavia, Bulgaria, Lithuania, Latvia, Estonia, the Greek and the Turkish republics – controlled territories in which large numbers of so-called "national minorities" resided. On June 28, 1919, the Polish Minority Treaty was concluded between President Woodrow Wilson and the Allied and Associated Powers, to protect the rights of minorities who made up nearly 40 percent of the total population of Poland at that time and consisted of Jews, Russians, Germans, Lithuanians, and others. Thirteen similar agreements were then drawn up with various successor governments, "in which they pledged to their minorities civil and political equality, cultural and economic freedom, and religious toleration."[41] Not only was there a fatal lack of clarity in how a national minority was to be defined, but the fact that the protection of minority rights applied only to the successor states of the defeated powers, and not to Great Britain, France, and Italy, which refused to consider the extension of the minority treaties to their own territories, created cynicism about the motivations of the Allied Powers in supporting minority rights in the first place. This situation led to anomalies whereby, for example, the German minority in Czechoslovakia could petition the League of Nations for the protection of its rights, but the large German minority in Italy could not. The position of Jews in all successor states was also unsettled: if they were a national minority, was it in virtue of their race, their religion, or their language that they were to be considered as such, and exactly which rights would this minority status entail?

For Arendt, the growing discord within and the political ineptitude of the League of Nations, the emerging conflicts among so-called national minorities themselves, as well as the hypocrisy in the application of the Minority Treaties, were all harbingers of developments in the 1930s. The modern nation-state was being transformed from an organ which would execute the rule of all for all its citizens and residents into an instrument of the nation as a narrow "imagined" ethno-national community. "The nation has conquered the state, national interest had priority over law long before Hitler could pronounce 'right is what is good for the German people'" (OT: 275).

The perversion of the modern state from an instrument of law into one of lawless discretion in the service of the nation was evident when states began to practice massive denaturalizations against unwanted minorities, creating millions of refugees, deported aliens, and stateless peoples across borders – special categories of human created through the actions of nation-states. In a territorially bounded nation-state system or in a state-centric international order, one's legal status is dependent upon protection by the highest authority which controls the territory upon which one resides and issues the papers to which one is entitled. One becomes a *refugee* if one is persecuted, expelled, and driven away from one's homeland; one becomes a *minority* if the political majority in the polity declares that certain groups do not belong to the supposedly "homogeneous" people; one is a *stateless* person if the state whose protection one has hitherto enjoyed withdraws such protection, nullifying the papers it has granted; one is a *displaced* person if, having been rendered a refugee, a minority, or a stateless person, one cannot find another polity to recognize one as its member and remains in a state of limbo, caught between territories, none of which desire one to be its resident. It is here that Arendt concludes:

> We become aware of the existence of a right to have rights (and that means to live in a framework where one is judged by one's actions and opinions) and a right to belong to some kind of organized community, only when millions of people emerge who had lost and could not regain these rights because of the new global political situation . . . The right that corresponds to this loss and that was never even mentioned among the human rights cannot be expressed in the categories of the eighteenth-century because they presume that rights spring immediately from the "nature" of man . . . the right to have rights, or the right of every individual to belong to humanity, should be guaranteed by humanity itself. *It is by no means certain whether this is possible.* (OT: 296–7; my emphasis)

Published in 1951, seven years before *The Human Condition* which appeared in 1958, this analysis of anti-Semitism both in terms of the crisis of the nation-state and the demise of the interwar state system, establishes what Martin Jay calls "the primacy of the political,"[42] which was central to Arendt's attempt to understand modern Jewish experience in Europe.[43]

Conclusion: From *The Origins of Totalitarianism* to the Genocide Convention

Whether it be through the language of political economy, of psychoanalysis, or of German philosophy and sociology, Arendt and Adorno and Horkheimer remained German – more accurately, Western

European – Jews in their reflections on anti-Semitism. For them, the Jewish faith was a private matter, guaranteed by the freedom of religious belief of the modern liberal state. The collective aspects of Jewish existence had become for their generation a matter of familial or social choice alone: one could go to synagogue or not; one could marry a Jew or not; one could raise one's children in the Jewish community or not. Of course, there were other thinkers and traditions more attuned to the collective dimension of Jewish existence in Germany, as well as its transmission through the Hebrew language, liturgy, and tradition. *Das Jüdische Lehrhaus,* directed by Franz Rosenzweig, and the Institut für Sozialforschung were housed in the same building.[44] Yet it was rare for the more traditional Jewish orientation to share universalist and universalizing impulses. This is precisely the legacy of Raphael Lemkin (1901–59), whose efforts to have the United Nations adopt the Genocide Convention transformed the memory of the Holocaust into a universal experience of humankind as such. Lemkin, as I will discuss in the next chapter, wanted the law to mediate the universal and the particular, and tried to reconcile the law of all nations with the irreducibly specific memories of nations and peoples facing extermination. It may be instructive in conclusion to briefly compare the dialectic of the universal and the particular for Lemkin, in contrast with Arendt and Adorno and Horkheimer.

Arendt's, Adorno's, and Horkheimer's decided attempts to explain the phenomenon of Nazi anti-Semitism, through categories that situate this phenomenon within the broader history of Western civilization and Enlightenment, cannot be separated from their moral and political commitments to envisage a world in which human equality and difference, tolerance and the acceptance of otherness would one day prevail. For all their dyspeptic, and often careless, dismissals of political liberalism, Adorno and Horkheimer are political liberals in the sense clarified for us by John Rawls.[45] The memory of the Holocaust and the destruction of European Jewry are transformed in their works into the utopian hope that an emancipated society may be housed within a republican framework. Put succinctly: their methodological universalism in explaining anti-Semitism cannot be separated from their belief that Jews can live a life of dignity, freedom, and tolerance only in a society that aspires to human emancipation and guarantees public freedoms to *all* its citizens.[46] In her emphasis on the good of politics and the dignity of the political, Arendt takes issue with this privatistic conception of liberal freedoms as negative liberties and seeks ultimately a republican correction to

38

liberal individualism; yet she does not reject the central tenets of modern political liberalism that is based on the recognition of fundamental human equality.

By contrast, transforming the persecution not only of the Jews, but of other peoples such as the Gypsies, the Poles, the Slovenes, and the Russians into a universal legacy for mankind, actionable under the law of nations, was Raphael Lemkin's desideratum. In the Preface to *Axis Rule in Occupied Europe*, he writes: "The practice of extermination of nations and ethnic groups as carried out by the invaders is called by the author 'genocide,' a term deriving from the Greek word *genos* (tribe, race) and the Latin *cide* (by way of analogy, see homicide, fratricide)."[47] These few famous lines offered a term for what Churchill, referring to the extermination of European Jewry, called "a crime without a name." Lemkin himself, it has been pointed out, did not insist on the uniqueness of the Holocaust but attempted to formulate "a broad theory and definition of genocide, in which the Holocaust served as prime example, not as an exception."[48]

Lemkin, who worked as an attorney in the Polish State Prosecutor's Office and fled to the United States in 1939 via Sweden, not only brought a legal imagination and perspective to the understanding of anti-Semitism and the extermination of the Jews; he also introduced the category of "the group" and emphasized that "The objectives of such a plan would be the disintegration of the political and social institutions, of culture, language, national feelings, religion, the economic existence of national groups, and the destruction of the personal security, liberty, health, dignity, and even the lives of individuals belonging to such groups."[49] I will conjecture that neither Arendt nor Adorno and Horkheimer, emerging as they did out of the more liberal and individualistic traditions of German-Jewish emancipation, would be as accepting as Lemkin was of the concept of the group or of the moral and political imperative to preserve groups. Groups, for them, would be worth defending only insofar as they served the prospects of the emancipation or freedom of their members. Nevertheless, in Arendt's prescient reflections on the minorities question in interwar Europe and on "the right to have rights," we sense anticipations of the problem of cultural groups and the protection of the cultural legacy of minorities that dominated Lemkin's work.

What we gain by evaluating Adorno and Horkheimer's and Arendt's explorations of Nazi anti-Semitism in comparative perspective, and by extending this evaluation briefly to touch upon the legacy of

Raphael Lemkin, is insight into the dialectic of the universal and the particular that inevitably and necessarily accompanies all reflections on the fate of European Jewry. And all such reflection remains a testimony to that unprecedented spiritual and intellectual legacy of the twentieth century's émigré intellectuals, brilliantly named by Martin Jay as "permanent exiles."

INTERNATIONAL LAW AND HUMAN PLURALITY IN THE SHADOW OF TOTALITARIANISM

Hannah Arendt and Raphael Lemkin

Ironies of Biography

Hannah Arendt and Raphael Lemkin were witnesses to the twentieth century. They both experienced the dislocating transformations of the European continent as a consequence of two world wars; they lost their states as well as their homes in this process, narrowly escaped the clutches of the Nazi extermination machine, and made it to the New World through sheer luck and fortuitous circumstance. Their thought is marked by the cataclysms of the last century, and they have in turn emerged as indispensable interlocutors for all of us in understanding this past.

There are also astonishing parallels in their early biographies. She was born in Hanover in 1906 (d. 1975) and grew up in Königsberg in East Prussia. After World War I, the Polish Corridor was created and cut East Prussia and Köngisberg off from the rest of Weimar; in 1945 Königsberg was occupied by the Soviets and was renamed "Kaliningrad." Lemkin was born in Bezwodene in 1900, then part of Tsarist Russia. Between the two world wars (1918–39) Bezwodene became part of Poland, and today is Bezvodna in Belarus. The experience of living on territories which changed political authority, while

This chapter originally appeared in *Constellations. An International Journal of Critical and Democratic Theory* 16/2 (June 2009): 331–51; it has also been reprinted in Seyla Benhabib, ed., *Politics in Dark Times: Encounters with Hannah Arendt*, pp. 219–47. It has been abbreviated and revised for inclusion in this volume.

their populations remained the same, may have made the disjunctions between territoriality, sovereignty, and peoplehood all too vivid for both.

Arendt was arrested by the Gestapo in the spring of 1933 and was forced to flee to Paris via Prague with her mother. During those very same years, Ralph Lemkin was a young clerk in the Polish State Prosecutor's office and had been collecting documents on Nazi war legislation, particularly those affecting cultural, linguistic, religious activities, and artifacts of cultural and religious groups. In 1933, he had sent a paper to a League of Nations conference in Madrid, in which he proposed that "the crimes of barbarity and vandalism be considered as new offences against the law of nations."[1] In 1939, he fled from Poland and reached Stockholm, where he continued to do extensive research on Nazi occupation laws throughout Europe. On April 18, 1941, he arrived in the United States via Japan. That very same year, Arendt and her second husband, Heinrich Blücher, arrived in New York via Portugal.

Yet, in contrast to Arendt, who acquired worldwide fame after her arrival in the USA with her many works and university appointments, Lemkin, after the general acclaim he received with the passage of the Genocide Convention by the United Nations in 1948, fell into obscurity and died a lonely death, destitute and neglected in New York in 1959.

It is certainly fascinating to speculate whether these Jewish refugees, who were caught up in the great dislocations of their time, ever met one another in some location or association in the United States. We just don't know. What is even more astonishing is the lack of any discussion in Hannah Arendt's work of Lemkin's great book on the concept of genocide;[2] nor is there any evidence that Lemkin knew Arendt's work on totalitarianism, which certainly was the most powerful historical documentation and philosophical analysis in the early 1950s of the unprecedentedly murderous character of the Nazi regime. Arendt and Lemkin appear to have existed in the same time and space coordinates without ever encountering one another. It becomes thus incumbent upon retrospective readers of their work to put together the pieces of the puzzle in this missed encounter.

This missed encounter can itself be viewed as a metaphor for the ways in which not only their lives but also their thought ran so close and yet remained so distant.[3] In 1944, Ralph Lemkin published *Axis Rule in Occupied Europe*, in which he demanded that a new category of the law of nations be formulated in order to reckon with and bring to justice war crimes committed by Nazis and their Allies against the many peoples of Europe. He was concerned that international law should recognize the unprecedented nature of genocide of the Jews and other peoples. In 1951, Hannah Arendt published *The Origins of Totalitarianism*, which also exposed the unprecedented political nature of totalitarianism as a novel form of political rule in history – in fact, as a transformation of the sphere of the political as such. Yet, unlike Lemkin, Arendt was quite skeptical that declarations of human rights, international conventions, and the like could help restore the destroyed political fabric of the world after World War II. In a passage which almost seems to take aim at Lemkin's efforts to pass the Genocide Convention, Arendt wrote:

> Even worse was that all societies formed for the protection of the Rights of Man, all attempts to arrive at a new bill of human rights were sponsored by marginal figures – by a few international jurists without political experience or professional philanthropists supported by the uncertain sentiments of professional idealists. The groups they formed, the declarations they issued show an uncanny similarity in language and composition to that of societies for the prevention of cruelty to animals. No statesman, no political figure of any importance could possibly take them seriously and none of the liberal or radical parties in Europe thought it necessary to incorporate into their program a new declaration of human rights. (*OT*: 292)

Did Arendt possibly have Lemkin in mind when she referred in dismissive terms of those "international jurists without political experience"? And could she have been referring to Eleanor Roosevelt, the tireless force behind the passage of the Universal Declaration of Human Rights in 1948, when she took a swipe at "professional philanthropists supported by the uncertain sentiments of professional idealists"? There are no references in Arendt's work, as far as I can tell,[4] to Raphael Lemkin.

Ironically, though, by 1963, when she writes *Eichmann in Jerusalem*, Arendt has not only accepted the categories of the Genocide Convention, but goes even beyond Lemkin to provide a philosophical condemnation of the crime of genocide in the light of her concept of human plurality. Genocide, in Arendt's view, destroys plurality and is a crime against the human condition as such. In the dramatic Epilogue to *Eichmann in Jerusalem*, she states that the "justice of what was done in Jerusalem would have emerged to be seen by all if the judges had dared to address their defendant in something like the

43

Genocide not just crime against direct victims, but against ALL of us.

following terms" (*EJ*: 277). In astonishingly pointed language, she then delivers her own verdict against Adolph Eichmann:

> You admitted that the crime committed against the Jewish people during the war was the greatest crime in recorded history, and you admitted your role in it . . . Let us assume, for the sake of argument, that it was nothing more than misfortune that made you a willing instrument in the organization of *mass murder*; there still remains the fact that you have carried out, and therefore actively supported, a policy of *mass murder*. (*EJ*: 277–9; emphasis mine)

I want to suggest that these two quotations – from *The Origins of Totalitarianism* and from *Eichmann in Jerusalem* – are like bookends marking the evolution of Arendt's thought from skepticism toward international law and human rights[5] in the 1950s toward a cautious confirmation of their role in shaping politics among nations in the 1960s. Between the 1951 publication of *The Origins of Totalitarianism* and the 1963 appearance of *Eichmann in Jerusalem*, post-World War II politics were transformed with the creation of the United Nations in 1946, the Universal Declaration of Human Rights in 1948, and the adoption of the Genocide Convention by the General Assembly that same year. Although Arendt never abandoned her belief in the necessity of the self-determination of peoples to guarantee individuals their human as well as citizens' rights, her faith in international law and institutions grew in the intervening years. The complex relationship between republican self-government and new developments in the international sphere, including international law, are part of the subtext of Arendt's reflections on the trial of Adolph Eichmann in Jerusalem.[6] And this new world constellation comes about, in no small measure, through Lemkin's tireless efforts in drafting and advocating the acceptance of the Genocide Convention.

Lemkin remained one of those "obscure international jurists," in her words, who single-handedly and tirelessly worked to craft and eventually saw adopted by the United Nations the Convention on Genocide on December 9, 1948. I shall argue in this chapter that with her claim that Eichmann must die because he "carried out a policy of not wanting to share the earth with the Jewish people and the people of a number of other nations," Arendt not only confirmed Raphael Lemkin's understanding of the crime of genocide as the "intent to destroy, in whole or in part, a national, ethnical, racial or religious group, as such,"[7] but gave it a firm ontological grounding in the human condition.

Arendt and Lemkin on Anti-Semitism

In tracing this transformation in Arendt's thought, we should begin by recalling that, as analyzed in the previous chapter, for Arendt, anti-Semitism was not an eternal aspect of the human condition or of human history. It originated with the interlacing of historical, socio-economic, political, and cultural circumstances around the rise of the modern nation-state, the emancipation of European Jewry, and the eventual rise of European imperialism. These political develop-ments and their consequences in turn fueled Arendt's profound pes-simism about the capacity of modern political and legal institutions in the European continent to resist anti-Semitism, and encouraged her skepticism about their ability to resolve the paradoxes that they themselves created.[8]

Raphael Lemkin, by contrast, was a jurist trained in the law of nations, and for him the rise of European anti-Semitism and the eventual destruction of European Jewry did not need to be explained in terms of the fate of the Jews alone. He considered genocidal anti-Semitism to be one episode *among others* in the long history of the cultural extermination of human groups; the Holocaust was to be singled out for its intensity and extent rather than its logic.

In chapter VIII of *Axis Rule in Occupied Europe*, Lemkin discusses the legal status of the Jews (ARiE: 75–8). He observes matter-of-factly that the definition of a Jew was based by Axis powers (among which are included not only Germany, but Italy, Hungary, Bulgaria, and Romania too) upon the Nuremberg laws. "A Jew is any person who is, or has been, a member of the Jewish faith or who has more than two Jewish grandparents" (ibid.). The latter are considered Jewish if they are, or have been, members of the Jewish faith. Lemkin is particularly attentive to differences in the treatment of Jews stem-ming from France, Norway, Belgium, and the Netherlands in the hands of the Nazis, in contrast with those hailing from the Eastern European territories; but after the deportation en masse to Poland of Western European Jews, he claims, these differences among different Jewish nationalities evaporated.

In contrast to Arendt's reflections, there is no social, economic, psychological, or cultural analysis of European anti-Semitism in Lem-kin's work, but, rather, a very detailed account of the race-policies of the Nazis and their attempts at the Germanization of the European continent. Whereas Arendt attempts to understand the causes of anti-Semitism, Lemkin focuses on the *consequences* of racialist Nazi ideology. Prejudice and genocide, among human groups – which in his unpublished Notes is extended as far as the colonization of the Aztecs and the Incas, the destruction of early Christians by the Romans, and, less controversially, to the genocide of Ottoman Armenians – appear rooted for him in a deep-seated anthropological predilection of the human species.[9] It is only the law that can counter this. "Only man has law," he is reported to have said.[10]

Arendt's and Lemkin's analyses of anti-Semitism, then, show little affinity: for her, the emergence of the Jewish Question in the heart of late nineteenth- and mid-twentieth-century Europe requires a full-scale diagnosis of the paradoxes of the modern nation-state system, whereas he sees deep-seated tendencies throughout human history toward the persecution of vulnerable groups, and among them the Jews. It is the goal of law to protect the vulnerable against the predator and the exploiter, but the law cannot eradicate evil from human hearts.

Lemkin retains his faith in the relative autonomy of legal institutions vis-à-vis the political process, but instead of documenting the folly of the League of Nations and of Minority Treaties, as Arendt does, he strives to put into legal coda the unfulfilled promises of this institution, in particular, with respect to minority rights and vulnerable peoples. In the 1950s both agree, however, somewhat naively, that the "rule of law" in the American Republic has reached the right balance between politics and the law.[11] Above all, they believe that political traditions in the United States have helped ameliorate the fatal confusions which recurred on the continent between the constitution of a state that guarantees equality before the law and equal rights to all its citizens regardless of their ethnic origin and the supremacy of the will of the nation, understood as a homogeneous ethno-cultural entity.

What were Lemkin's crucial innovations in international law with the introduction of the concept of "genocide"? I will argue that underlying this legal concept is an "ontology of the group." While little noted in the literature on Lemkin, this concept has two origins: one is the legal category of Minorities, as defined by President Wilson's 14 Points, and the other is a Herderian belief in the group as the *conditio sina qua non* of all human artistic and cultural achievement.[12] Arendt, by contrast, only harbors skepticism toward such group concepts. Yet, like Lemkin, she believes in the ontological value and irreducibility of *human plurality*. It is because we inhabit the world with others who are *like* us and yet always different *from* us that the world is perspectival and can only manifest itself to us from a particular vantage point. Nevertheless, plurality need not be constituted through the "ascribed" groups of ethnicity, nationhood, race, or religion alone. Quite to the contrary. It is only when ascription is transcended through association and human beings come together for a joint purpose in the public sphere that plurality, which is the human condition, is most strikingly revealed. I shall argue that Arendt's philosophical grounding of the concept of plurality provides the concept of genocide with one of its strongest moral and existential underpinnings.[13]

The Genocide Convention

According to the Genocide Convention, adopted on December 9, 1948:

> genocide means any of the following acts with intent to destroy, in whole or in part, a national, ethnical, racial or religious group, as such: (a) Killing members of the group; (b) Causing serious bodily or mental harm to members of the group; (c) Deliberately inflicting on the group conditions of life calculated to bring about its physical destruction in whole or in part; (d) Imposing measures to prevent births within the group; (e) Forcibly transferring children of the group to another group.[14]

Not only in terms of historical research but in terms of more technical legal considerations as well, Lemkin's various definitions of genocide are elastic, and exhibit an " 'instability' between the historical and the legal, between the cultural and the 'ethnical,' between intent and consequence."[15] Debates as to the degree of intent which must accompany certain acts to be deemed genocidal – the definition of the group which is subject to extermination; whether social classes should or should not be considered as groups; what degree of destruction of the cultural legacy of the group constitutes genocidal intent as distinct from forced assimilation, ethnic cleansing, or displacement – are all puzzles that have accompanied these words from their inception and will continue to do so.[16] But Lemkin not only brought legal imagination and perspective to the understanding of anti-Semitism and the extermination of the Jews; he also introduced the category of *the group* and insisted that a genocidal plan would be characterized by the following:

47

The objectives of such a plan would be the disintegration of the political and social institutions, of culture, language, national feelings, religion, the economic existence of *national groups*, and the destruction of the personal security, liberty, health, dignity, and even the lives of individuals belonging to *such groups*. Genocide is directed against *the national group as an entity*, and the actions involved are directed against individuals, not in their individual capacity, but as members of *the national group*. (*ARiE*: 79; emphasis mine)

The famous chapter IX of *Axis Rule in Occupied Europe* is dedicated to showing why Nazi and Axis actions in occupied Europe constitute a crime that requires a *new* conception. Admittedly, given his insistence that genocide against groups has been a constant feature of human history, it is at times unclear whether Lemkin thinks that this is an *old* crime which requires a *new* name, or a *new* crime, which differs from historical precedents so radically, that it must be called by a *new* name. He thinks it is the latter (*ARiE*: 79). Lemkin is concerned to prove that the Nazis are waging an unprecedented total war since they make no distinction between the nation and the state: "the nation provides the biological elements for the state" (*ARiE*: 80, 90).[17] Such total war is the antithesis of the Rousseau-Portalis Treaty[18] which ought to have governed war among sovereign states and which was, he believes, implicit in the Hague Regulations of 1907: "This doctrine holds that war is directed against sovereigns and armies, not against subjects and civilians" (ibid.). The Nazis violated this principle not only by waging total war, but even prior to war, through their policies of Aryanization of the German race (by forbidding mixed marriages with Jews and others; by employing euthanasia on the feeble-minded and the retarded; through efforts at the Germanization of peoples such as the Dutch, Norwegians, and Luxembourgers, and the Germanization of the soil alone of people *not related* to Germans by blood such as Poles, Slovenes, and Serbs, and, finally, when it came to the Jews, through their total extermination (ibid.: 81–2).

Lemkin is first and foremost concerned to establish that there are no existing instruments of international law to deal with such crimes. The Hague Convention on "Respecting the Laws and Customs of War on Land" (signed on October 18, 1907), has rules addressing "some (but by no means all) of the essential rights of individuals; and these rules do not take into consideration the interrelationship of such rights with the whole problem of nations subjected to virtual imprisonment." (*ARiE*: 90). The Hague rules deal with "the sovereignty of a state," but not with preserving "the integrity of a people" (ibid.).

In a subsequent essay, Lemkin names genocide a "composite crime."[19] By his own account, as early as 1933, he formulated two new categories of crime in international law – the crime of *barbarity*, "conceived as oppressive and destructive actions directed against individuals as members of a national, religious, or racial group" (ibid.: 91), and the crime of *vandalism*, "conceived as malicious destruction of works of art and culture because they *represent the specific creations of the genius of such groups*" (ibid.; emphasis mine). In 1944, he is convinced that neither these terms nor the Hague Conventions are adequate to deal with the crime being perpetrated by Axis powers.

Yet why is the destruction of the life, works, culture, and life-form of a national group more heinous than the destruction of the individuals belonging to this group? According to Lemkin, insofar as "the actions involved are directed against individuals, not in their individual capacity, but as members of *the national group*" (*ARiE*: 79), they violate the *moral* principle that innocents shall not be harmed, the *legal* principle that the law punishes individuals for what they do, not for what or who they are, as well as *the laws of war and peace* that innocent civilians must be spared and must not be treated as collateral damage. There is an added dimension of legal criminality and moral culpability when destruction is aimed at the *national group as such*. To make this point, Lemkin returns here to the Minority Treaties of the interwar period and observes that "National and religious groups were put under a special protection by the Treaty of Versailles and by specific minority treaties, when it became obvious that national minorities were compelled to live within the boundaries of states ruled by governments representing the majority of the population" (*ARiE*: 90–1). Not only the life and well-being, but also the "honor and reputation" of such groups were to be protected by the legal codes at that time (ibid.: 91). Already, then, legal developments in the interwar years anticipated the need for special protection of the life and well-being as well as the honor and reputation of such groups.

But why privilege the national/ethnic/religious group in this fashion? In a passage that remains frequently uncommented upon, Lemkin lays bare what I will call his "ontology of groups":

> The world represents only so much culture and intellectual vigour as are created by its component national groups. Essentially the idea of a nation signifies constructive cooperation and original contributions, based upon genuine traditions, genuine culture, and a well-developed national psychology. The destruction of a nation, therefore, results in

the loss of its future contributions to the world. Moreover, such destruction offends our feelings of morality and justice in much the same way as does the criminal killing of a human being: the crime in one case as in the other is murder, though on a vastly greater scale. (*ARiE*: 91)

This passage is noteworthy for a number of reasons: Lemkin is quite unconcerned about the definition of a national group, considering it almost self-evident and using it interchangeably with *ethnos* (*ARiE*: 79); he often includes race and religion as well as social groupings as being in need of protection (*ARiE*: 93).[20] The Genocide Convention speaks of a "national, ethnical, racial or religious group," without much specification as such. Whether one considers Lemkin's own formulations or refers to the text of the Genocide Convention, it is the "ascriptive" group, the group into which one is *born* or into which one is *thrown* (to speak with Martin Heidegger), that constitutes his reference point. Such groups are not created; they are found. They are not invented but discovered.

Most significantly, Lemkin's understanding of the group is cultural-ist,[21] defined in terms of the "genuine traditions, genuine culture, and well-developed national psychology" (*ARiE*: 91). Culture, in turn, is viewed fairly conventionally as "high culture," as "original contributions" to the world. In a popular piece addressed to a large audience in the *American Scholar*, Lemkin writes:

> We can best understand this when we realize how impoverished our culture would be if the peoples doomed by Germany, such as the Jews, had not been permitted to create the Bible, or to give birth to an Einstein, a Spinoza; if the Poles had not had the opportunity to give to the world a Copernicus, a Chopin, a Curie; the Czechs, a Huss, a Dvořák; the Greeks, a Plato and a Socrates; the Russians, a Tolstoy and a Shostakovich.[22]

Is there a distinction to be made, then, between cultures which contribute to world civilization and others which have not or cannot? Is there a lurking assessment then between "genuine traditions" and "genuine culture" and "non-genuine," inauthentic traditions and cultures? And would such distinctions affect the claim of some cultures to be entitled to be preserved and protected more than others? Is Lemkin's ontology of the group based upon an implicit hierarchy of cultures and their contributions?

My goal here is not to engage in postmodernist skepticism about holistic concepts of groups and culture against Lemkin. Even beyond postmodern skepticism, however, the definition of the group that is deemed worthy of legal recognition remains a contentious matter in all debates on group rights, and has consequences for *which* collective rights groups are deemed to be entitled to, as opposed to the individuals who are members of such groups.[23] Lemkin's own understanding of the national group has two sources: from a legal point of view, he reverts to the instruments of the Minority Treaties of the interwar period, which, as we saw above through Arendt's analysis too, were themselves hardly unproblematic. Philosophically, Lemkin is heir to a romantic and nationalist Herderian tradition that sees national groups, broadly conceived, as sources of a unique perspective on the world, as originators of a mode of disclosing the world.[24]

This privileging of national groups leads Lemkin to conclude that:

> genocide is a problem not only of war but also of peace. It is an especially important problem for Europe, where differentiation into nationhood is so marked that despite the principle of political and territorial self-determination, certain national groups may be obliged to live as minorities within the boundaries of other states. If these groups should not be adequately protected, such lack of protection would result in international disturbances, especially in the form of the disorganized emigration of the persecuted, who would look for refuge elsewhere. (*ARiE*: 93)

Lemkin's thought here slides from the crime of genocide to the peacetime protection of minority rights, which, as he admits, is a matter of civil and constitutional and not criminal law (ibid.). But whereas for Hannah Arendt, the division of people within a nation-state into minorities amid a majority, is *the source* of the problem itself, Lemkin sees strengthening protection for minority rights to be necessary in peace time as well. He thereby tries to use legal means to address political questions which are properly matters of state organization that concern the design of political constitutions and institutions – whether these be federalist or unitary.

Arendt presents a rather different understanding of the value of the group. For her, the group is not ascribed but formed; it is not discovered, but constituted and reconstituted through creative acts of human association. The value of the group does not lie first and foremost in its "original contributions" to world culture and its "genuine traditions" but, rather, in its manifestation of human diversity, in its disclosing a new perspectival outlook on the world.[25] The world is disclosed for us through diversity and plurality.

contrast Lemkin & Arendt

Plurality as a Fundamental Category in Arendt's Work

No passage better expresses the concept of plurality in Arendt's work than the following:

> If it is true that a thing *is* real . . . only if it can show itself and be perceived from all sides, then there must always be a plurality of individuals or peoples . . . to make reality even possible and to guarantee its continuation. In other words, the world comes into being only if there are perspectives . . . If a people or a nation, or even just some specific human group, which offers a unique view of the world arising from its particular vision of the world . . . is annihilated, it is not merely that a people or a nation or a given number of individuals perishes, but rather that a portion of our common world is destroyed, an aspect of the world that has revealed itself to us until now but can never reveal itself again. Annihilation is therefore not just tantamount to the end of the world; it also takes its annihilator with it.[26]

As Patricia Owens observes:

> [W]ars of annihilation that aim to wipe out a particular group attack the basic fact of human plurality and violate the 'limits inherent in violent action.' With genocide we are not 'just' talking about large numbers of dead but something that is potentially immortal. The public, political world, the political constitution of a people, the outcome of people's living together, and debating their common affairs is also destroyed with genocide.[27]

Genocide violates "an altogether different order," writes Arendt in *Eichmann in Jerusalem* (*EJ*: 272).

The category of plurality is no less ontological in Arendt's thought than that of the group is in Lemkin's. For both authors, these categories represent some element and principle which is part of the order of being human in the universe. Arendt names this "the human condition," that is, "the basic conditions under which life on earth has been given to man."[28] Plurality is the fact that corresponds to our irreducible sameness as members of the same species and that at the same time expresses our irreducible difference from one another. "Plurality is the condition of human action because we are all the same, that is, human, in such a way that nobody is ever the same as anyone else who ever lived, lives, or will live" (*The Human Condition*: 8). This plurality is the precondition of the possibility of all political life: because we are members of the same species who have

52

speech and reasoning, or who are capable, of *legein* – reasoned speech – we can communicate with one another, build a world together as well as destroy one another. And since we are all subject to similar bodily needs and face likewise the struggle with nature, we face the "circumstances of justice," that is, of how to establish just institutions under conditions of vulnerability and scarcity.

Plurality is also what enables diversity and perspectivality:

> In acting and speaking, men show who they are, reveal actively their unique personal identities and thus make their appearance in the human worlds, while their physical identities appear without any activity of their own in the unique shape of the body and sound of the voice. The disclosure of "who" in contradistinction to "what" somebody is – his qualities, gifts, talents and shortcoming, which he may display or hide – is implicit in everything somebody says and does. (*The Human Condition*: 179)

We live in a world constituted by narratives about the "who" as well as the "what" of action; this web of narratives is the medium through which the multiplicity and diversity of perspectives on human affairs converge and conflict, are woven together and torn apart.

These ontological theses of Hannah Arendt's are well known.[29] Her concept of plurality enables Arendt to escape both the ascriptivism and the culturalism of Lemkin's concept of the group. Groups for Arendt are enduring associations, rooted in the human capacity to create a world in common that is shareable yet diverse, that is communicable yet open to misunderstanding, and that appears as one yet is refracted through many different narratives and perspectives. While from a philosophical point of view, there can be little question about the brilliant acuity to Arendt's analyses, from a legal point of view, from the standpoint of the jurist, the protean aspect of Arendt's concept of plurality may be too volatile. The juridification of the category of the group brings with it inevitable ontological as well as sociological problems.

Ironically, her skepticism toward group concepts and her dynamic concept of plurality enable Arendt to deliver a trenchant account of the crime of genocide as constituting a "crime against the human condition," as such. This, I believe, is the meaning of the passage from *Eichmann in Jerusalem*, the first part of which is quoted on p. 44 above:

> And just as you supported and carried out a policy of not wanting to share the earth with the Jewish people and the people of a number of

other nations – *as though you and your superiors had any right to determine who should and who should not inhabit the world* – we find that no one, that is, no member of the human race, can be expected to share the earth with you. This is the reason, and the only reason, you must hang.[30] (*EJ*: 277–9; emphasis mine).

Genocide is "an attack upon human diversity as such, that is, upon a characteristic of the "human status" without which the words "mankind" or "humanity" would be devoid of meaning" (*EJ*: 268–9).

It is hard not to see in these passages of searing eloquence a belated vindication of those such as Lemkin whom Arendt seemed to dismiss more than a decade ago as "those few international jurists without political experience or professional philanthropists supported by the uncertain sentiments of professional idealists" (*OT*: 292) but who, through their tireless efforts, transformed the meaning of the "human status." Abandoning her bitter irony of *The Origins of Totalitarianism* in 1951, Arendt in *Eichmann in Jerusalem*, in 1963, embraces and honors Lemkin's legacy, although it remains a mystery why she does not credit Lemkin by name.

Brief Epilogue: Arendt and Lemkin on *Universal Jurisdiction*

For Lemkin, no less than for Arendt, embracing the concept of genocide raised the question of jurisdiction. In *Axis Rule in Occupied Europe*, Lemkin is ready to include the crime of genocide as amended under the Hague Regulations (93). He later insists, however, that this crime must be independent of any prior treaty or set of regulations. Furthermore, he notes that "the adoption of the principle of *universal repression* as adapted to genocide by countries which belong now to the group of non-belligerents or neutrals, respectively, would likewise bind these latter countries to punish the war criminals engaged in genocide or to extradite them to countries in which these crimes were committed" (ibid.: 92; emphasis mine). Universal repression makes the culprit liable not only in the country in which he committed the crime, but also "in any other country in which he might have taken refuge" (ibid.: 94). Astonishingly, Lemkin shows himself to be little concerned with difficulties which may arise with the application of the principle of universal repression, such as the capacity of prosecutors in other countries to be able to collect evidence, provide for adequate defense of the defendants, escape the semblance of "victor's justice," and a myriad other procedural and substantive details which may go wrong in a criminal trial. By contrast, these and other details haunted Arendt with regards to the trial of Adolph Eichmann and cast doubts for her on its full legality.

For Lemkin, "genocide offenders should be subject to the principle of universal repression as should other offenders guilty of the so-called *delicta juris gentium* (such as, for example, white slavery and trade in children, piracy, trade in narcotics and in obscene publications, and counterfeiting of money)" (ibid.: 94). There is something deeply unsatisfactory about singling out the radicalness of the crime of genocide on the one hand, and comparing it to piracy, trade in narcotics and in obscene publications, and so on, on the other. The only crime to which genocide can be compared, insofar as it too is a crime against the human status and the human condition, is slavery, and this is what Lemkin was not willing to do.

In *Eichmann in Jerusalem*, Arendt notes that the analogy between genocide and piracy is not new, and that the Genocide Convention expressly rejected the claim to universal jurisdiction and provided instead that "persons charged with genocide . . . shall be tried by a competent tribunal of the States in the territory of which the act was committed or by such international penal tribunal as may have juris-diction" (*EJ*: 262).[31] With the recognition of the crime of genocide as a *crime against humanity*, Arendt believes that the path had been cleared to entertain the likelihood that "international penal law" will develop. Quoting from Chief Justice Robert Jackson in the Nurem-berg Trials, she points out that international law is viewed as an "outgrowth of treaties and agreements between nations and of accepted customs," and as long as that is the case she believes that "in consequence of this yet unfinished nature of international law," it is ordinary trial judges who have to render justice by facing the unprecedented with the "help of, or beyond the limitation set upon them through, positive, posited laws" (ibid.: 274). Arendt does not consider the negative consequences of "judges making law," though, on the whole, she is very sensitive that law, whether domestic or international, be seen by a self-governing people to be its law, and not be imposed upon it by other instances and authorities.[32]

Lemkin, on the other hand, in 1948 was fearful that an interna-tional criminal court would mean "too great an affront to state sovereignty."[33] Ironically, Arendt was willing to go beyond him in the principle as well as the practice of the persecution of the crime of genocide. Undoubtedly, though, both would have greeted enthusiasti-cally the establishment of an International Criminal Court with the jurisdiction to try those accused of crimes against humanity and of genocide through the Treaty of Rome. They would also have been dismayed that their adoptive country, for whose constitutional traditions they had such reverence – the United States – first signed and then withdrew from the Treaty of the International Criminal Court. But, as the historian Mark Mazower notes, the tensions between Lemkin and the drafters of the Universal Declaration around the issue of "domestic jurisdiction" were there from the beginning and Lemkin had good reasons to be cautious. "Partly," notes Mazower, "this arose over the anxieties that the United States – where the Senate was already jittery about foreign meddling in domestic affairs, especially in the South – would certainly not ratify a future covenant on human rights if confronted with something as binding as the Genocide Convention."[34]

These ambivalencies and tensions with respect to the transformation of the international norm of sovereignty, already present in the early years of the establishment of the United Nations, pose a challenge to our contemporary world, very much as the violation of the laws of war and peace, the collapse of the League of Nations, the nation-state system in Europe, and the Holocaust did for Arendt and Lemkin. The following chapters will trace these changes in the international legal order, particularly in the domain of human rights, and explore their implications for the norms and practice of state sovereignty (see chapters 6 and 7 of this volume).

ANOTHER UNIVERSALISM
On the Unity and Diversity of Human Rights

Husserl and the Crisis of Western Reason

Between 1934 and 1937, as Europe was plunging toward a new war, an ailing Edmund Husserl composed the series of reflections, notes, and lectures that would be posthumously published as *The Crisis of European Sciences and Transcendental Phenomenology*.[1] Full of foreboding and pathos amid the dark clouds gathering over the European continent, Husserl gave voice to a sense of civilizational crisis: "The true struggles of our time, the only ones which are significant, are struggles between humanity which has already collapsed and humanity which still has roots but is struggling to keep them or find new ones" (*Crisis*: 15). For Husserl, these struggles were not primarily political ones among the totalitarian ideologies of Nazism, Soviet-style communism, versus liberal democracy; they were, in the first place, philosophical[2] (*Crisis*: 15).

What haunted Husserl then and might well challenge us now is none other than the claims to universality of Western philosophy and rationalism. If that form of inquiry, which originated in the Greek

---

This chapter is based on my Presidential Lecture, delivered at the Eastern Division meetings of the American Philosophical Association in December 2006; it was printed in the *Proceedings and Addresses of the American Philosophical Association* 81/2 (November 2007): 7–32. It has been revised for inclusion in this volume. I am deeply grateful to Kenneth Baynes, Richard Bernstein, Rainer Forst, Thomas A. McCarthy, Robert Post, Amelie Rorty, James Sleeper, Matthew Noah Smith, Tamar Gendler, Shelly Kagan, and the participants of the Yale Political Theory Colloquium on December 7, 2006, for their comments and criticisms of earlier drafts of this chapter.

pursuit of *theoria*, has no claim to universality, if it is the manifestation of just one more cultural life-world among others, then it cannot "be decided," as Husserl put it, "whether European humanity bears within itself an absolute idea (sic!) rather than being merely an empirical anthropological type like 'China' or 'India'" (*Crisis*: 16). For Husserl, reflection on the crisis of the European sciences was essential not only for understanding Europe's spiritual-political malaise; it meant having the courage to defend the legacy of philosophical rationalism since the Greeks to be not only the cognitive form of inquiry of a historically contingent life-world – the West – but as having a claim to universality for all of humanity, for other life-forms that were now, in Husserl's words, increasingly "Europeanizing themselves."

In a lecture presented before the Vienna Cultural Society on May 7 and 10, 1935, during the composition of the *Crisis of the European Sciences*, Husserl was even blunter:

> [We] pose the question: How is the spiritual shape of Europe to be characterized? Thus we refer to Europe not as it is understood geographically, as on a map, as if thereby the group of people who live together in this territory would define European humanity. In the spiritual sense the English dominions, the United States, etc., clearly belong to Europe, whereas the Eskimos or Indians presented as curiosities at fairs, or the Gypsies, who constantly wander about Europe, do not. Here the title "Europe" clearly refers to the unity of a spiritual life, activity, creation, with all its ends, interests, cares and endeavors, with its products of purposeful activity, institutions, organizations.[3]

These attempts by an aging Husserl, who passed away on April 27, 1938, to retrieve a sense of the West's commonalty by demarcating its spiritual and philosophical legacy not only from the high civilizational worlds of China and India, but from the "lesser worlds" of Eskimos, Gypsies, and "Indians" (by which he meant North and South American indigenous peoples), are poignant in the highest degree. Husserl's is a form of extreme Eurocentrism, which, without even so much as a blush, finds it necessary to rank entire life-worlds and cultural totalities according to whether or not they are capable of attaining "the entelechy of humanity" (Husserl) – that is, universal philosophical reason. Perhaps it is the cruelest of ironies that the Nazis – who were to enter Poland a year and a half after Husserl's death – thought that Europe's Jews, to whom Husserl belonged, far from being the spiritual descendants of the Greeks, bore rather more affinity to the Gypsies, another dark people without a land and wan-

58

dering among the nations of the world. The concentration camps of Europe devastated the Sinti and the Roma along with the Jews. It was Husserl's good fortune not to have experienced the worst and to have died with his faith in European rationalism intact.

Universalism and Human Rights: An Indefensible Legacy?

Why recall this episode at all? Why dust off a volume composed during such a fraught period of history? Certainly, I have no intention of defending Husserl's project of a transcendental phenomenology or his search for some "absolute idea" borne by Western humanity! Nevertheless, his late reflections articulate a question that is still very much with us: what is universalism? In what respects, if any, is the legacy of Western rationalism a universal one? Husserl's answer to these questions is an *essentialist* one: it takes the form of identifying *logos* – in his words – as the *entelechy* of humanity and to claim that other cultural life-forms, which certainly deserve respect for their achievements,[4] are nevertheless *inferior* to the occidental life of *theoria* or the spirit of contemplation.

These questions have become all the more pressing in our times. Whereas for Husserl it was the impending rise of fascism and the retreat of Europe from rational liberalism that was of concern, we are confronted with the galloping spread to all corners of the world of "our" Western way of life which often, however, uses the shields of Western reason and Enlightenment to bring other peoples and cultures under the influence of an inegalitarian global capitalism, whose effects are manifestly neither rational nor humane. The legacy of Western rationalism has been used and abused in the service of institutions and practices that will not stand scrutiny by the very same reason that they claim to spread. As the globe grows together materially into one world, it becomes all the more urgent to understand how claims to universality can be reconciled with assertions of religious and cultural difference; how the unity of reason can be reconciled with the diversity of life-forms.

The public vocabulary through which these questions are articulated most forcefully is the *language of human rights*.[5] The spread of human rights, as well as their defense and institutionalization, have become the uncontested language, though not the reality, of global politics. It is in terms of the language of human rights that I, too, wish to pose the question of universalism anew in this chapter. I will argue that there is one fundamental moral right, the "right to have rights"[6] of every human being, that is, to be recognized by others, and to recognize others in turn, as persons entitled to moral respect and legally protected rights in a human community. Human rights, I will maintain, articulate moral principles protecting the communicative freedom of individuals; while such moral principles are distinct from the legal specification of rights as justiciable claims, nevertheless, there is a necessary and not merely contingent connection between human rights as moral principles and their legal-juridical form.

There is wide-ranging disagreement in contemporary thought about the philosophical justification as well as the content of human rights. Indeed, it has been remarked that "in recent years, as political commitment to human rights has grown, philosophical commitment has waned."[7] Some argue that human rights constitute the "core of a universal thin morality" (Michael Walzer), while others claim that they form "reasonable conditions of a world-political consensus" (Martha Nussbaum). Still others narrow the concept of human rights "to a minimum standard of well-ordered political institutions for all peoples"[8] (John Rawls) and caution that there needs to be a distinction between the list of human rights included in the Law of Peoples, and defensible from the standpoint of a global public reason, and the Universal Declaration of Human Rights of 1948.

These different justifications of human rights inevitably lead to a certain variation in content and to "cherry-picking" among various lists of rights. Michael Walzer, for one, suggests that a comparison of the moral codes of various societies may produce a set of standards "to which all societies can be held – negative injunctions, most likely, rules against murder, deceit, torture, oppression and tyranny."[9] But this way of proceeding would yield a relatively short list. "Among others," notes Charles Beitz, "rights requiring democratic political forms, religious toleration, legal equality for women, and free choice of partner would certainly be excluded."[10] From the standpoint of many of the world's moral systems, such as ancient Judaism, medieval Christianity, Confucianism, Buddhism, and Hinduism, Walzer's "negative injunctions against oppression and tyranny" would be consistent with great degrees of inequality among genders, classes, castes, and religious groups.

Another suggestion is that a *non-parochial* view of human rights, while it may not be endorsed necessarily by all conventional moralities, may, in fact, find favor in the eyes of most conceptions of *political and economic justice* in the world: understood thusly, human rights would constitute the core of a *political* rather than *moral* overlapping consensus. Martha Nussbaum's defense of human rights follows this strategy.[11] I agree that we can view the public law documents of our world such as the Universal Declaration of Human Rights, the International Covenant on Civil and Political Rights, the International Covenant on Economic, Social and Cultural Rights, and the Geneva Conventions of 1951 and their Protocol of 1967, as embodying such "a political overlapping consensus."[12] Nevertheless, as I develop further in the next chapter, Nussbaum's method of philosophical deduction, which ties in rights concepts all too narrowly to a philosophical anthropology of human capabilities, is problematic.

Certainly, the most provocative defense for limiting human rights "to a minimum standard of well-ordered political institutions for all peoples" has been John Rawls's. Rawls lists the right to life (to the means of subsistence and security); to liberty (to freedom from slavery, serfdom, and forced occupation, and to a sufficient measure of liberty of conscience to ensure freedom of religion and thought); to personal property and to "formal equality as expressed by the rules of natural justice (that is, that similar cases be treated similarly)"[13] as the basic human rights. The rights to liberty of conscience and association are pared down in *The Law of Peoples* (1999) such as to accommodate "decent, hierarchical societies," which grant *some* liberty of conscience to other faiths but not *equal liberty of* conscience to minority religions that are not state-sanctioned. Article 18 of the Universal Declaration of Human Rights, by contrast, which guarantees "the right to freedom of thought, conscience and religion," including the right to change one's religion, "to manifest one's religion or belief in teaching, practice, worship and observance," is much more egalitarian and uncompromising vis-à-vis existing state religions than is Rawls's right to the "non-egalitarian liberty of conscience."

Most significantly, Rawls passes over without comment the all-too crucial Article 21 of the Universal Declaration which guarantees everyone "the right to take part in the government of his country, directly or through freely chosen representatives," and which stipulates "the will of the peoples shall be the basis of the authority of government."[14] There is no *basic human right to self-government* in the Rawlsian scheme.[15]

Given that the Universal Declaration of Human Rights (UDHR) is the closest document in our world to international public law, how can we explain this attempt on the part of many philosophers to restrict the content of human rights to a fraction of what is internationally agreed to – at least on paper? I am not precluding the possibility that these documents themselves may be philosophically confused, produced as a consequence of political compromises – as was the UDHR, which was the subject of continuous negotiation between the delegations of the United States and the Soviet Union.[16] Nevertheless, they do set certain public norms and standards, which are underwritten by the vast majority of the states in the world. As James Griffin has argued, it is at least necessary to consider seriously the "discrepancies between the best philosophical account of human rights and the international law of human rights."[17]

I wish to argue that it is necessary to shift both the *justification* strategy and the derivation of the *content* of human rights away from minimalist concerns[18] toward a more robust understanding of human rights in terms of the "right to have rights." Let me note that while I owe the phrase "the right to have rights" to Hannah Arendt, in her work this right is viewed principally as a *political* right and is narrowly identified with the "right to membership in a political community." I will instead propose a conception of the "right to have rights," understood as the claim of each human person to be recognized as a moral being worthy of equal concern and equally entitled to be protected as a legal personality by his or her own polity, as well as the world community. In thus reformulating Arendt's conception, I endorse a discourse-theoretic account of rights as also formulated by Rainer Forst, who writes: "The moral basis for human rights . . . is the respect for the human person as an autonomous agent who possesses a right to justification . . . Human rights secure the equal standing of persons in the political and social world, based on a fundamental moral demand of respect."[19]

In what follows, I begin by looking more closely at the term "universalism"; then I develop a discourse-theoretic account of human rights. This, in turn, leads to the question whether there are some minimal assumptions about human nature and rationality, which must underlie any normative account of human rights. Universalism cannot simply, without residue, be reduced to juridico-political principles alone. Certain normative commitments are crucial. I argue that justificatory universalism and moral universalism are deeply intertwined.

The Many Dimensions of Universalism

Let me begin by distinguishing among essentialist universalism, justificatory universalism, moral universalism, and juridical universalism.[20]

1. _Universalism_ may signify the belief that there is a fundamental human nature or human essence which defines who we are as humans. Some say, as did most philosophers of the eighteenth century, that human nature consists of stable and predictable passions and dispositions, instincts, and emotions, all of which can be rationally discovered and analyzed. Thomas Hobbes, David Hume, and Adam Smith, but also Claude-Adrien Hélvètius and Baron Paul-Henri Dietrich d'Holbach come to mind here. Others may argue that there is no fixed human nature (Jean-Jacques Rousseau), or that even if there were, it would be irrelevant for determining what is most essential about us as humans (Immanuel Kant): namely, our capacity to formulate and live by universalizable moral principles. Still others may repudiate empirical psychology, philosophical anthropology, and rationalist ethics, and maintain that what is universal about the human condition is that we are doomed to choose for ourselves and to create meaning through our actions in a universe devoid of such standards and values. Although many philosophical universalists are essentialists, they need not be. As the example of Jean-Paul Sartre shows, they can be existentialists as well.

2. Universalism in contemporary philosophical debates has come to mean, most prominently, a _justification strategy_. Hermeneuticists, strong contextualists, postmodern skeptics, and power/knowledge theorists all question whether there can be an impartial, objective, and neutral philosophical reason; all maintain that justificatory strategies –which they regard as pretenses to philosophical objectivity – are trapped within historical horizons and are beholden to cultural, social, and psychological currents of power that are often barely acknowledged (cf. Michel Foucault, Jean-François Lyotard, and the early Jacques Derrida).

   These contextualist critics are opposed by _justificatory universalists,_ most of whom are not essentialists: some entertain very few rock-bottom beliefs about human nature and psychology, but they all share strong beliefs in the normative content of human reason – that is, in the validity of procedures of inquiry, evidence, and questioning which have been the cognitive legacy of Western philosophy since the Enlightenment. Impartiality; intersubjective verification of results, argument, and data; consistency of belief, and self-reflexivity are the minimum conditions of this normative content. (Karl Otto-Apel, Jürgen Habermas, Hilary Putnam, Robert Brandom, and John Rawls are in this sense "justificatory universalists.")

3. Universalism, still others argue, is not primarily a term of *cognitive* inquiry; equally significantly, it has a (moral) meaning. I would define it as the principle that all human beings, regardless of race, gender, sexual orientation, bodily or physical ability, ethnic, cultural, linguistic, and religious background are entitled to equal moral respect. The hard question in philosophical ethics continues to be whether such a *moral universalism* can be defended without some commitment to cognitive universalism, either in the sense of essentialism or justificatory universalism.

4. Finally, universalism can be understood in (juridical) terms. Many who are skeptical about providing definitive accounts of human nature and rationality may nonetheless urge that the following norms and principles *ought* to be respected by all legal and political systems claiming legitimacy: all human beings are entitled to certain basic human rights, these juridical universalists say, including, minimally, the rights to life, liberty, security and bodily integrity, some form of property and personal ownership, due process before the law and freedom of speech and association, including freedom of religion and conscience. Some would add socio-economic rights, such as the right to work, health care, disability and old-age benefits to this list; others would insist on including democratic as well as cultural self-determination rights.[21]

I will argue that any legal and political justification of human rights, that is, the project of *juridical universalism*, presupposes recourse to *justificatory universalism*. The task of justification, in turn, cannot proceed without the acknowledgment of the communicative freedom of the other, that is, of the right of the other to accept as legitimate only those rules of action of whose validity she has been convinced with reasons. Justificatory universalism then rests on *moral universalism*, that is, equal respect for the other as a being capable of communicative freedom. Justificatory universalism, however, need not presuppose a full-fledged theory of human nature or a comprehensive moral, religious, or scientific worldview: an account of human agency in terms of the "generalized" and "concrete" other will suffice. This means that juridical universalism without some defense of moral universalism is incoherent. However, these are not relationships of "entailment." Moral universalism does not *entail or dictate* a specific *list of human rights* beyond the protection of the communicative freedom of the person;

nor does justificatory universalism do so. But without the recognition of such communicative freedom, the enterprise of justification itself is meaningless. Philosophical differences will still persist in articulating the content of such recognition. My position is distinctive in interpreting such communicative freedom in relation to the "right to have rights."

Let me further clarify my claims concerning entailment relations between moral, legal, and justificatory universalisms. I am not engaging in some search for indubitable foundations, for a solid and stable ground upon which to build a full-fledged theory of human rights. We can think of foundationalism as an inverted pyramid: a single point at the foundation and a top which fans out into an expanding triangle. There have been devastating philosophical criticisms of such projects, beginning with Hegel's *Phenomenology of Spirit*, extending to the work of American pragmatists, such as Charles Sanders Peirce and John Dewey, and most recently as carried out by Wilfred Sellars, Robert Brandom, and John McDowell. I take this critique and the repudiation of philosophical foundationalism to be philosophically justified and proceed on this assumption without providing further independent arguments.[22]

In this chapter, I practice a form of "presuppositional analysis." Any justification of human rights, I contend, will presuppose some conception of human agency, of human needs, of human reason, as well as making some assumptions about the characteristic of our socio-political world. While Alan Gewirth and James Griffin[23] build their justification of human rights upon a conception of human agency, the approach to human rights initiated by John Rawls, with his project of developing "public reason," presupposes that the late-modern political world is characterized by inevitable pluralisms and burdens of judgment, as well as by the presence of distinct societies such as liberal democracies, decent hierarchical, and burdened societies, along with outlaw states. It is indeed hard to see how else one can proceed but by making some such assumptions.

By engaging in presuppositional analysis, I will attempt to show that communicative freedom is what we must presuppose in any meaningful account of human rights. I will then expand this concept of communicative freedom into an account of human agency. Distinctive differences between my account and those of Griffin's, in particular, will then be visible.

65

Human Rights and the Justification Question

Recall here Alasdair MacIntyre's provocative claim:

> the best reason for asserting so bluntly that there are no such things as rights is indeed precisely of the same type as the best reason we possess for asserting that there are no witches, and the best reason we possess for asserting that there are no unicorns: every attempt to give good reasons for believing that there are such rights has failed.[24]

Echoing Jeremy Bentham's quip that belief in natural rights is "nonsense on stilts,"[25] MacIntyre gives voice to a long tradition of skepticism toward talk of "natural rights," "human rights," or "basic rights." Such criticisms are based on the mistake of identifying human rights with the social imaginary of early bourgeois thinkers.[26] Historically, the widespread use of the terms "property" and "propriety," to designate rights in general, served to demarcate a sphere of individuals' claims and entitlements and gave them an aspect of inviolability.[27] At the same time this language has marred discussions of rights down to our own days.

We need neither repeat the naturalistic fallacy nor the paradigmatic use of property rights to defend rights claims in general. I will argue that rights claims are of the following sort: "I can justify to you with good reasons that you and I should respect each others' reciprocal claim to act in certain ways and not to act in others, and to enjoy certain resources and services." Some rights claims are about *liberties*, that is, to do or to abstain from doing certain things without anybody else having a moral claim to oblige me to act or to withhold from acting in certain ways. Liberty rights generate duties of forbearance. Other rights claims are about *entitlement to resources*. Such rights, as the right to an elementary school education or to secure neighborhoods, for example, entail obligations on the part of others, whether they be individuals or institutions, to act in certain ways and to provide certain material goods. As Jeremy Waldron observes, such rights issue in "cascading obligations."[28]

For the Kantian morally constructivist tradition, rights claims are not about what *exists*; rather, we ask whether our lives together within, outside, and betwixt polities ought not to be guided by mutually and reciprocally guaranteed immunities, constraints upon actions, and by legitimate access to certain goods and resources. Rights are not about what there *is* but about the kind of world we reasonably *ought* to want to live in.

66

In his *Metaphysics of Morals*, Kant proposed that there is one basic right: "Every action which by itself or by its maxim enables the freedom of each individual's will to co-exist with the freedom of everyone else in accordance with a universal law is *right*" (*gerecht*).[29] Note that Kant's formulation is not about a list of basic rights that is said to precede the will of the republican sovereign. Rather, the Kantian principle establishes how a juridico-civil order can come into existence, which would be in compliance with the moral law of respect for the freedom of each. The Kantian "principle of right," like the natural rights discourse of the tradition, basically states that only that political order can be considered legitimate that is based upon a system of general laws that binds the will of each equally. *Generality*, *formal reciprocity*, and *equality* are features of the "principle of right." Your freedom as a moral being can be restricted only by reasons that would be generally and reciprocally applicable to each. A polity based on the principle of rights respects you as a moral being.

KANT

A discourse-theoretic justification of the principle of right would differ from Kant's in the following ways. Instead of asking what each of us could will without self-contradiction to be a universal law for all, in discourse ethics we ask: which norms and normative institutional arrangements could be considered valid by all those who would be affected if they were participants in special moral argumentations called discourse? (T. A. McCarthy). The emphasis now shifts *from* what each can will to be valid for all via a thought experiment, *to* those justificatory processes through which you and I, in dialogue, must convince each other of the validity of certain norms – by which I mean "general rules of action." You have a fundamental right to justification and "any moral justification of the rights of human beings must be able to redeem discursively the claim to general and reciprocal validity raised by such rights."[30]

D.T

How then can we justify talk of human rights without falling either into the traps of naturalistic fallacy or possessive individualism? My answer is: "In order to be able to justify to you why you and I ought to act in certain ways, I must respect your capacity to agree or disagree with me on the basis of reasons the validity of which you accept or reject. But to respect your capacity to accept or reject reasons the validity of which you may accept or reject means for me to respect your capacity for communicative freedom." I am assuming that *all* human beings who are potential or actual speakers of a natural or symbolic language are capable of communicative freedom, that is, of saying "yes" or "no" to an utterance whose validity claims they

67

comprehend and according to which they can act.[31] Human rights are moral principles that protect the exercise of your communicative freedom and that require embodiment in legal form.[32]

Certainly, the exercise of communicative freedom is an exercise of agency, of formulating what goals and ends we wish to pursue and how to effectuate such pursuits. Unlike agent-centric human rights theories, however, which are still the most commonly subscribed to accounts of human rights, in the discourse-theoretic model, we proceed from a view of the human agent as an individual embedded in contexts of communication as well as interaction. The capacity to formulate goals of action is not prior to the capacity to be able to justify such goals with reasons to others. Reasons for actions are not only grounds which motivate me; they are also accounts of my actions as I project myself as a "doer" unto a social world which I share with others, and through which others recognize me as a person capable of, and responsible for, certain courses of action. Agency and communication are two sides of the same coin: I only know myself as an agent, because I can anticipate being part of a social space in which others recognize me as the initiator of certain deeds and the speaker of certain words for which I must be able to provide an account. But even this process of providing an account is not subsequent or posterior to the formulation of my goals of action. I can view myself as a doer of deeds and speaker of words only insofar as I can formulate an account to myself and of what it is that I wish to do and how to find the right words to express what I mean. The capacity for providing such accounts presupposes an internalization of the standpoint of the other(s) in whose eyes and ears my acts will accomplish something and my words will mean certain things. Being able to take the standpoint of the other is necessary to be able to formulate a coherent account of oneself as an agent – as a doer as well as a narrator. It is the weakness of all agent-centric accounts of human rights that they abstract from the social embeddedness of agency in such shared contexts of speech and action, and instead focus on the isolated agent as the privileged subject for reasoning about rights.[33]

First and foremost, as a moral being capable of communicative freedom you have a fundamental *right to have rights*. In order to exercise communicative freedom, your capacity for embedded agency needs to be respected. You need to be recognized as a member of an organized human community in which your words and acts situate you within a social space of interaction and communication. You have a "right," that is, a moral claim to be recognized by others as

68

"a rights-bearing person," entitled to a legally instituted schedule of rights.[34] Others can only constrain your freedom as a moral being through reasons that satisfy the conditions of formality, generality, and reciprocity for all.

The right to have rights further involves the acknowledgment of your identity as a generalized as well as a concrete other.[35] If I recognize you as a being entitled to rights only because you are like me, then I deny your fundamental individuality which makes you different. If I refuse to recognize you as a being entitled to rights because you are so other than me, then I deny our common humanity.

The standpoint of the "generalized other" requires us to view each and every individual as a being entitled to the same rights and duties we would want to ascribe to ourselves. In assuming this standpoint, we abstract from the individuality and the concrete identity of the other. We assume that the other, like ourselves, is a being who has concrete needs, desires, and affects, but what constitutes his or her moral dignity is not what differentiates us from each other, but rather what we, as speaking and acting and embodied beings, have in common. Our relation to the other is governed by the norms of *formal equality and reciprocity*: each is entitled to expect from us what we can expect from him or from her. In treating you in accordance with these norms, I confirm in your person the rights of humanity and I have a legitimate claim that you will do the same in relation to me.

The standpoint of the "concrete other," by contrast, requires us to view each and every being as an individual with an affective-emotional constitution, concrete history, and individual as well as collective identity, and in many cases as having more than one such collective identity. In assuming this standpoint, we bracket what constitutes our commonality and focus on individuality. Our relation to the other is governed by the norms of *equity* and *complementary reciprocity*. Our differences in this case complement rather than exclude one another. In treating you in accordance with these norms, I confirm not only your humanity but your human individuality. If the standpoint of the generalized other expresses the norm of respect, that of the concrete other anticipates experiences of altruism and solidarity.

Concepts of the generalized and the concrete other do not describe human nature; rather, they are phenomenological accounts of human experience. Admittedly, the standpoint of the generalized other, in the very universalistic form that I have given to it, presupposes the egalitarian experiences of modernity. I am not maintaining, in some Hegelian fashion, that these views are the necessary end products of the course of history. Rather, they are contestable, fraught, and fragile experiences through which the standpoint of "generalized other," as extending to all of humanity, becomes a practical possibility but certainly not a political actuality.

Such reciprocal recognition of each other as beings who have the right to have rights involves political struggles, social movements, and learning processes within and across classes, genders, nations, ethnic groups, and religious faiths. Universalism does not consist in an essence or human nature that we are all said to have or to possess, but rather in experiences of establishing commonality across diversity, conflict, divide, and struggle. Universalism is an aspiration, a moral goal to strive for; it is not a fact, a description of the way the world is.[36]

Let me emphasize how this justification of human rights through a discourse-theoretic account of communicative freedom differs from others. In the first place, the justification of human rights is viewed as a dialogic practice and is not mired in the metaphysics of natural rights theories or possessive individualist selves. This justification of human rights also differs from *agent-relative* accounts, because in such accounts human rights are viewed as enabling conditions of the exercise of agency, as described in some fashion. This then leaves unanswered the question why the claim that some condition or another is essential to the exercise of *your* agency should impose a moral obligation upon *me* to respect that claim. By contrast, in the discourse model, we argue that my recognition of *your* right to have rights is the very precondition for you to be able to contest or accept *my* claim to rights in the first place. *My* agent-specific needs can serve as a justification for *you* only if I presuppose that *your* agent-specific needs can likewise serve as a justification for *me*. And this means that you and I have recognized each other's right to have rights.

namaste and all···

Skepticism Toward Discourse-Theoretic Justifications

Does not this discourse-theoretic justification of human rights prove either too much or too little? Are not my formulations dependent upon some understanding of what constitutes "good reasons" in discourses? And, surely, the contextualist will continue, such shared understandings can hardly be non-controversial, so your justification strategy is mired in circularity. It presupposes an understanding of "good reasons," such as to preclude moral points of view incompatible with the non-recognition of communicative freedom. To face this serious objection, let me first observe that discourses, to be distinguished from bargaining, cajoling, brainwashing, or coercive manipulation, are dependent upon certain formal conditions of conversation: these are the *equality* of each conversation partner to partake in as well as initiate communication, their *symmetrical* entitlement to speech acts, and *reciprocity* of communicative roles – each can question and answer, bring new items to the agenda, and initiate reflection about the rules of discourse itself. These formal preconditions, which themselves require reinterpretation within the discursive process, impose certain *necessary* constraints upon the *kinds of reasons* that will prove acceptable within discourses, but they *never can*, nor should they be required to, provide *sufficient* grounds for what constitute good reasons. Indeed there is a circularity here, but this is not a vicious circle. It is the hermeneutic circularity of practical reason which Aristotle had noted long ago in his *Ethics* to be an essential feature of all reasoning in morals and politics: we always already have to assume some understanding of equality, reciprocity, and symmetry in order to be able to frame the discourse model in the first place, but each of these normative terms are then open to reflexive justification or recursive validation within the discourse itself. Such recursive validation of the preconditions of discourse has been misunderstood by many as indicating a vicious circle. These charges ignore the hermeneutical structure of practical reason and wish to have practical reason proceed as if it were theoretical reason, that is, from uncontested first premises.

This limitation of the range of what can or cannot count as good reasons in terms of the necessary conditions of recursively validated discursive structures will still not convince some;[37] nevertheless, let me emphasize that communicative freedom is what makes the practice of normative justification at all possible, for if human beings cannot assent to or reject each others' claims on the basis of reasons the validity of which they can evaluate, then there can be no justificatory enterprise at all. Even if the reasons we invoke in such a practice are utilitarian or Kantian, Nietzschean, or Christian, in doing so we must always already presuppose the capacity of our conversation partner to assent or dissent from our claims on the basis of reasons the validity of which she comprehends. "Justificatory universalism" is at the heart of reason as a reason-giving enterprise and so is the recognition of the other as a being capable of communicative freedom and of the right to have rights.

The motivation for moral discourses arises when the certitudes of our life-worlds break down through conflict, dissent, and disagreement, when there is conflict as well as contention, misery as well as lack of solidarity. Discourses are not simply hypothetical thought experiments or conversation chambers that we can choose to enter into or exit at will; they are reflexive dialogues the need for which emerges out of the very real problems of our life-worlds. It is when everyday certitudes disappear that we assume the attitudes of reflective and critical distance, which are essential for discourses. In this sense, Husserl is right: there is an intrinsic connection between the commitment to reason as a life-form founded on contingent practices of reason-giving and justification, and the view of the human person as a free being entitled to respect.

There is an unbreakable bond, then, between reason understood as a justificatory enterprise, as reason-giving, and the justification of human rights. Justificatory universalism presupposes moral universalism – the respect for the other as a being capable of communicative freedom. I am not grounding the claim that human beings *ought* to be considered as beings entitled to rights upon their rationality, which, as we know, the natural law tradition considered to be an expression of the divine in human beings. Rather, I have argued that the right to have rights, and the moral right of the human being to be considered as a being entitled to juridico-civil rights, are enabling conditions of the exercise of communicative freedom. This communicative freedom, in turn, is presupposed by every justificatory process.

Human rights and the various public law documents in our world define both a *minimum* to be maintained and a *maximum* to be aspired to. There will always be debate about their meaning as well as their comprehensiveness; therefore, any list we provide of them is necessarily incomplete. New moral, political, and cultural struggles will bring forth rights to be added to the list and to extend the maximum that humans can aspire to. For example, technological developments in human cloning, gene therapy, and gene manipulation are likely to lead to some basic rights protecting human beings' biological and species integrity in the near future.[38] Precisely because they emerge out of such struggles and learning processes, human rights documents cannot simply embody an "overlapping consensus" or "minimum conditions of legitimacy"; they give voice to the aspirations of a profoundly divided humanity by setting "a common standard of achievement for all peoples and all nations" (Universal Declaration, Preamble).

72

How can one make the transition from these highly abstract and formal considerations of the right to have rights to the specific rights regimes, legal systems, charters, and conventions of existing polities? What about the legal form of human rights?[39] In jurisprudence as well as moral philosophy there have long been two dominant positions in response to this question: natural rights vs. legal positivism. The natural rights position can count Aristotle, the Stoics and St Thomas Aquinas, the social contract theorists of modernity, such as Locke and Rousseau, as well as Leo Strauss, among its advocates. They argue that no political or legal order can be considered legitimate that does not subscribe to, respect, or enshrine in its constitution certain rights which human beings are entitled *qua* human beings and which are thus unalterable and unrescindable. In the language of modern constitutionalism, these rights are "entrenched."

Legal positivism, a complex position which some trace to the Sophists such as Thrasymachus, to Machiavelli, to H. L. A. Hart as well as Carl Schmitt, contends that legal systems are not susceptible to judgments based on "extra-legal" standards of articulation – whether these be moral, metaphysical, naturalistic, or scientific. Any legal system, insofar as it is a coherent articulation of norms, carries within itself its own standards of judgment, evaluation, subordination, and subsumption – in short, its own rules of recognition, which make it function as the legal system that it is. The idea of entrenched norms, such as natural rights are considered to be, and which are supposed to precede any legal system, is unacceptable from this point of view.

The language of human rights straddles this divide. The discourse of democracies, in particular, is necessarily caught in the tension generated by the context- and community-transcending validity dimension of human rights, on the one hand, and the historically formed, culturally generated, and socially shaped codifications and legislation of existing juridico-civil communities, on the other. The point is not to deny this tension by embracing only one or another of these moral alternatives but to negotiate their interdependence, by resituating or reiterating the universal in concrete contexts. This is a project I have called "interactive universalism" in *Situating the Self* and "democratic iterations" in subsequent works.[40] It is around the negotiation of the unity and diversity of human rights, that is, the articulation of the relation between their *moral core* and their *legal form*, that the most salient differences between my approach and other contemporary positions will become apparent.[41]

In the following chapters, I will develop a strategy for going beyond this long-standing opposition of natural rights theories and legal positivism by distinguishing between "the principle of rights" and "the schedule of rights."[42] Basic human rights, resting on the moral principle of the communicative freedom of the person, are also legal rights, that is, rights that require embodiment and instantiation in a specific legal framework. The principle of rights is realized in a duly constituted order of the rule of law which views all citizens and residents as individuals entitled to equal protection of the law and to a schedule of rights, enumerated often in the form of bills of rights and declarations of rights. As Ronald Dworkin has observed, human rights straddle that line between morality and justice; they enable us to judge the legitimacy of law.[43]

But how is this schedule of rights to be determined? There are actually two issues here: first, as I will discuss below, there are some rights theories that consider their *juridification* to be irrelevant or secondary (Amartya Sen). The communicative model of rights developed here differs from these positions. Second, there are attempts to proceed from a philosophical view of human nature or agency to a *specific* schedule of rights, and to argue that any legitimate legal and political order would need to respect such rights (Martha Nussbaum). As distinguished from Nussbaum's, my position is that the legal form of human rights can present legitimate variations in juridical and constitutional interpretations and contextualizations, provided that these variations result from the exercise of public autonomy through structures of self-governance. Without self-governance, human rights remain hollow. There is an intrinsic, and not merely contingent, connection between human rights and democratic self-determination.[44] The principle of rights binds the will of the democratic sovereign because the equality of all under the law must be recognized for self-government to be a meaningful practice at all. Once this democratic equality of law-giving citizens is presupposed, then the schedule of rights in each polity can be determined by the discursive articulation of legislative processes. Unlike in natural rights theories, therefore, it is not assumed that rights are "pre-political" claims of individuals, sitting or standing outside polities, so to speak. But nor do I assume that the legal system can be governed by its internal normative standards alone; democratic legitimacy cannot be reduced to mere legality. Democratic legitimacy derives from the institutions and channels of discursive justification circulating in all spheres of society and through which the people can understand themselves as law-giving as well as law-obeying consociates. Their communicative right to have rights is fully realized only when they are viewed as moral and political persons standing under laws of which they are authors as well as subjects. I will characterize processes of interplay between democratic will- and opinion-formation, on the one hand, and constitutional principles and international law, on the other hand, as "democratic iterations." Through democratic iterations, citizens articulate the specific content of their schedule of rights, as well as making these rights their very own. To develop this communicative model of the right to have rights and the centrality of democratic iterations will be the task of the next three chapters.

Human Rights and Global Democratic Iterations

In 1935, as Husserl surveyed the intellectual-political landscape of a Europe hurtling toward another world war, the fragile institution of the League of Nations was in decay, owing to, among other things, the hypocrisies created by the various minority and statelessness treaties that had accompanied the demise of the Austro-Hungarian, Russian, and Ottoman Empires, as well as the German Kaiserreich. For Husserl, faith in Western reason, through force, had to replace the expectation that institutional structures could embody the principles of reason and freedom, of peace and justice, in more tangible fashion. Yet the 1948 Universal Declaration, and the era of human rights that has followed it, reflect the moral learning experiences not only of Western humanity but of humanity at large. The world wars were fought not only in the European continent but also in the colonies, in Africa and Asia. The national liberation and anti-colonization struggles of the post-World War II period, in turn, inspired principles of self-determination. The public law documents of our world are distillations of such collective struggles, as well as of collective learning processes. It may be too utopian to name them steps toward a "world constitution," but they are more than mere treaties among states. They are global public law documents which, along with many other developments in the domain of *lex mercatoria*, are altering the terrain of the international domain. They are constituent elements of a global and not merely international civil society. In this global civil society, individuals are rights-bearing not only in virtue of their citizenship within states but in virtue of their humanity *simpliciter*. Although states remain the most powerful actors, the range of their legitimate and lawful activity is increasingly limited. We need to rethink the law of peoples against the background of this newly emergent and fragile global civil society, which is always being threatened by war, violence, and military intervention. The shrinking world public sphere, while increasing contact across cultures, also creates bewilderment as to how to explain deep divergences.

There is a fundamental relationship between complex cultural dialogues[45] taking place among peoples in a global civil society and processes of democratic iteration. Only when members of a society can engage in free and unrestrained dialogue about their collective identity in free public spheres can they develop narratives of self-identification, which unfold into fluid and creative reappropriations of their own traditions. By contrast, totalizing discourses about "our culture" vs "theirs" inhibit the free flow of individual and collective cultural narratives because these might produce subversive effects, by destabilizing the legitimizing collectivities in whose name power is exercised. Cultures are narratively constituted through contentious accounts of self–other differentiations. The other is not outside our culture, but constitutive of it. Intercultural conversations and intracultural ones are deeply intertwined.

Human rights are also enabling conditions, in the legal and political senses, of "uncoerced democratic iterations" among the peoples and cultures of the world. Such iterations cannot be understood as agreements frozen in time and space, but only as a continuing conversation, a complex dialogue, which challenges the assumption of completeness of each culture, by making it possible for its members to look at themselves from the perspectives of others. Since the goal is not an irreversible agreement but the enlargement of perspectives, the consequence of such dialogues is to educate us to the range of acceptable variation in the interpretation and contextualization of human rights. This calls for a broadening of our understanding of the unity and diversity of human rights on a global scale.

— 5 —

IS THERE A HUMAN RIGHT TO DEMOCRACY?
Beyond Interventionism and Indifference

Minimalism About Human Rights?

In a recent article, Joshua Cohen has helpfully distinguished among two kinds of "minimalism about human rights." The first is "substantive," the second, "justificatory" minimalism.[1] *Substantive* minimalism concerns the content of human rights, and is "more broadly, about norms of global justice," and limits human rights to what was once known as "negative liberty." Michael Ignatieff's *Human Rights as Politics and Idolatry*,[2] but also Thomas Nagel's "The Problem of Global Justice" may be considered prime examples of this position.[3] "Justificatory minimalism," by contrast, is about how to present "a conception of human rights, as an essential element of a conception of global justice for an ethically pluralistic world – as a basic feature of . . . 'global public reason'."[4]

This is an important distinction. The attractiveness of "justificatory minimalism" flows out of a desire to find an overlapping consensus in the international domain that would be based not on comprehensive worldviews and doctrines that are often exclusionary or sectarian in outlook; rather, such a global overlapping consensus would need to be "free standing" in Rawlsian language, and that means justifiable in terms of general public political principles. In a world

This chapter is a much revised version of the 2007 Lindley Lecture delivered at the University of Kansas and published under the same title by the university in 2008. I thank David Alvarez Garcia for discussions concerning Joshua Cohen's recent work on Rawls and human rights.

77

where the concept of human rights has been much used and abused to justify all sorts of political actions and interventions, such caution is certainly welcome. A free-standing global overlapping consensus is intended to enhance the prospects of world peace by assuring that the terms of such an understanding would be acceptable to all peoples on the basis of reasons that they could endorse from within their particular worldview, religious outlook, and the like.

Yet this laudable concern with liberal toleration and peaceful coexistence can also lead to liberal indifference, and, even more so, to an unjustified toleration for the world's repressive regimes such as many "decent, hierarchical peoples" (Rawls) may be and often are. Joshua Cohen's position vis-à-vis this implication of Rawls's work is complex. Unlike Rawls, Cohen argues that "any reasonable conception of collective self-determination that is consistent with the fundamental value of membership and inclusion, will . . . require some process of interest representation and official accountability, even if not equal political rights for all."[5] In other words, even if the scope of representation and accountability defended by Cohen goes beyond the "consultative hierarchy" considered sufficient by Rawls, Cohen still considers the recognition of *equal* political rights not to be necessary for collective self-determination to be satisfied. How plausible is this limitation? How cogently can one distinguish "interest representation" and "official accountability" from democratic equality? Why compromise on "equal political rights for all"?[6]

As I have argued in the previous chapter, I wish to shift both the *justification strategy* and the derivation of the *content* of human rights away from *minimalist* concerns toward a more robust understanding of human rights in terms of the right to have rights. I have defended a discourse-theoretic justification which seeks to synthesize the insights of discourse ethics with the Arendtian "right to have rights," thereby hoping to point the way toward a fuller defense of human rights within a global justice context.[7]

Is the discourse-theoretic account really independent of strong assumptions about human nature and rationality in its conception of human rights?[8] Whereas defenders of a Rawlsian approach may argue that my mode of proceeding amounts to justifying human rights in the light of a comprehensive moral doctrine, that is, discourse ethics, others such as Martha Nussbaum and Amartya Sen would disagree with my insistence that human rights, although they articulate moral principles, must assume legal form as well. This chapter is dedicated to considering these criticisms.

I begin with a sharper delineation between a discourse ethics-based justification strategy and the approaches of Nussbaum and Sen; I then argue that Cohen's claim that there is no human right to democracy is indefensible and self-contradictory.

Human Rights: Moral Claims and Legal Form

Martha Nussbaum suggests that a *non-parochial* view of human rights, while it may not be endorsed by all conventional moralities, may find favor in the eyes of main conceptions of *political and economic justice* in the world: understood thusly, human rights would constitute the core of a *political* rather than *moral* overlapping consensus.[9] Nevertheless, Nussbaum's method of philosophical deduction, which grounds rights concepts all too narrowly in a philosophical anthropology of human capabilities, is problematic. No distinction is made in her account between rights as "moral principles" and rights as "legal entitlements," on the one hand, and "the principle of rights" and "the schedule of rights," on the other.

To clarify: in my view, rights articulate moral claims on behalf of persons, and even on behalf of non-human beings such as animals and the environment that can be deeply and irretrievably affected by our actions. Although to raise a moral rights claim puts pressure on political and legislative institutions to generate a justiciable legal entitlement, not all such rights claims result in specific legal entitlements. For example, to speak of the rights of endangered species is a moral claim that can eventually be translated into a legal entitlement. *Whether* this takes the form of forbidding whaling off the coast of Japan or instituting positive measures, such as to protect the Gold Eagle in the United States, is an open question to be decided by democratic peoples. Moral rights do not directly dictate the specific content of legal entitlements. This is a point which is blurred in Nussbaum's account.

The distinction between the "principle of right" and the "schedule of rights" is related to the differentiation between the moral form of rights and their legal content, but is <u>not identical</u> with it. When a person's right to have rights is recognized in a duly constituted regime of the rule of law through the acknowledgment of that person as a member,[10] then the "principle of right" is acknowledged; but this leaves open the question as to *what level of variation* in the enumeration, content, and interpretation of rights is permissible among different "schedules of rights." Many legislatures, which we would consider legitimate by widely shared standards of democratic authorization, transparency, and public accountability, for example, can nevertheless proceed from a different schedule of rights. By "permissible," here I mean normatively defensible.[11] Nussbaum envisages a one-to-one correspondence between a philosophically derived list of human rights, based upon her moral theory of human capabilities, and the legal enactments of specific legislatures. She thereby neglects how legitimate variations in the interpretation, contextualization, and application of human rights can emerge across self-governing polities.[12]

In "Elements of a Theory of Human Rights," Amartya Sen criticizes Nussbaum's attempt to identify an "overarching 'list of capabilities'," on the grounds that such a "canonical list," as well as the weight to be attributed to the various items on this list, cannot be chosen without a further specification of context. More importantly, Sen sees in such a procedure "a substantive diminution of the domain of public reasoning."[13] Sen wishes to consider human rights as "primarily ethical demands," which relate to the "significance of the freedoms that form the subject matter of these rights" (ibid.). Although he refrains from an exhaustive listing of these freedoms himself, for Sen freedoms are actualizations of capabilities, both in the sense of opportunities and also of processes requisite for such capabilities to unfold. "Rather, freedom, in the form of capability, concentrates on the *opportunity* to achieve combinations of functionings," he writes (ibid.: 334).

By situating human rights so centrally within an *ethical* theory of freedom and capabilities in this early article, Sen disregards the political history of rights which were always closely tied to claims to legitimacy and just rule. Rights are not simply about strong moral entitlements which accrue to individuals; they are also claims to justice and legitimacy which enframe our collective existence as well. We cannot simply reduce rights to the language of moral correctness. Violating a right is different from inflicting a moral harm on a person. We can do the latter, that is, inflict moral harm on a person, without engaging in the former, that is, the violation of their rights; certainly, some violations of rights, but not all, are also forms of moral harm. For example, by humiliating you in front of your family, friends, and your loved ones, I inflict moral harm upon your dignity as a person; but I have not thereby violated your "human right to dignity," which I would be doing if I were to subject you to torture and other forms of "cruel and unusual punishment." All violations of basic human

80

rights, by contrast, that impinge upon the communicative freedom of the person also inflict moral harms. Thus, if I hinder you from exercising your capacity to express your opinion freely within the boundaries set by the law, then I have not only violated your right to freedom of expression, but I have also harmed your moral capacity as a person capable of communicative freedom to engage in dialogue with others. I do not see, from Sen's account in "Elements of a Theory of Human Rights," that we can make such necessary distinctions between "moral harm" on the one hand and "rights violations" on the other.

In his magisterial later work, *The Idea of Justice*, Sen is more sensitive to the matter of the juridification of rights and their central significance in disputes about political legitimacy.[14] He endorses H. L. A. Hart's view against Bentham's narrow dismissal of rights as "nonsense on stilts" (see p. 228 below). Sen writes:

> Whereas Bentham saw rights as a "child of law", Hart takes the view of seeing human rights as, in effect, *parents of law*: they motivate specific legislation . . . Hart is clearly right – there can be little doubt that the idea of moral rights can serve, and has often served in practice, as the basis of new legislation.[15]

But Sen contends that if human rights are "seen as powerful moral claims," then there can be different routes in promoting and realizing them. Formal legislation is only one way among many, and many human rights may be best realized not through the legislative route at all.[16]

While it is hard to disagree with these eminently reasonable claims, I sense that there is still a confusion in Sen's account of human rights. Sen writes of "the ethical importance of a stammerer's liberty not to be slighted or ridiculed in public meetings" as a demand that would not be a good subject of punitive legislations, but that should be protected "through the influence of education and public discussion on civility and social conduct." But what kind of a human right of the stammering individual is being violated in this case: certainly the right not to be discriminated against on account of a disability and not to be coerced and abused because of such disability. But is there a "human right" against being humiliated in public through slight or ridicule? Would it not be more appropriate rather to name this a negative moral duty, that is, a duty not to violate the dignity of another human being by subjecting them to disrespect and ridicule? In what sense is there a "human right" *not to be humiliated in public*

81

or *in private* for that matter? Is this not a matter of a moral duty we owe to others of respecting them (and ourselves); a moral duty which can only be translated into the language of human rights when some justiciable violation of human equality, dignity, or worth occurs? Again, what are the rules and procedures for such transition or translation from moral duties to justiciable rights claims? Sen's concept of human rights, defined as "ethical claims constitutively linked with the importance of human freedom," ignores these distinctions.[17]

The lack of a clear distinction between rights as moral claims and their legal form is common to both Nussbaum's and Sen's approaches for different reasons. In this respect the discourse-theoretic justification of rights differs from both.

Discourse-Theory of Human Rights and the Rawlsian Objection

What about the Rawlsian argument, then, that the discourse-theoretic justification presented above is by no means a minimalist one and that in fact it presupposes a comprehensive moral theory? Let us recall that Rawls's principal motivation in limiting the list of human rights to certain essentials is to formulate a "political conception" of rights that *would* or *could* be endorsed by all the known and recognized moral, religious, scientific, and so on comprehensive worldviews in the global community. If the core of political liberalism is to formulate political conceptions of rights and justice that citizens within a national community would or could endorse despite their widely divergent comprehensive views, analogously, the core of public reason on a global scale is to formulate a "minimalist conception of human rights," which would or could be endorsed by peoples subscribing to divergent religious and moral traditions. Joshua Cohen spells this out clearly: "Justificatory minimalism is animated by an acknowledgment of pluralism and embrace of toleration. It aspires to present a conception of human rights without itself connecting that conception to a particular ethical or religious outlook."[18]

Is a discourse-theoretical approach open to the objection that it represents a narrow ethical outlook? I believe not, but there will be several steps to this answer: some methodological and some substantive. First, there is a methodological divide between the Rawlsian and discourse-theoretic approaches about the use of counterfactual thought experiments and/or dialogue situations. The justification strategy proposed by the discourse-theoretical approach respects the pluralism of worldviews not by counterfactually imagining, let us say, what a Buddhist and a Catholic may hypothetically agree to as construed by the theorist, but by framing and encouraging a *real rather than a virtual dialogue* between a Buddhist and a Catholic person such that a reasonable agreement between them may result. The emphasis in discourse ethics is on the constraints necessary for the dialogic procedure to function, which admittedly ought to be "thin" enough not to be identifiable with any particular moral or religious worldview and yet "thick" enough to guide the conversation toward rationally justifiable agreement, even if such agreement is to be understood as a regulative principle and not as an actual state of affairs. This is at least my aspiration in defending discourse-ethics. Discourse ethics is intimately related to political and institutional practices of communication, justification, contestation, and further argumentation.

There is a further methodological problem in the Rawls-Cohen approach: When the constituent addressees of global public reason are identified as worldviews or peoples rather than as individuals, what results is a "methodological holism." The premises behind such holism are as follows: (i) cultures are clearly delineable wholes; (ii) cultures are congruent with population groups and a non-contested description of the culture of a human group, beyond multiple narratives, is possible; (iii) even if cultures and groups do not stand in one-to-one correspondence, and even if there is more than one culture within a human group and more than one group that may possess the same cultural traits, this poses no problem for politics or policy. In the words of Terence Turner, such a view "risks overemphasizing the internal homogeneity of cultures in terms that potentially legitimize repressive demands for communal conformity; and by treating cultures as badges of group identity, it tends to fetishize them in ways that put them beyond the reach of critical analysis."[19]

A Rawlsian would argue that without such theoretical simplification the representation of these positions would be overly complex; after all, political philosophy is concerned with "ideal," not with "non-ideal" theory. But from the standpoint of social science or social theory, the methodological assumptions guiding such ideal constructions are not neutral. The Rawlsian position ends up by abstracting from the *lived history* of traditions and worldviews that are themselves dominated by frequent clashes of interpretation to such a radical extent that points of overlap between such worldviews and the liberal tradition, and among these worldviews themselves, are underestimated.[20] Rawls has made it amply clear that in proceeding in such fashion he also wishes to avoid normative cosmopolitanism by insisting that peoples, construed along idealized devices of representation and not individuals, are the agents of justice in a global context.

To understand how wrong-headed this line of argumentation is, particularly in an international context, take a country like Turkey as an example: close to 99 percent of the population of Turkey are Muslim. If we wished to represent this country in terms of the religious beliefs of its citizens, we would be completely mistaken. Much like the rest of the world, since the sixteenth and seventeenth centuries, Ottoman Turkey has encountered modernity, and has struggled with the compatibility of Islam and modernity, in a process which has left neither the Turkish understanding of modernity nor that of the Turkish understanding of Islam unchanged. Many arguments about human rights, equality, and democratic representation have been part of the political vocabulary of reform and transformation since at least the early nineteenth century. How can a Rawlsian methodology account for the complex coexistence of clashing worldviews and their transformations within the same country? (See also chapter 9 below on the "scarf affair.")

In case it is argued that Turkey is a special case because of its close and sustained encounter with the West for many centuries, consider Malaysia: at the present an authoritarian form of Islamic orthodoxy rules in this country. But Malaysian history exhibits Buddhist and Confucian as well as forms of liberal secular thinking. These traditions often constitute resources for dissidents to draw upon in opposing the regime. How is this complex history to be represented in a Rawlsian law of peoples? I fear that it is not represented at all. The assumption that, in reasoning about global human rights, the relevant units are comprehensive worldviews simply reduces peoples and their histories to a holistic counterfactual, which then results in the flattening out of the complex history of discourses and contestations within and among peoples.

Far from exhibiting liberal tolerance, this approach displays liberal ignorance. These methodological assumptions reinforce a liberal-nationalist understanding of the world of international relations. They lead us to assume that individuals from other cultures and traditions have not entertained similar kind of debates and concerns about human rights, justice, and equality throughout their histories, as we have in ours. It ignores thereby complex cultural conversations that have taken place throughout human history, and the fact that secular

Enlightenment liberal ideas have themselves become a part of the cultural discourse of many peoples and traditions of the world since their inception in Western modernity. By not giving this complex conversation its due, the minimalist approach preaches liberal tolerance but results in liberal indifference.

Democracy as a Human Right

In "Is There a Human Right to Democracy?" Joshua Cohen concludes in the negative. For him, a philosophical account of human rights considers these as "entitlements that serve to ensure the bases of membership."[21] "Just membership," in his account, is distinct from "mere membership"; while *just* membership does entail democratic self-government, *mere* membership does not.[22] According to Cohen:

> the central feature of the normative notion of membership is that a person's good is to be taken into account by the political society's basic institutions: to be treated as a member is to have one's good given due consideration, both in the process of arriving at authoritative collective decisions and in the content of those decisions.[23]

A society is self-determining if its political arrangements satisfy three conditions: political decisions result from and are accountable to a process in which everyone's interests are represented; there are rights of dissent for all; and public officials justify their decisions in terms of a widely held notion of the common good.[24]

Yet if, as Cohen admits, to have one's good to "be given due consideration" entails freedom of opposition and dissent, and if membership is not simply a matter of benevolent despotism but of proper representation, how can the right of dissent and opposition be protected in the absence of democratic institutions? What does *decent* representation mean without ongoing institutions of representation? Without an enduring commitment to the independence of institutions which express opinions about the good of the members of a community, that itself may or may not be consonant with that of the regime or of the majority, how can Cohen's demanding conception of membership be satisfied? Cohen does not provide a single empirical example of what such a regime might look like. Of course, in normative argumentation he is not required to do so. But we do not find the equivalent of the Rawlsian example of "Kazanistan" in Cohen's work. And indeed we cannot, for Cohen's understanding of membership is more ambitious than Rawls's and it is harder for him to find plausible socio-historical and cultural examples to satisfy this theoretical construction. Cohen's normative account of membership inevitably leads him to endorse more robust forms of self-government than he is willing to admit; his own account sets him on the slippery slope toward democratic self-governance whether through representative or more participatory forms of institutions.

Cohen is aware of this slippery slope and boldly asserts that since democracy involves a rigorous commitment to egalitarianism, and since such egalitarianism cannot be made compatible with major moral and religious worldviews such as Confucianism, Islam, Buddhism, and so on, a *human* right to democracy cannot be an aspect of a global conception of justice. Its defense is not "free-standing" but involves recourse to controversial individualistic and egalitarian moral assumptions. He asks:

> Is the equal right to participate that I have associated with democracy a human right? And is the democratic conception of persons as free and equal . . . a plausible component of a conception of human rights comprised within global public reason? We know that the conception of persons as free and equal is not universally accepted by different ethical and religious outlooks.[25]

As I have argued, however, this appeal to what other traditions and worldviews may or may not consent to, would or would not consider acceptable, is itself based upon a faulty device of representation and a thin methodology. It repeats the Rawlsian mistake that in reasoning about such matters we must proceed from idealized and ahistorical constructions of moral and religious worldviews and ignore the messy history of concrete collectivities in whose lives such worldviews always clash, compete, and dialogue with one another. It is of course a poignant historical irony that, just as philosophers had built arguments as to why there could not be a universal human right to democracy, in 2007, Buddhist monks in Myanmar and Tibet abandoned their monasteries and risked death, torture, and reprisals by challenging the oppressive Burmese and Chinese regimes on behalf of human rights and democracy. Contrary also to nearly a decade of speculation since the events of September 11, 2001, about the incompatibility of Islam and democracy, in the spring of 2011 countries such as Egypt, Libya, and Tunisia erupted with demands to end authoritarian rule, establish respect for human rights, hold free parliamentary elections, and so on.[26]

In *The Idea of Human Rights*, Charles Beitz also considers Joshua Cohen's claims. I will return to Beitz's general argument in greater detail below. Regarding Cohen's arguments, Beitz notes that there are several respects in which self-determining but non-democratic societies may entail certain kinds of disadvantages, even dangers, for their citizens. All individual interests may not be given equal weight and "higher offices may be restricted to members of an established church, and representatives of the dominant group may have preferred access to the public arena."[27] Furthermore, even if "The idea of self-determination requires that political decisions be responsive to people's interests . . . it is not inherent that this responsiveness should be guaranteed through fixed procedures that harness outcomes to expressions of individual preferences" (183). But, if this is so, then paternalism or benevolent despotism may not be excluded, since the idea of a shared common good and people's interests may be interpreted by authorities in such hierarchical societies without much heed to the views of minority ethnic or religious groups or other dissenters.

Beitz's agreement with Cohen's position, therefore, is not a wholehearted one but he is nevertheless led to it:

> Since human rights must be both universal and action-guiding, the proper inference from the fact that there are circumstances in which the absence of democratic institutions would not generate (even *pro tanto*) reasons for outside agents to act is that the doctrines of human rights should not embrace such a right.[28]

This is a curious claim. Is the absence of plausible grounds to justify outside interference itself sufficient to deny that a human right to democracy exists even if no specific agent is obligated to intervene? Is intervention the only reasonable and even obligatory response in such cases? Furthermore, does it matter who is intervening, by what means, and on whose behalf?[29] More importantly, aren't prudential considerations of political morality being unduly employed in this context to deny a right as significant as that of democratic self-governance?[30]

One further and important distinction between my position and those of Nussbaum, Sen, and Cohen is the sharp differentiation they each make between human rights as "urgent requirements of political morality," in Cohen's words,[31] whose "force does not depend on their expression in enforceable law," and my insistence that human rights must assume legal form. I wish to argue that human rights embody moral principles which need contextualization and specification in the form of legal norms. How is this legal content is to be shaped?

Self-Government and the Range of Rights

Let us return to the question of the legitimate range of rights: if we agree on the centrality of a principle such as "freedom of religious expression," are we committed to accepting that minority religions are entitled to rights to public expression equally with the majority, as I would argue, or can we maintain that freedom of religious expression is compatible with some reasonable restrictions upon its exercise, as Rawls has claimed? How can we provide a satisfactory answer and from within which set of constraints? It is at this point that the human right to self-government becomes crucial, and why I would claim, contra Rawls and Cohen (and Beitz), that it is a basic human right. *My thesis is that without the right to self-government which is exercised through proper legal and political channels, we cannot justify the range of variation in the content of basic human rights as being legitimate* (see chapter 7 below for a full elucidation of this claim). If the difficulty with Martha Nussbaum's conception of human rights is that no distinction is made between the philosophical account of human rights and their legal embodiment, the weakness of the Rawlsian "minimalist position" about human rights is that one is forced to accept whatever a legal regime stipulates to be the content of human rights as legitimate, as long as such a regime meets certain minimum criteria of being a *decent, well-ordered society*. Among other things, this is compatible with the denial of equal freedom of religion, expression, and association to religious and ethnic minorities, and with gross inequalities in the treatment of women.

Only if the people are viewed not merely as subject to the law, but also as authors of the law, can the contextualization and interpretation of human rights be said to result from public and free processes of democratic opinion and will-formation. Such contextualization, in addition to being subject to the various legal traditions in different countries, attains democratic legitimacy insofar as it is carried out through the interaction of legal and political institutions with free public spaces in civil society. When such rights principles are appropriated by people as their own, they lose their parochialism as well as the suspicion of Western paternalism often associated with them. I call such processes of appropriation "democratic iterations."[32]

Suffice it to say at this point that *democratic legitimacy* reaches back to principles of *normative justification,* though the two are not identical.[33] As I will argue in chapter 7, democratic iterations do not alter conditions of the normative validity of practical discourses that are established independently of them; rather, democratic iterations enable us to judge as *legitimate or illegitimate* processes of opinion and will-formation through which rights claims are contextualized and contested, expanded and revised through actual institutional practices in the light of such criteria. Such criteria of judgment enable us to distinguish a *de facto consensus* from a *rationally motivated* one.

Given then the centrality of the right of democratic self-determination, exercised in and through the free public institutions of civil and political societies, the discourse theorist will concede to Rawlsians that her justification of human rights is not a minimalist one either in the procedural or substantive senses. The values of private and public autonomy play a crucial role in this discourse-theoretic account. We treat each human person as a moral being capable of acting on the basis of reasons the validity of which she has accepted or, as the case may be, rejected; furthermore, democratic self-governance is a confirmation of one's standing as a free and equal being living under laws the legitimacy of which she can always challenge, contest and question. This view expresses a "political" conception of human rights and is not metaphysical. Rather, the very idea of human rights suggests that we are beings capable of private and public autonomy whose interests in such autonomy must be respected.

Human Rights and the Pitfalls of Interventionism

We should free human rights discourse from the interventionist rhetoric that has so often accompanied it in recent times. Undoubtedly, much of the philosophical reticence in defending a human right to democracy is related to the wish to distance oneself from the disastrous foreign policy of the G. W. Bush administration (2001–9), when the language of human rights was deployed as a fig leaf to justify pre-emptive and interventionist foreign policy ambitions.[34]

Nevertheless, in appealing to civil society and the public sphere as the privileged arenas for norm-articulation and democratic iterations, isn't one ignoring the frequent cases of such grave human rights abuses that intervention via the use of military force may be essential to maintain any allegiance to human rights and cosmopolitanism?

Chapter II (7) of the United Nations Charter permits wars of self-defense on the part of members, while Article 51 of the United Nations Charter authorizes military action in the event of an armed attack against a member of an organization such as NATO.[35] Both Articles were appealed to after the 2001 attack on the World Trade Center. Furthermore, the Genocide Convention obliges states to undertake military action such as to prevent genocide, slavery, and ethnic cleansing – provided that the UN Security Council authorizes such actions. As most students of international affairs admit, however, we are now poised on a slippery slope, when judges seem to be creating law, while statesman are clamoring for the need to make new laws in this arena.[36] The grounds for humanitarian intervention are expanding into the principle of "the obligation to protect" (Kofi Annan). But it is all too unclear exactly which parties are responsible for such an obligation to protect. If the United Nations is responsible, then it would be necessary to revise the current practice of considering military intervention on behalf of the United Nations legitimate only when authorized by the permanent members of the Security Council. In such cases, the obligation to protect is often hostage to the veto power of the five permanent members of the council, whose own standing as permanent members goes back to a balance of powers dating from the end of World War II. This situation is hardly adequate to reflect the global realities of our time and the emergence of such powers as Germany, Brazil, India, and Japan to world prominence. These contradictions and institutional flaws are[37] pulling the United Nations to and fro in opposite and confused directions, with no clear resolution in sight.

We have entered uncharted waters in the international arena. On the whole, I am opposed to the creeping interventionism behind the formula of the duty to intervene, placing my hope for as long as possible, and for as long as necessary, in the forces of civil society and civilian organizations to spread cosmopolitan norms and move all societies closer together toward compliance with the Universal Declaration of Human Rights.[38] My commitment to global civil society actors in this arena should not be mistaken for neo-liberal anti-statism. Within the boundaries of existing polities, the state is the principal public actor that still has the responsibility to see to it that human rights norms are both legislated and actualized. However, many states have willingly undertaken to commit themselves to various public human rights documents, with the consequence that they are also subject to evaluations by a range of transnational actors and groups, some of which are set up by the UN treaty bodies and others of which are activist NGOs that see themselves as the principal agents of spreading legal respect for and monitoring compliance with human rights.

When, why, and under what conditions military intervention to stop massive human rights violations is justifiable remains a question in political ethics. By "political ethics," I mean the balancing between intentions and consequences, between an ethics of responsibility and an ethics of conviction (Max Weber). Particularly when states are considered the unique agents of intervention and when intervention means the use of military force, *only* the prevention of genocide, slavery, and ethnic cleansing can justify such acts. Regime change is not justified. For members of a global community there are nevertheless myriad other ways in which to work across borders to spread democracy, civil society, and a free public sphere. The range of activities of global citizens goes far beyond military intervention and the use of force.

As cases of recent interventions, as well as failure to intervene, in Kosovo, Rwanda, Iraq, Darfur, and others prove, the Genocide Convention and the United Nations Charter alone are not adequate for this task in guiding the world community. There is need for a new Law of Humanitarian Interventions which is clearer about the conditions under which intervention by the UN in the affairs of a country is justified. Nevertheless, such cases will continue to confront one with hard choices and will always entail the exercise of political judgment. As Allen Buchanan asked, "is illegal international legal reform" in the international arena possible through unauthorized interventions?[39] Such questions impose upon citizens, leaders, and politicians the "burden of history." I think that philosophy can neither guide us all the way down in such deliberations, nor guarantee that our good intentions will not be destroyed by contingent events and turn into their opposite. Nor should it do so. Nevertheless, as Kant observed,[40] there is a distinction between the "political moralist," who misuses moral principles to justify political decisions, and a "moral politician," who tries to remain true to moral principles in shaping political events. The discourse of human rights has often been exploited and misused by "political moralists"; its proper place is to guide the moral politician, be they citizens or leaders. All that we can offer as philosophers is a clarification of what we can regard as legitimate and just in the domain of human rights themselves.

Charles R. Beitz's *The Idea of Human Rights* is the most sensitive and detailed treatment of human rights from the standpoint of a newly developing global practice. Beitz views human rights as a "public political project with its own distinctive purposes, forms of action, and culture" (13) that are part of the "global normative order." This order, in turn, is defined as a "body of norms that are more or less widely accepted as regulative standards for conduct in various parts of global political space" (209). In examining the discourse of human rights in the light of international treaty and customary law, in his close attention to the institutional practice and culture of human rights, and the successful reformulation of the Rawlsian doctrine of human rights as standards of international legitimacy within a Society of Peoples, Beitz's work breaks new ground. His is a "practical or a functional conception," which takes "the functional view of human rights in international discourse and practice as basic" (103). What then is this functional conception? Beitz writes: "appeals to human rights, under conditions that will need to be specified, can provide reasons for the world community or its agents to act in ways aimed at reducing infringements or contributing to the satisfaction of the rights in societies where they are insecure" (106). In this two-level model, states are the primary bearers of responsibilities with respect to compliance with human rights and "the international community and those acting as its agents (are) the guarantors of these responsibilities" (108). Yet this manner of stating the problem does not only makes state responsibility central to human rights doctrine; it places the question of intervention and the permissible forms of intervention right at the heart of human rights doctrine. Certainly, Beitz is sensitive to the role of non-state agents and institutions as well as to developments in global civil society for spreading human rights, but unfortunately not enough. His is still very much a state-centric vision of the international order and, in two instances, Beitz's liberal political impulses are curbed by reasons of deference to the international order of sovereign states. First, since he assumes that to defend a human right to democracy would mean, under certain circumstances which are imprecise, that *some* state agent or another ought to or may intervene in the affairs of a society to establish democracy, Beitz denies that democracy is a human right and accepts Joshua Cohen's formulation.

In the second case, with respect to the question whether women's rights as defended by the Convention on the Elimination of All Forms of Discrimination Against Women (CEDAW) are not too radical vis-à-vis existing conceptions of moral orders in the world, Beitz is careful. CEDAW requires states to take steps to "eliminate discrimination against women by any person, organization or enterprise," and "'to modify or abolish existing laws, regulations, customs and practices' that sustain discrimination anywhere in society" (186). Beitz observes that in this respect CEDAW is quite radical and would force one to contemplate "large scale changes in policy and social practice but also in prevailing social norms in some of the world's societies" (190). Doesn't this open the door then to intolerance at best, and to intervention in the affairs of other societies at worst? Beitz concedes that if "human rights are supposed to be matters of international concern, and if there are no feasible means of expressing this concern in political action, then perhaps to this extent women's human rights doctrine overreaches" (195). Still, not willing to give up his liberal sympathies for the full equality for women, or for the functional doctrine of human rights, Beitz suggests that perhaps we need to shift the paradigm of human rights from a "juridical" one to a conception of political value (195). This is an interesting suggestion which opens up a complex view of the interaction between the juridical and political conceptions of human rights, but which is not elaborated upon by Beitz.

In the next two chapters, I will document transformations in the institutions and practices of state sovereignty and will develop a model of "jurisgenerative politics," with the purposes of integrating the juridical and political dimensions of human rights. Jurisgenerative cosmopolitan politics may offer a way out of the impasse encountered by the most sophisticated contemporary liberal defenses of human rights, such as Joshua Cohen's and Charles Beitz's.

— 6 —

TWILIGHT OF SOVEREIGNTY OR THE EMERGENCE OF COSMOPOLITAN NORMS?
Rethinking Citizenship in Volatile Times

Transformations of Citizenship

In several works in the last decade, I have documented the disaggregation of citizenships rights, the emergence of an international human rights regime, and the spread of cosmopolitan norms.[1] National citizenship is a legal and social status, which combines some form of collectively shared identity with the entitlement to social and economic benefits, and the privileges of political membership through the exercise of democratic rights. I have argued that in today's world the civil and social rights of migrants, aliens, and denizens are increasingly protected by international human rights practices. The establishment of the European Union has been accompanied by a Charter of Fundamental Rights and Freedoms and by the formation of a European Court of Justice.[2] The European Convention for the Protection of Human Rights and Fundamental Freedoms, which encompasses states which are not members of the EU as well, permits the claims of citizens of adhering states to be heard by a European Court of Human Rights. Parallel developments can be seen on the American continent, through the establishment of the Inter-American System for the Protection of Human Rights and the Inter-American Court of

This chapter was published in *Citizenship Studies* 11/1 (February 2007): 19–36. It has been revised for inclusion in this volume. It has also been reprinted in *Democracy, States, and the Struggle for Global Justice*, Heather Gautney, Omar Dahbour, Ashley Dawson, and Neil Smith (New York and London: Routledge, 2009), pp. 79–99.

Human Rights. African states have accepted the 1981 African Charter on Human and Peoples' Rights through the Organization of African Unity, and to date it has been ratified by 49 states.[3]

Despite these developments, the link between national citizenship and the core entitlement of democratic participation, such as voting rights, are retained by permitting only nationals to exercise them in most cases; but in this domain too changes are visible throughout the European Union: a recent article by Kees Groenendijk of the Council on Migration, concludes that:

> Of the 29 European States covered in this paper, 17 allow some catego-
> ries of resident non-nationals to participate in local elections . . . These
> states are Belgium, Denmark, Estonia, Finland, Hungary, Ireland,
> Lithuania, Luxembourg, the Netherlands, Norway [which is not an
> EU member SB], Portugal, Slovakia, Slovenia, Spain, Sweden, six
> cantons in Switzerland [which is not an EU member SB], and the
> United Kingdom. Eight of these states (Denmark, Hungary, Norway,
> Portugal, Slovakia, Sweden, six cantons in Switzerland and the United
> Kingdom) allow non-nationals (EU nationals and third-country nation-
> als) to vote in elections for regional or national representative bodies.
> Five of these 17 states (Belgium, Estonia, Hungary, Luxembourg, and
> Slovenia) do not allow third-country nationals to stand as candidates
> in municipal elections.[4]

These trends are not limited to Europe. Increasingly, Mexico, and Central American governments such as El Salvador and Guatemala as well, are permitting those who are born to citizen parents in foreign countries to retain voting rights at home and even to run for office; the practice of recognizing dual citizenship is becoming wide-spread. In South Asia, particularly among economic elites who carry three or more passports and navigate three or more national econo-mies, the institution of "flexible citizenship" is taking hold.[5]

Yet these changes in modalities of political belonging have been accompanied by other, more ominous, forms of exclusion: first, the condition of refugees and asylum seekers has not benefited equally from the spread of cosmopolitan norms. While their numbers the world over have increased as a result of the global state of violence,[6] most liberal democracies since September 11, 2001, and even before then, had already shifted toward criminalizing refugee and asylum seekers, either on the grounds that they were lying to gain access to economic advantages in more affluent countries or that they were potential security threats. The politics of refuge and asylum have become sites of some of the world's most intense global distributional,

95

as well as racialized, confrontations. Even within the European Union, the establishment of refugee-processing transit camps (RPTCs) outside the borders of the EU, to catch refugees and illegal migrants before they land on European soil, have been advocated by the UK and Denmark, and are in operation in Spanish-held territories in North Africa and, until the outbreak of civil war there in the spring of 2011, in transit camps in Libya.

Furthermore, as Hannah Arendt observed more than half a century ago, "the right to have rights" remains an aporetic longing.[7] For who is to grant the right to be a member, the right to belong to a community in which one's right to have rights is to be protected by all? Within a permanently divided humanity, it is first and foremost membership in a polity in which one's right to have rights is defended through the solidarity of all, that the aporias of statelessness may be resolved. Our defense of the right to have rights must combine then the liberal vision of citizenship as entitlement to rights, with the republican-democratic vision of membership to be attained through full democratic participation.

The disaggregation of citizenship rights through the extension of cosmopolitan norms, the continuing liminality of refugees and asylum seekers, and the increasing criminalization of migrants as a consequence of the global state of confrontation between the forces of political Islam and the USA, in particular, have led a number of scholars to interpret these recent trends in quite a different light from the views I express here. For some, the spread of an international human rights regime and of cosmopolitan norms sounds like a Pollyannaish narrative which does not account for the growing condition of global civil war (Giorgio Agamben; Michael Hardt and Antonio Negri).[8] For others, while these trends toward a cosmopolitan order are real, one needs to consider the more radical political potentials of the present as well (Etienne Balibar; David Held).[9]

The very great disparity among these diagnoses of our contemporary condition, which extend from predictions of global civil war and a permanent state of exception, to the utopia of citizenship beyond the state and to transnational and global democracy, may itself be an indication of the volatile and obscure moment we are traversing. What has become crystal clear is that the changing world security situation since September 11, 2001, has destabilized the principle of formal sovereign equality of states. The spread of cosmopolitan norms and transformations of sovereignty inevitably accompany one another. The rise of an international human rights regime, which is one of the hallmarks of post-Westphalian transformations in sovereignty, also heralds alterations in the jurisdictional prerogative of nation-states. Jean L. Cohen has thus observed:

> Talk of legal and constitutional pluralism, societal constitutionalism, transnational governmental networks, cosmopolitan human rights law enforced by "humanitarian intervention," and so on are all attempts to conceptualize the new global legal order that is allegedly emerging before our eyes. The general claim is that the world is witnessing a move to cosmopolitan law . . . But . . . if one shifts the political perspective, the sovereignty-based model of international law appears to be ceding not to cosmopolitan justice but to a different bid to restructure the world order: the project of empire.[10]

So, which is it: the rise of cosmopolitan norms or the spread of empire? Indeed, it is crucial to unravel this ambivalent potential: while the emergence of cosmopolitan norms are intended to protect individuals' status as rights-bearing persons in a global civil society, there are dangers as well as opportunities created by the weakening of state sovereignty. The fact that the internationalization of human rights norms and the weakening of state sovereignty are developing in tandem with each other, decidedly does not mean that the one can be reduced to the other; the genesis of these trends as well as their normative logics are distinct.[11] Nor should concerns about the weakening of state sovereignty, some of which I share, lead one to reject the spread of human rights norms for fear that they can be used to justify humanitarian interventions.

The Changing Shape of Sovereignty

Since these transformations are altering norms of state sovereignty, as well as impacting the actual capacity of states to exercise sovereignty, it is important at the outset to distinguish between *state sovereignty* and *popular sovereignty*. The concept of "sovereignty" ambiguously refers to two moments in the foundation of the modern state, and the history of modern political thought in the West since Thomas Hobbes can plausibly be told as a contentious struggle between these poles: first, sovereignty means the capacity of a public body, in this case the modern nation-state, to act as the *final* and *indivisible* seat of authority with the jurisdiction to wield not only "monopoly over the means of violence," to recall Max Weber's famous phrase, but also to distribute socio-economic justice and manage the economy.

Sovereignty also means, particularly since the French Revolution, *popular sovereignty*, that is, the idea that the people are subjects and objects of the law, or the makers as well as obeyers of the law. Popular sovereignty involves representative institutions, the separation of powers, and the guarantee not only of liberty and equality, but of the "equal value of the liberty of each." Etienne Balibar has expressed the interdependence between state sovereignty and popular sovereignty thus:

> state sovereignty has simultaneously "protected" itself from and "founded" itself upon popular sovereignty to the extent that the political state has been transformed into a "social-state" . . . passing through the progressive institution of a "representation of social forces" by the mechanism of universal suffrage and the institutions of social citizenship.[12]

My question is: how does the new configuration of state sovereignty influence popular sovereignty? Which political options are becoming possible? Which are blocked? Today we are caught not only in the reconfiguration of sovereignty but also in the *reconstitutions of citizenship*. We are moving away from citizenship, understood exclusively as national membership, toward a *citizenship of residency* which strengthens the multiple ties to locality, to the region, and to transnational institutions.

I will argue that cosmopolitan norms enhance the project of popular sovereignty while prying open the black box of state sovereignty.[13] They challenge the prerogative of the state to be the highest authority dispensing justice over all that is living and dead within certain territorial boundaries. In becoming party to human rights treaties, states themselves limit their own prerogatives. Very often this can lead to conflicts between the will of majorities and international norms, as we can observe with regard to women's rights, the rights of cultural, ethnic and linguistic minorities, and environmental standards, among other examples. But such contentions have become all too frequent precisely because the world is moving toward new forms of post-Westphalian politics of global interdependence.

Separate from the influence of cosmopolitan human rights norms, and to be distinguished from it, is the undermining of state sovereignty through the demands of global capitalism. Global capitalism is indeed creating its own form of "global law without a state" (Günther Teubner), as well as sabotaging the efforts of legislators to conduct open and public deliberations on legislation that impacts the global movements of capital and of other resources. Furthermore, many states are privatizing their own activities by disbursing authority over prisons and schools to private enterprises and companies.[14] My thesis is that, whereas cosmopolitan norms lead to the emergence of *generalizable human interests and the articulation of public standards of norm justification*, global capitalism is leading to the *privatization and segmentation of interest communities* and the *weakening of standards of public justification through the rise of private logics of norm generation*. The result is the deterioration of the capacity of states to protect and provide for their citizens.

This chapter first documents in broad strokes three kinds of transformations taking place in the relationship of territoriality and jurisdiction: transnational migrations, the emergence of global law, and the rise of fast-track legislation. The two latter trends are leading to the undermining of popular sovereignty and the privatization of state sovereignty, while transnational migrations are both enabled by and contribute to the spread of cosmopolitan norms. I then conclude with normative considerations on democratic iterations, through which cosmopolitan norms and the will of democratic majorities interact via public argumentation and deliberation.

Deterritorialization and Law: Colonialism vs Transnational Migrations

The modern state formation in the West begins with the "territorialization" of space. The enclosure of a particular portion of the earth and its demarcation from others through the creation of protected boundaries, and the presumption that all that lies within these boundaries, whether animate or inanimate, belongs under the dominion of the sovereign is central to the territorially bounded system of states in Western modernity. In this Westphalian model, territorial integrity and a unified jurisdictional authority are two sides of the same coin; protecting territorial integrity is the obverse side of the power of the state to assert its jurisdictional authority (*dominium*).

The modern absolutist states of Western Europe were governed, in Carl Schmitt's terms, by the "Jus Publicum Europaeum" as their international law.[15] However, this model was unstable from its inception, or, in Stephen Krasner's famous phrase, "sovereignty is hypocrisy."[16] Already the discovery of the Americas in the fifteenth century, the imperialist ventures into India and China, the struggle for domination over the Indian Ocean, and the nineteenth-century

99

colonization of Africa destroyed this form of state sovereignty and international law by chipping at the peripheries.[17] Not only the West's confrontation with other continents, but also the question of whether the non-Christian Ottoman Empire belonged to the "Jus Publicum Europaeum," showed the limitations of this order. Though Schmitt himself is not far from idealizing this moment in the evolution of "the law of the earth," his own account documents its inherent limits and eventual dissolution.[18] The "deterritorialization" of the modern state goes hand in hand with its transformation from early bourgeois republics into European empires, whether they be those of England, France, Spain, Portugal, Belgium, the Netherlands, or Italy.

The evolution of bourgeois republics into empires destroys the overlap of territorial control with jurisdictional authority that governs, at least in principle, the motherland. Europe's colonies become the sites of usurpation and conquest in which *extra-juridical spaces*, removed from the purview of liberal principles of consent, are created. As Edmund Burke was to express it pithily with respect to "administrative massacres" in India, and during the impeachment by the British House of Commons of Warren Hastings, who was responsible for them, this needed to be done so that "breakers of the law in India might [not] become 'the makers of law for England.'"[19]

With the rise of bourgeois and democratic republics, the "subject" of the absolutist state is transformed into the "citizen." As the Westphalian paradigm of sovereignty meets its limits outside Europe, it is constitutionalized at home by social struggles for increased accountability, universal suffrage, expanded representation, democratic freedoms, and social rights. These struggles are the sites of popular sovereignty, and of demands to make the state apparatus responsive and transparent to its citizens. In ways that much scholarship has not even begun to fathom, popular sovereignty struggles at home, the spread of modern citizenship, and imperialist ventures abroad go hand in hand.[20]

This legacy of empire has come back today to haunt the resource-rich countries of the northern hemisphere through the rise of transnational migrations. Transnational migrations also produce an uncoupling of territoriality, sovereignty, and citizenship, but in ways quite different from colonialism. Whereas in the nineteenth and twentieth centuries, European imperialism spread forms of jurisdiction into colonial territories, and shielded them against democratic consent and control, contemporary migratory movements give rise to overlapping jurisdictions which are often protected by international norms.

In 1910, roughly 33 million migrants lived in countries other than their own; by the year 2000, their number had reached 175 million;[21] In 2010, that number was estimated to be 214 million (Cf. <http://www.migrationinformation.org/datahub/comparative.cfm>). From 1910 to 2000, the population of the world grew from 1.6 to 5.3 billion, roughly threefold; at the end of 2011 it is estimated to reach 7 billion. Migrations, by contrast, increased almost sixfold over the course of the same 90 years. Strikingly, more than half of this increase occurred in the last three decades of the twentieth century, between 1965 and 2000. In this period, 75 million people undertook cross-border movements to settle in countries other than those of their origin. It is noteworthy that from 2000 to 2010 alone, world migration grew by 40 million.[22]

Transformations in patterns of migration are leading more and more individuals to retain ties with their home countries and not to undertake total immersion in their countries of immigration. The ease provided by globalized networks of transportation, communication, electronic media, banking, and financial services are producing guest workers, seasonal workers, dual nationals, and diasporic commuters. Migrations no longer bring with them total immersion and socialization in the culture of the host country – a process poignantly symbolized by the assignment to immigrants to the USA of new family names in Ellis Island.

Today nation-states encourage diasporic politics among their migrants and ex-citizens, seeing in the diaspora not only a source of political support for projects at home, but also a resource of networks, skills, and competencies that can be used to enhance a state's own standing in an increasingly global world. Notable examples of such diasporas are the large Indian, Chinese, and Jewish communities across the globe. Their continuing allegiance to the so-called "home country" is carefully cultivated.

Migrations thus lead to a pluralization of allegiances and commitments and to the growing complexity of the identity of nationals who, more often than not, in today's world, are also ex-, post- and neo-colonials. We are witnessing the increasing migration from periphery to center, encouraged by wide differentials in standards of living between regions of the world, and facilitated by the large presence of family and kin already at the center of what was once the Empire. Indians, Pakistanis, Kashmiris, and Sri Lankans in the UK; Algerians and Moroccans in France; Surinamese and Moluccans in the Netherlands; Latin Americans in Spain; Libyans in Italy are all population groups whose history is deeply bound up with European empires.

The Westphalian state which extended toward the rest of the world now finds that its borders are porous in both directions, and that not only does the center flow to the periphery, but the periphery flows toward the center.

State sovereignty, which has always meant some capacity and prerogative to protect borders, now more than ever depends upon skillful negotiations, transactions, agreements, and controlling flows in cooperation with other states. Of course, states and regions differ widely in their ability to assert their sovereignty and to throw their weight around. The poorer economies of Central America, South Asia, and Africa are less able to police their borders; the world's largest refugee populations are also settled in some of the world's poorest regions such as Chad, Pakistan, and Ingushtia.[23]

Migrations are the site of intense conflicts over resources as well as identities. In the contemporary world, strong states militarize and increasingly criminalize migratory movements. The poor migrant becomes the symbol of the continuing assertion of sovereignty. Migrants' bodies, both dead and alive, strew the path of states' power.

Transnational migrations reveal the pluralization of sites of sovereignty in that, with changing patterns of acculturation and socialization, migrants begin to live in multiple jurisdictions. Although they are increasingly protected by cosmopolitan norms in the form of various human rights treaties, they are still vulnerable to a system of state sovereignty which privileges national citizenship while restricting dual and multiple citizenship regimes.

Militarization and criminalization are defensive responses which states use to reassert their sovereignty in the face of transnational migrations. But is it possible to think about sovereignty in terms other than those suggested by the model of autochthonous impermeability? Is it conceivable to think of sovereignty in relational terms? Is it possible to disaggregate sovereignty's functions and yet create modalities of cooperation?[24] Can we still maintain the ideal of popular sovereignty and democratic rule if the state-centered model of sovereignty is itself becoming dysfunctional?

Deterritorialization of Law: Global Capitalism

Transnational migrations reveal the dependence of states upon the worldwide movement of peoples as well as each other's policies. Since every inch of the face of the world, with the exception of the North and South Poles, are now controlled and governed by a state which has territorial jurisdiction, cross-border movements initiated by migrants as well as by refuge and asylum seekers, bring to light the fragility as well as the frequent irrationality of the state system. Vis-à-vis people's cross-border movements, the state remains sovereign, albeit in much reduced fashion. Vis-à-vis the movement of capital and commodities, and information and technology, across borders, the state today is more hostage than sovereign.

A great deal has been written in recent years about globalization as a worldwide phenomenon and the corresponding diminished capacity of states. I am persuaded by the argument that to understand this phenomenon it is analytically more useful to use the term "stateness," that is, the dynamic capacity of states to react to and control their environments in multiple ways.[25] There is tremendous variation across the globe in the capacity of "stateness." The affluent democracies of North America, Europe, Australia, and New Zealand, to some extent can manipulate, tame, and channel the forces of global capitalism as well as the worldwide flow of information, communication, and transportation technologies – although the worldwide economic crises since 2008 reveal that their capacities to do so are limited too. Viewed comparatively, this is obviously much less true for many states in North Africa, the Middle East, Latin America, and Asia. The rise to global prominence of China, India, and Brazil, as well as the Asian "tiger" economies, is in large measure due to the capacity of these states to channel economic globalization to their own advantage.

In her analysis of Southeast Asian economies, Aihwa Ong gives a compelling example of the ways in which global capitalism is creating jurisdictional spaces that escape democratic controls. New forms of "multinational zones of sovereignty" in the form of growth triangles (GTs) are spreading throughout South Asia and Central America. These "straddle borders between neighboring states such as to maximize the locational advantage and attract global capital."[26] The three GTs formed by linking neighboring countries are Indonesia-Malaysia-Singapore (Sijori), Indonesia-Malaysia-Thailand, and Brunei-Indonesia-Malaysia-Philippines. Transnational corporations such as Nike, Reebok, and the Gap now employ millions of women who work 12 hours a day and make less than $2.00 a day. Ong observes that these

> growth triangles are zones of special sovereignty that are arranged through a multinational network of smart partnerships and that

103

exploit the cheap labor that exists within the orbit of a global hub such as Singapore. It appears that GT workers are less subject to the rules of their home country and more to the rules of companies and to the competitive conditions set by other growth triangles in the region.[27]

A parallel account is provided by Carolin Emcke of the workings of the *maquiladoras* in Central America. These are established by foreign capital in El Salvador, Guatemala, and Costa Rica under the protection of respective governments, often as tax-free zones to attract foreign investment. They protect the zones they occupy through the use of private security guards and forces, crush any attempt to organize the labor force, and fiercely defend themselves against international and even national control and supervision. They resemble medieval warlords who have taken the native populations hostage.[28]

Whether it is the Growth Triangles of Southeast Asia or the *maquiladoras* of Central America, this form of economic globalization results in the disaggregation of states' sovereignty, with their own complicity. As in the case of colonization and imperialism, there is an uncoupling of *jurisdiction and territory* in that the state transfers its own powers of jurisdiction, whether in full knowledge or by unintended consequence, to non-statal private and corporate bodies. The losers in this process are the citizens from whom state protection is withdrawn or, more likely, who never had strong state protection in the first place, and who become dependent upon the power and mercy of transnational corporations and other forms of venture capitalists.

Despite the great variation across countries with respect to the interactions of the global economy and states, one generalization can be safely made: economic globalization is leading to a fundamental transformation of legal institutions and of the paradigm of the rule of law. Increasingly, globalization is engendering a body of law that is self-generating and self-regulating and that does not originate solely, or maybe even primarily, through the legislative or deliberative activity of national legislators.

Law Without a State?

In his influential article, "'Global Bukowina': Legal Pluralism in the World Society," Günther Teubner has argued that, "Today's globalization is not a gradual emergence of a world society under the leadership of interstate politics, but is a highly contradictory and highly fragmented process in which politics has lost its leading role."[29] As examples of global law without a state, Teubner cites *lex mercatoria*, the transnational law of economic transactions; labor law, in the formulation of which enterprises and labor unions, acting as private actors, become law-makers; and the technical standardization and professional self-regulation as engaged in worldwide by the relevant parties without the intervention of official politics.

This emergent body of law is "a legal order," even if it has no specific point of origination in the form of law-producing institutions, and, even less, a single and visible law-enforcing agency. The boundaries of global law are not set by national borders but by "'invisible colleges,' 'invisible markets and branches,' 'invisible professional communities,' 'invisible social networks.'"[30] Territorial boundaries and jurisdictional powers are once more uncoupled.

As Teubner acknowledges, this form of law has serious democratic deficits. "It is a law that grows and changes according to the exigencies of global economic transactions and organizations. This makes it extremely vulnerable to interest and power pressures from economic processes, because it is 'indeterminate' and can change in its application from case to case."[31] Soft law is law without the characteristics traditionally associated with the rule of law, namely, transparency, predictability, and uniformity of application. These features of the rule of law, however, are not merely procedural characteristics; they act as guarantees of the equality of persons and citizens before the law. Global law, by contrast, is not equality-guaranteeing and equality-protecting; rather, it is law which enables global corporations and other bodies to carry out their transactions speedily in an increasingly complex environment, by generating self-binding and self-regulating norms in contrast to what is regarded as the slower, clumsier, and often unpredictable actions of national legislatures.

There are important clashes and tensions between these features of *lex mercatoria* and human rights law or cosmopolitan norms: both the Growth Triangles and the *maquiladoras* are characterized by a *suspension* of human rights norms in such zones of special economic and business privilege. Furthermore, individuals working in these zones are not only, or even primarily, the citizens of the countries in which such zones operate; very often they are themselves transnational migrants from neighboring countries, whose human rights are regularly trampled upon. Thus Malaysians, Thai, Burmese, and

105

others work in Indonesia, and illegal Chinese laborers abound in the *maquiladoras* of Central America. While, without a doubt, the flow of global capital is responsible for encouraging the flow of transnational migrations, we see that the norms which ought to protect migrants and the laws which enable global capitalism are not compatible; in fact, often, they are antagonistic. *Lex mercatoria*, the law of international commercial transactions, and human rights law often collide and conflict.[32]

That economic globalization threatens core features of the rule of law and thereby also challenges the prospects for liberal democracy is emphatically argued by William E. Scheuerman in *Liberal Democracy and the Social Acceleration of Time*:

> Contemporary capitalism is different in many ways from its historical predecessors: economies driven by huge transnational corporations that make effective use of high-speed communication, information, and transportation technologies represent a relatively novel development. The relationship of capitalism to the rule of law is thereby transformed as well ... As high-speed social action "compresses" distance, the separation between domestic and foreign affairs erodes, and the traditional vision of the executive as best suited to the dictates of rapid-fire foreign policy making undermines basic standards of legality in the domestic sphere as well.[33]

The transformation of the rule of law gives rise to fast-track legislation, pushed through by national legislators without adequate debate and deliberation; the power of deliberative bodies is eclipsed and that of the executive increases:

> The main problem posed by globalization is less that transnational business can only preserve its autonomy by limiting state power to exercise the rule of law than that the democratic nation-state can only hope to maintain its independence in relation to global business by counteracting the virtually universal competitive rush to provide transnational firms with special rights and privileges.[34]

States are pushed into the "race to the bottom," to embrace neoliberal reforms, cutting back on the welfare state, and relaxing labor and environmental legislations.

Law without a state? Or race to the bottom? In the first part of this chapter I asked: the spread of cosmopolitan norms or imperialism? Again, we seem confronted by alternatives and disjunction. Surely, these are not the only alternatives which globalization processes confront us with, but, in either case, the model of liberal sovereignty – based upon the unity of jurisdiction administered over a defined territory, assuring citizen's equality through the administration of the rule of law and guaranteeing social welfare through economic redistribution – increasingly appears as if it were the memory of a quaint past. It is important to emphasize that sovereign states are players with considerable power in this process: they themselves often nurture and guide the very transformations that curtail and undermine their own powers.[35]

Whether it be through changing patterns of transnational migrations, or through the emergence of Growth Triangles and new forms of global law without the state in the accelerated and fluid global marketplace, or through the pressure to adapt state bureaucracies to the new capitalism, an epochal change is under way, in which aspects of state sovereignty are being dismantled chip by chip. State jurisdiction and territoriality are uncoupled and new agents of jurisdictional authority are emerging in the form of multinational corporations. In some cases, the state disburses its own jurisdiction to private agencies in order to escape the territorial control of popular legislators – take the activities of the private security agency called Blackwater during the Iraq War, and now named 'Xe'. The social contract is increasingly frayed.

If the analysis presented above is partially accurate, does the "twilight of state sovereignty" mean the end of citizenship and of democratic politics, the displacement of the political, or maybe even its eventual disappearance in the evolution of world societies? What are the normative consequences of these transformations?[36] What light does this social-theoretic analysis shed on the political philosophies of the present period?

Twilight of Sovereignty and Global Civil Society

Just as the capacity of nation-states to exercise their "stateness" varies considerably, so do their reactions to the shrinking sphere of state autonomy and activity. Vis-à-vis the economic, ecological, legal challenges, and the growing fluidity of worldwide migrations, the states of Europe have chosen *the cooperative restructuring of sovereignty*. To be juxtaposed to this cooperative restructuring of sovereignty is the *unilateral reassertion of sovereignty*. At the present time not only the United States, but China, Iran, and India are going down this route, not to mention Russia, North Korea, and Israel. The strategy here is to strengthen the state via attempts to gather all the markers of sovereignty in the public authority, with the consequence of increased militarization, frequent disregard for international law and human rights, regressive and hostile relations with neighbors, and criminalization of migration. The third alternative is the *weakening* of the already fragile institutions of *state sovereignty* in vast regions of Africa, Central and Latin America, and South Asia. In these cases, global market forces further destabilize fragile economies; they break up the bonds between the large armies of the poor and the downtrodden and their local elites. The latter now are engaged in networking with their global counterparts, thus leaving the masses of their own countries to the mercy of *maquiladoras*, paramilitaries, drug lords, and criminal gangs. The state withdraws into a shell, as has happened in the Ivory Coast, in the Congo, in the Sudan, in El Salvador, in some parts of Mexico, in Burma, and so on. Under such conditions, popular sovereignty takes the form, at best, of guerilla warfare and, at worst, of equally criminal groups fighting to gain a piece of the pie. Neither the contraction of "stateness" nor its militarized reassertion re-enhance popular sovereignty.

The volatile and often ambivalent configurations of institutions such as citizenship and sovereignty, which have defined our understanding of modern politics for the last 360 odd years since the Treaty of Westphalia (1648), have understandably given rise to conflicting commentaries and interpretations in contemporary political thought. These can be characterized as theories of empire, theories of transnational governance, and theories of post-national citizenship.

Empire, according to Michael Hardt and Antonio Negri, is the ever-expanding power of global capital to bring farther and farther reaches of the world into its grip. Unlike the extractive and exploitative empires of the past, however, the new empire encourages the spread of human rights norms; it pushes the new technologies of networking throughout the world, thus destroying the walls of separation and generating a new global connectivity consonant with this new age.[37]

Since the webs of empire are so ubiquitous, sites of resistance to it are diffuse, decentered, and multiple. The "multitude" resists the total penetration of life-worlds by empire in organizing demonstrations against the G-7, the World Bank, the Gulf War, the Iraq War, and the violation of international law. The multitude focuses on power as a global phenomenon and attempts to generate a counterforce to empire.[38]

108

The metaphors of networking, entanglement, binding, spread of communicative forms, and the like which underlie this social-theoretical analysis are one-sided precisely because they present a world without institutional actors and without structured centers of resistance.[39] Relatedly, the multitude – Hardt's and Negri's revolutionary subject – is not representative of the citizen. The multitude is not even the carrier of popular sovereignty since it lacks the drive toward the constitutionalization of power, which has been the desiderata of all popular movements since the American and French Revolutions. The multitude gives expression to the rage of those who have lost their republics: the multitude smashes institutions and resists power. It does not engage in what Hannah Arendt has called *constitutio libertatis*.[40] By contrast, popular sovereignty aims at widening the circle of representation among all members of the demos into an enduring form; popular sovereignty aims at the control of state power via the separation of powers between the judiciary, the legislative, and the executive; popular sovereignty means creating structures of accountability and transparency in the public exercise of power. This is a far cry from the politics of the multitude.

This aspect of the legitimate exercise of power is well emphasized in contemporary debates by theorists of *transnational governance* such as Anne-Marie Slaughter and David Held. At the roots of empire's extension, argue advocates of transnational democracy, lies a problem of legitimation. We are in the grips of forces and processes that resemble the galloping horseman without a head. Decisions are made in exclusive board meetings of the IMF, WTO, and the World Bank, affecting the lives of millions, while nation-states refuse to sign multilateral treaties such as the Kyoto Convention, as in the case of the USA, or the Rome Treaty that has lead to the establishment of the International Criminal Court. Theorists of the multitude seem to confuse politics with carnival. Only transnational institutions can build permanent structures to counteract the forces of empire.

According to advocates of global governance, by contrast, we need transparent and accountable structures of world regulation and coordination. Some of these structures are already in place through the networking of experts working on economic, judicial, military, immigration, health, and communication issues, they observe. These form horizontally networked sites of information, coordination, and regulation. The future of global citizenship depends on becoming actively involved in such transnational organizations and working toward global governance. Whether this implies world government or not is at this stage beside the point: what matters is to increase structures of global accountability and regulation.[41]

In the version of the global governance thesis advocated by Anne-Marie Slaughter, who focuses less on the normative possibilities for democratic governance beyond borders but more on the horizontal networks linking government officials in judicial, regulatory, and administrative organizations across state boundaries, a realm of law "beyond the state" has already been created and the reach of global law is extended through the power of regulatory organizations which are themselves part of national institutions.

Whereas followers of the late Niklas Luhmann, such as Günther Teubner, see structures of global governance resulting *per impossibile* through the self-regulating interlocking of anonymous systems of norm-generation that act as each other's environment, Anne-Marie Slaughter places her faith in the networking of actual elites in the judiciaries across the world, in administrative bureaucracies, regulatory agencies, and the like. The hope is that new norms and standards for public behavior will result through such interlockings.

Defenders of global governance have a point: the current state of global interdependence requires new modalities of cooperation and regulation. Arms control, ecology, combating disease and epidemics, and fighting the spread of poverty must be global joint ventures that require the cooperation of all people of good will and good faith in all nations of the world. As David Held in particular has argued powerfully, the goal is not only to form new institutions of transnational governance but to render existing ones such as the WTO, IMF, and AID more transparent, accountable, and responsive to their constituencies' needs. This in turn can only happen if popular movements within donor and member countries force the elites who govern these institutions toward democratic accountability. It is naive to assume, as Günther Teubner and Anne-Marie Slaughter at times seem to, that the good faith of elites or the miraculous sociological signals of anonymous systems alone will move such structures toward democratization and accountability. They won't. Transnational structures need to be propeled toward a dynamic where they can be controlled by public law.

Here, however, we reach a dilemma: precisely because state-centered politics have become so reduced in effectiveness today, new theoretizations of the political have emerged. Yet my critique of the models of empire and transnational governance seems to presuppose a form of popular sovereignty, a *global demos*, which is nowhere in existence. Where is the popular sovereign who can counter empire or who can be the bearer of new institutions of transnational governance?

Today we are caught not only in the reconfiguration of sovereignty but also in the *reconstitutions of citizenship*. We are moving away from citizenship, understood as national membership, increasingly toward a *citizenship of residency*, which strengthens the multiple ties to locality, to the region, and to transnational institutions. In this respect defenders of post-national citizenship are correct. The universalistic extension of civil and social rights, and, in some cases, of political participation rights as well, to immigrants and denizens within the context of the European Union is heralding a new institution of citizenship. This new modality decouples citizenship from national belonging and rootedness in a particular cultural community. Not only in Europe, but all around the globe, we see the rise of political activism on the part of non-nationals, post-nationals, and ex-colonials. They live in multicultural neighborhoods, they come together around women's rights, secondary language education for their children, environmental concerns, jobs for migrants, representation on school boards and city councils, and legalizing the status of undocumented workers. This new urban activism, which includes citizens as well as non-citizens, shows that political agency is possible beyond the member/non-member divide. The paradoxes of the "right to have rights" are ameliorated by those who exercise their democratic-republican participation rights with or without possessing the correct papers.

Nor is the local alone the site of post-national citizenship. New modalities of citizenship and a nascent public sphere are also emerging at the global level through the meetings of the World Social Forum in which activists from all nations, representing women's, ecology, ethnic rights, cultural self-determination, and economic democracy groups, as well as NGOs and INGOs, gather together to plan strategy and policy. They are, in many cases, the ones who articulate and bring to global awareness problems to which transnational structures of governance have to respond. These citizens' groups and social activists are the transmitters of local and global knowledge and know-how; they generate new needs and demands that democracies have to respond to. They are members of the new global civil society. This new global civil society is not only inhabited by multinational and transnationals, whether public and private, but also by citizens, movement activists, and constituents of various kinds. This emergent global civil society is quite complementary to republican federalism,

111

which in my opinion constitutes the only viable response to the contemporary crisis of sovereignty.[42]

Republican Federalism and Democratic Sovereignty

I will define "republican federalism" as the constitutionally structured reaggregation of the markers of sovereignty, in a set of interlocking institutions each responsible and accountable to the other. There is, as there must be in any structuring of sovereignty, a moment of *finality*, in the sense of decisional closure, but not a moment of *ultimacy*, in the sense of being beyond questioning, challenge, and accountability. As Judith Resnik notes, the development of international law and of cosmopolitan human rights treaties are creating new modalities for the exercise of federalism:

> federalism is also a path for the movement of international rights across borders, as it can be seen from the adoption by mayors, local city councils, state legislatures, and state judges of transnational rights including the United Nations Charter and the Convention to Eliminate all Forms of Discrimination Against Women (CEDAW) and the Kyoto Protocol on global warming. Such actions are often trans-local – with municipalities and states joining together to shape rules that cross borders.[43]

I call such processes of "law's migration" (Resnik) across state boundaries and institutional jurisdictions, whether institutionalized or popular, "democratic iterations." Democratic iterations can take place in the "strong" public bodies of legislatures, the judiciary and the executive, as well as in the informal and "weak" publics of civil society associations and the media.

Democratic iterations are processes of linguistic, legal, cultural, and political repetitions-in-transformation – invocations that are also revocations.[44] Through such iterative acts a democratic people, considering itself bound by certain guiding norms and principles, reappropriates and reinterprets these, thus showing itself to be not only *subject* to the laws but also their *author. Popular sovereignty no longer refers to the physical presence of a people gathered in a delimited territory, but rather to the interlocking in global, local and national public spheres of the many processes of democratic iteration in which peoples learn from one another.*[45]

There will be an inevitable tension between the border- and boundary-transcending discourses of democratic iterations and state

112

sovereignty. In fact, democracy is the process through which the popular sovereign tries to tame state sovereignty by making it responsive, transparent, and accountable to the people. The spreading cosmopolitan norms, which aim to protect human beings as such, not only in virtue of their national membership status but as citizens of a global civil society, and claims to popular sovereignty, mutually reinforce one another. Whereas, in the case of the decline of state sovereignty, it is the receding of the public exercise of state power that is of concern, in the case of the augmentation of popular sovereignty, international and cosmopolitan norms subject the public agencies that exercise power to increasing scrutiny. First and foremost, state institutions are submitted to heightened public and juridical scrutiny, thus aiding the assertion of popular sovereignty. The supposed conflict between the spread of cosmopolitan norms and popular sovereignty is based upon a mistaken equation of state with popular sovereignty.

Cosmopolitan norms give rise to the cross-border interlocking and coordination of democratic iterations among those who are organized in human rights, women's rights, ecology, and indigenous rights movements. By contrast, *lex mercatoria* and other forms of law without the state, preferred by the agents of global capitalism, strengthen private corporations vis-à-vis public bodies. Thus, in the case of the North American Free Trade Agreement, firms are granted rights hitherto generally limited to nation-states alone. Chapter II (B) of the Treaty allows private businesses to submit complaints against member-states to a three-member tribunal. One of the members is chosen by the affected state, another by the firm, and the third jointly by the parties. As Scheuerman observes, "NAFTA thereby effectively grants states and corporations equal authority in some crucial decision-making matters." And he adds, "In a revealing contrast the procedures making up NAFTA's labor 'side agreement' deny similar rights to organized labor."[46]

There is an interesting parallel here to the growing power of individuals to bring charges for human rights violations against states that are signatories to the European Convention for the Protection of Human Rights and Fundamental Freedoms in front of the European Court of Human Rights. In this case, as well, states are defendants and no longer immune from legal prosecution. In both cases, the "black box" of state sovereignty has been pried open, but with very different normative presuppositions: in the case of NAFTA and other forms of global commercial law, states become liable to prosecution by corporate bodies which do not represent *generalizable*

113

interests but only their particular interests and those of their constituents. Interestingly, they also disempower organized labor and environmental groups from enjoying similar jurisdictional privileges in bringing charges against various corporate parties.

In the case of charges brought against states for human rights violations, by contrast, there is a potential *generalizable interest* shared by all citizens and residents of a state alike; namely, to prevent the use of torture and other forms of the widespread violation of human rights. Human rights trials against sovereign states even go beyond the generalizable interest of the national citizens involved and establish universalizable norms of human rights that would protect individuals everywhere and in any part of the world. There is a context-transcending power to these human rights iterations that feeds into the normative power of cosmopolitan norms.

The boundaries of the political have shifted today beyond the republic housed in the nation-state. The deterritorialization of law brings in its wake a displacement of the political. It is clear that only multiple strategies and forms of struggle can reassert the ruptured link between popular consent and the public exercise of power, which is the essence of democratic sovereignty. Transnational structures of governance are fundamental in order to tame the forces of global capitalism; but the accountability of transnational elites can only be demanded by their own constituencies when they mobilize for post- and trans-national citizenship projects. The interlocking networks of local and global activists form an emergent global civil society, in which new needs are articulated for a worldwide public, new forms of knowledge are communicated to a world public opinion and new forms of solidarity across borders are crafted.

Popular sovereignty cannot be regained today by returning to the era of the "black box" of state sovereignty: the formal equality of sovereign states must mean the universalization of human rights norms across state boundaries, respect for the rule of law, and the spread of democratic forms of government all over the globe. It is an insult to the dignity and freedom of individuals everywhere to assume, as so many today are tempted to do, that human rights and cosmopolitan norms, such as the prohibition of crimes against humanity, are products of Western cultures alone whose validity cannot be extended to other peoples and other cultures throughout the world. Not only is this a very inadequate view of the spread of modernity as a global project, but it is also a philosophical conflation of genesis and validity, that is to say, of the conditions of origin of a norm with the conditions of its validity. Global human rights and cosmopolitan

114

norms establish new thresholds of public justification for a humanity that is increasingly united and interdependent.[47] New modalities of citizenship, not only in the sense of the privileges of membership but also in the sense of the power of democratic agency, can only flourish in the transnational, local as well as global spaces, created by this new institutional framework. The multiplying sites of the political herald transformations of citizenship and new configurations of popular sovereignty.

For some, the increasing tensions between the state sovereignty and a cosmopolitan vision of human rights are harbingers of ominous developments: first, there is the argument, advocated by many on the left, that any denial of the principle of the sovereign equality of states provides a green light for increasing interventionism; others, more mindful of the contradictions inherent to the world society of states, plead for reform of the United Nations.[48]

Among those who take the need for building new institutions of global governance to heart, there are also distinctions among cosmopolitans and regionalists. While cosmopolitans are more open toward the project of a world federation of states, and dispute the degree and form of federalism or federationalism needed, regionalists advocate a multi-layered system of governance. In some of his recent essays, Jürgen Habermas, for example, has pleaded for a centralized authority – a reformed UN to have jurisdiction over matters of world war and peace and the implementation of human rights, while pleading for regional organizations (such as the EU) to repool sovereignty for the sake of socio-economic, ecological, and immunological cooperation.[49]

I welcome the resurgence of institutional imagination in contemporary discussions and consider my contribution in this essay to be a humble one of analytical and normative clarification: we need to differentiate between state and popular sovereignty, while exploring their interdependence. The nation-state, until recently, has been a very successful host to the project of popular sovereignty. But economic, military, immunological, and climate-related forces, as well as the explosion of new means of electronic communication and worldwide migrations, have weakened the institutions of the nation-state to such a point that without a "repooling of the markers of sovereignty" in new institutional forms, popular sovereignty cannot be actualized. Far from considering themselves authors as well as subject of their own laws, more and more people are becoming prey to the forces of global capitalism that rob them increasingly of their citizens' as well as human rights. The old regime of state sovereignty, which already in the very construction of the UN was poised between the conflicting demands of sovereign state equality and the realization of the universal principles of human rights, today has been further destabilized by global forces. We need not reject the principle of popular sovereignty, but we need to reconfigure a new regime of global state sovereignties. Despite all its problems, the European Union remains the most impressive example of such a reconfiguration of the markers of sovereignty in the spirit of republican federalism.[50] Hopefully, there will be others too.

CLAIMING RIGHTS ACROSS BORDERS
International Human Rights and Democratic Sovereignty

For Jürgen Habermas, on his eightieth birthday

The New Legal Landscape

The status of international law and of transnational legal agreements and treaties with respect to the sovereignty claims of liberal democracies has become a highly contentious theoretical and political issue.[1] In his highly controversial decision that struck down the death penalty for juvenile delinquents, Justice Kennedy cited the United Nations Convention on the Rights of the Child and the African Charter on the Rights and Welfare of the Child, among other documents.[2] In his dissenting opinion, Justice Scalia thundered: "The basic premise of the court's argument – that American law should conform to the laws of the rest of the world – ought to be rejected out of hand." Seeing this as an all-or-nothing equation, Justice Scalia drove to a *reductio ad absurdum*:

> The Court should either profess its willingness to reconsider all these matters in the light of views of foreigners, or else it should cease putting

An earlier version of this article has appeared in the *American Political Science Review* 103/4 (November 2009): 691–704. I am grateful to the Wissenschaftskolleg in Berlin for awarding me a fellowship from January to July 2009, during which time I completed this essay, and to Axel Wodrich, a visiting student at Yale University, for his meticulous comments on an earlier draft.

forth foreigners' views as part of the *reasoned basis* of its decisions. To invoke alien law when it agrees with one's own thinking, and ignore it otherwise, is not reasoned decision making, but sophistry.[3] (Emphasis in the original)

What indeed is the status of foreign and international law in a world of increasing interdependence? Isn't legal epistemology enriched by looking across the border and even the ocean?[4] What is the source of the anxieties and fears invoked by so many in recent years within the US context, in particular about the problematic relation of transnational legal norms and democratic sovereignty? Citing a foreign ruling does not convert it into a binding precedent but may be wise judicial reasoning.[5] While recent European discussions focus on global law with or without a state, global constitutionalism, a global *res publica*, juridification (*Verrechtlichung*) or constitutionalizaton (*Konstitutionalisierung*) in a world society,[6] there is increasing reticence on the part of many who argue that prospects of a world constitution and the global harmonization of legal traditions and jurisdictions are neither desirable nor salutary.[7] What sense can we make of this new legal landscape? Like Swift's giant Gulliver, states have been pinned down by hundreds of threads of international law, some of which they can free themselves from, while others, much like those tying the giant, prevent them from escaping their bonds. The controversy over international law has become the site of conflict over the future viability of democracies in a world of growing interdependence.

The first part of this chapter considers more closely several strands of critique of these legal transformations. I distinguish the *nationalist* from *democratic sovereigntiste* criticisms, and both from diagnoses which see in the present system of the universalization of human rights norms either the *Trojan horse of a global empire*, or *neocolonialist* intentions which abuse the doctrine of humanitarian interventions to assert imperial control over the globe. Both sets of critics ignore "the jurisgenerativity of law," and, in particular, the power of those most prominent cosmopolitan norms, namely, universal human rights, to empower local movements. While democratic sovereigntistes are wrong in minimizing the extent to which human rights norms contribute to improving democratic self-rule,[8] global constitutionalists are also wrong in minimizing the extent to which even the most cosmopolitan norms, such as human rights, require local contextualization, interpretation, and vernacularization by self-governing peoples.

118

The conclusion considers the impact of CEDAW (Convention on the Elimination of all Forms of Discrimination against Women) upon women in some Muslim countries, and analyzes how rights claims migrate across borders to produce forms of democratic iterations which extend across countries and legal traditions. These considerations are not offered in the spirit of what empirical political scientists would name a "case study," but rather they are offered to show how the very abstract concerns of normative political thought engaged in this essay may also shape the actions and movements of political agents waging contemporary struggles.[9] The neglect of social movements as actors of social transformation and of jurisgenerative politics has led to a naive faith in legal experts, international lawyers, and judges as agents of democratic change. They may be that as well; but, surely, these processes may create democratization without political actors. By contrast, I am interested in how social movements seek to empower themselves by introducing new subjectivities into the public sphere; by articulating new vocabularies of claim-making, and by anticipating new forms of togetherness.

Varieties of Sovereigntism

Sovereigntiste territorialism of the kind espoused by some members of the US Supreme Court is characterized, in Harold Koh's words, "by commitments to territoriality, national politics, deference to executive power, and resistance to comity or international law as meaningful constraints on national prerogative."[10] Sovereigntiste territorialism in our days suffers from a *sociological deficit* so massive that it almost amounts to a loss of touch with reality: the picture of the world that it proceeds from, namely, that of discrete nation-states, at whose borders foreign and international law stops, is radically out of step with legal, economic, administrative, military, and cultural reality and practice.[11]

The *normative* objections raised by sovereigntistes toward global legal developments are more weighty, and cannot be explained away in terms of the historically ingrained attitudes of American exceptionalism and American ambivalence toward international law.[12] These objections can in turn be separated into the *nationalist* and *democratic* variants. The *nationalist* variant traces the law's legitimacy to the self-determination of a discrete, clearly bounded people whose law expresses and binds its collective will alone.[13] The *democratic* variant says that laws cannot be considered legitimate unless a

119

self-determining people can see itself both as the author and the subject of its laws. For the democratic sovereigntiste, it is not paramount that the law express the will of a nation, of an *ethnos*, but that there be clear and recognized public procedures for how laws are formulated and in whose name they are enacted and how far their authority extends.

The *democratic sovereigntiste* argument has many adherents, among them Thomas Nagel, Quentin Skinner, Michael Walzer, and Michael Sandel.[14] Many, who would disagree with the sociological world picture of nationalist sovereigntisme, would nevertheless argue that recent trends toward a harmonized global legal system are normatively dangerous and undesirable. Consider, for example, Thomas Nagel's "The Problem of Global Justice."[15] Nagel takes the nation-state to be the indispensable framework within which questions of justice can arise, and considers foreign and international law to be no more than quasi-contractual commitments entered into voluntarily by discrete sovereign entities. Over and beyond the moral duties we owe each others as human beings, argues Nagel, there are no "thicker" obligations across borders that would place us in relationships of justice with other non-nationals with whom we can engage or not, depending on our disposition and interest, in building enduring projects of mutual benefit and cooperation. The global economy, much like the global legal system, on this view, consists of a series of discretely undertaken contractual obligations by individual states with other entities such as states and corporations, and often, as is the case with international treaties, with multiple other states and corporations. Yet neither the global economy nor the global legal system is a "system of cooperation" in the Rawlsian sense of the term, that is, an enduring form of human association whose members willingly undertake to work and live with one another under a framework of clearly demarcated rules for distributing benefits and liabilities. According to Nagel's "political conception of justice":

> sovereign states are not merely instruments for realizing the preinstitutional value of justice among human beings. Instead, their existence is precisely what gives the value of justice its application, by putting the fellow citizens of a sovereign state into a relation that they don't have with the rest of humanity, an institutional relation which must be evaluated by the special standards of fairness and equality that fill out the content of justice.[16]

For Nagel, too, the sociological and the normative dimensions of sovereigntisme are deeply intertwined. Since Nagel assumes that neither the global economy nor the world legal system is a system of cooperation in the Rawlsian sense, he reduces the problem of global justice to the moral duties which individuals owe one another as a matter of moral principle. Many critics of Nagel, such as Joshua Cohen and Charles Sabel, as well as Thomas Pogge, begin by correcting Nagel's world picture about international law and institutions in order to draw different normative conclusions.[17]

The terrain of the global legal system has now become the new battleground for the future of democracy. Discussions of global justice among political theorists have so far largely focused on distributive justice claims and on how to assess the normative wrongs of the current world system; the status of international law has rarely been addressed.[18] But the objections of democratic sovereigntistes to the legal universalists and world constitutionalists need to be taken seriously. We should be concerned that the rush to embrace global constitutionalism, with or without a state, is leaving the question of democratic legitimacy unanswered. Post-democracy and a techno-elitist democracy, attenuated through the systems of anonymous governance initiated by global specialists, are becoming increasingly attractive.[19]

Critics of International Law

In addition to the nationalist and democratic sovereigntiste positions considered above, there are three additional and well-articulated objections to these developments. They are to be distinguished from the first group in that they situate current legal developments in broader socio-economic and political contexts: first, is *the neo-Marxist critique*, according to which cosmopolitan law is but an epiphenomenon of economic globalization and of the spread of empire;[20] second, is the charge that recent actions by the UN Security Council are creating a worldwide *emergency condition,* through which the deformalization of law and extra-judicial political measures are gaining influence;[21] and, finally, there is the claim that humanitarian interventions and the prosecution of crimes against humanity through the International Criminal Court, in particular, are *neo-colonial* tools of world domination.[22]

This latter claim is particularly important for elucidating the ambivalent connection between the recent actions of the UN Security Council and cosmopolitan norms of human rights. Formulae such as "the obligation" or "the responsibility" to protect, which have been

121

increasingly endorsed by the Secretary General of the UN and which are logical consequences of viewing every individual as a being entitled to rights within the global civil society, are becoming slippery slopes toward the creation of an international emergency situation, legitimizing more and more humanitarian interventions. As Mahmood Mamdani puts it in biting terms: "The new humanitarian order, officially adopted at the UN's 2005 World Summit, claims responsibility for the protection of vulnerable populations . . . Whereas the language of sovereignty is profoundly political, that of humanitarian intervention is profoundly anti-political . . . The international humanitarian order, in contrast, does not acknowledge citizenship. Instead it turns citizens into wards."[23]

There is a great deal in these objections that should be taken seriously and that ought to give one pause: however, advocates of the neo-imperial capitalist hegemony thesis recapitulate a well-known Marxist trope which views the discourse of human rights as the ideological veneer enabling the spread of free-commodity relations.[24] Certainly, there is a historical as well as conceptual link between the universalization of market forces and the rise of the individual as a self-determining and free being, capable of disposing over her actions as well as goods. *But human rights norms are not norms of person, property, and contract alone, and they cannot be reduced to norms protecting free-market transactions.* Human rights norms such as freedom of speech, association, and assembly, are also citizens' rights, subtending and enabling collective action and resistance to the very processes of rapacious capitalist development which post-colonial Marxist critics of "humanitarian intervention" also decry. Many of the international human rights covenants contain, in fact, provisions *against* the exploitative spread of market freedoms, in that they protect union and associational rights, rights of free speech, equal pay for equal work, and workers' health, social security, and retirement benefits. Global capitalism, which creates special free-trade zones, is often directly in violation of these human rights covenants.

The charge that the defense of these cosmopolitan rights has unwittingly given rise to a *responsibility to protect* and hence to neo-colonial domination in the form of humanitarian interventions is complicated:[25] a very good example of this slippery slope from the *responsibility* to protect to the *duty* to intervene, by military force if necessary, occurred during the great typhoon that hit Myanmar-Burma in spring 2008. Bernard Kouchner, the former President of Médecins Sans Frontières and the former foreign minister of

France, argued that the nations of the world had a duty to intervene even against the will of the secretive Myanmar military junta. Robert Kaplan, the conservative thinker, concurred and suggested that the US Navy could move up the river delta to Myanmar and that, once it did so, the mission of humanitarian aid to the victims of the cyclone could easily morph into one of "nation-building." Only this time, one would be self-conscious about this task and apply the "Pottery Barn" principle outright: "If you break it, you own it"![26]

It would be foolish to deny, therefore, the ambivalences, contradictions, and treacherous double meanings of the current world situation, which often transform cosmopolitan intents into hegemonic nightmares. Nevertheless, the hermeneutics of suspicion in the face of these new developments will only take us so far because, with very few exceptions,[27] there is also a refusal on the part of these critics to consider law's normativity and jurisgenerativity, and instead to reduce law to its facticity, that is, to the fact that law can be enforced by state sanctions, and, if necessary, through violence.

One way to introduce some clarity into this debate is to focus on a *family* of global norms which enjoys widespread support and which constitutes the building blocks of any project of world constitutionalism and global legal harmonization. These are international human rights norms, originating with the Universal Declaration of Human Rights of 1948. A democratic sovereigntiste such as Nagel and a world-constitutionalist such as Habermas both agree that in addition to international law concerning the prohibition and conduct of war among states, human rights constitute the foundations of the international system.[28] The strategy of Habermas's general answer to Nagel is that the constitutionalization of international law need not take the form of a social contract for the formation of a world state which would transcend the political autonomy of existing states.[29] Instead, Habermas argues that "Today any conceptualization of a juridification of world politics must take as its starting point individuals *and states* as the two categories of *founding subjects of a world constitution*"[30] (emphasis in the text). Habermas insists that such a multi-level juridical order "should *not* lead to a mediatization of the world of states by the authority of a world republic which would *ignore the fund of trust accumulated in the domestic sphere and the associated loyalty of citizens to their respective nations*" (my emphasis; ibid.). By "mediatization" or "mediation," Habermas has in mind the necessity to consult a supranational authority, which would arise *if* world constitutionalism were understood, analogously to the creation of a world state or world republic. There are, however, more democratic modes of mediating international norms and national ones, which would not involve subordinating the national to the supranational. Such mediatization takes place through "democratic iterations" which interpret, consider, and contextualize the national in the light of the cosmopolitan, giving both sets of norms new and unexpected hermeneutic context. The present chapter concretizes more precisely what such mediatization between international norms and the "associated loyalty of citizens of respective nations" to their respective nations might involve.

The Rise of Cosmopolitan Norms and Jurisgenerativity

It is now widely accepted that since the Universal Declaration of Human Rights (UDHR), we have entered a phase in the evolution of global civil society which is characterized by a transition from *international* to *cosmopolitan* norms of justice. This is not merely a semantic change. While norms of international law emerge through treaty obligations to which states and their representatives are signatories, cosmopolitan norms accrue to individuals considered as moral and legal persons in a worldwide civil society. Even if cosmopolitan norms also originate through treaty-like obligations, such as the UN Charter and the various human rights covenants can be considered to be for their member-states, their peculiarity is that they limit the sovereignty of states and their representatives and oblige them to treat their citizens and residents in accordance with certain human rights standards.[31] States have now engaged in a process of "self-limiting" or "self-binding" their sovereignty, as evidenced by the very large number of signatories to the various human rights covenants which have come into existence since the Universal Declaration of Human Rights of 1948.[32]

To get a sense of the intensity and velocity with which these challenges have come upon us, consider a list of the human rights declarations which have been signed by a majority of the world's states since the UDHR in 1948:[33] the United Nations Convention on the Prevention and Punishment of the Crime of Genocide, adopted by Resolution 260 (III) A of the UN General Assembly on December 9, 1948 (Chapter II); the 1951 Convention on Refugees (which entered into force in 1954);[34] the International Covenant on Civil and Political Rights (ICCPR; opened to signature in 1966 and entered into force in 1976, with 167 out of 195 countries being parties to it as of

124

2011);[35] the International Covenant on Economic, Social and Cultural Rights (ICESCR; entered into force the same year and with 160 state parties as of June 2011),[36] and the Convention on the Elimination of all Forms of Discrimination Against Women (CEDAW; signed in 1979 and entered into force in 1981, with 186 state parties as of June 2011).[37] These are some of the best known among many other treaties and conventions.

By focusing on global human rights norms, as opposed to developments in global commercial, administrative, or entertainment law, or upon other institutions such as the International Criminal Court, I wish to counter as sharply as possible the democratic sovereigntiste objections to these developments. While I would endorse a *legal cosmopolitan* position that considers each human being as a person entitled to basic human rights,[38] my argument is that many critics of cosmopolitanism view the new international legal order as if it were a smooth "command structure," and they ignore the jurisgenerative power of cosmopolitan norms.

By "jurisgenerativity," a term originally suggested by Robert Cover,[39] I understand the law's capacity to create a normative universe of meaning which can often escape the "provenance of formal lawmaking." "The uncontrolled character of meaning exercises a destabilizing influence upon power," writes Cover. "Precepts must 'have meaning,' but they necessarily borrow it from materials created by social activity that is not subject to the strictures of provenance that characterize what we call formal lawmaking. Even when authoritative institutions try to create meaning for the precepts they articulate, they act, in that respect, in an unprivileged fashion."[40] Laws acquire meaning in that they are interpreted within the context of significations which they themselves cannot control. There can be no rules *without* interpretation; rules can only be followed insofar as they are interpreted;[41] but there are also no rules which can control the varieties of interpretation each rule can be subject to within all different hermeneutical contexts.[42] It is in the nature of rules in general and law in particular that the horizon of interpretation transcends the fixity of meaning. Law's normativity does not consist in its grounds of formal validity, that is in its legality alone, though this is crucial. Law can also structure an extra-legal normative universe by developing new vocabularies for public claim-making; by encouraging new forms of subjectivity to engage with the public sphere, and by interjecting existing relations of power with anticipations of justice to come. Law anticipates forms of justice in the future to come. Law is not simply an instrument of domination and a method of coercion, as theorists from Thomas Hobbes to Michel Foucault have argued; "the force of law" (to use a phrase of Jacques Derrida's),[43] involves anticipations of justice to come which it can never quite fulfill but which it always points toward.

Democratic sovereigntists ignore the fact that international human rights norms can empower citizens in democracies by creating new vocabularies for claim-making, as well as by opening new channels of mobilization for civil society actors who then become part of transnational networks of rights activism and hegemonic resistance.[44] Conflict of norms in the new legal universe that we have entered into are unavoidable and may be even desirable, so global constitutionalists are wrong in minimizing the necessity for mediating international norms through the will-formation of democratic peoples. Even human rights norms require interpretation, saturation, and vernacularization; they cannot just be imposed by legal elites and judges upon recalcitrant peoples; rather, they must become elements in the public culture of democratic peoples through their own processes of interpretation, articulation, and iteration.

Jurisgenerativity and Democratic Iterations

How is the jurisgenerative capacity of cosmopolitan norms at play, then, in the current state system? It will be important here to distinguish between a *normative- philosophical* analysis of the relationship between cosmopolitan human rights norms, endorsed through various covenants, and the *institutional channels* through which such covenants shape and influence the signatory states' legislation and political culture.

Human rights covenants and declarations articulate general principles that need contextualization and specification in the form of legal norms. How is this legal content to be shaped? Fundamental human rights, although they are based on the moral principle of the communicative freedom of the person, are also rights that require justiciable form, that is, rights that require embodiment and instantiation in a specific legal framework. Human rights straddle that line between morality and justice; they enable us to judge the legitimacy of law.[45]

In negotiating the relationship between general human rights norms, as formulated in various human rights declarations, and their concretization in the multiple legal documents of various countries, we may invoke the distinction between a *concept* and a *conception*.[46]

We need to differentiate between a *moral concept* such as fairness, equality, and liberty – let us say – and *conceptions* of fairness, equality, and liberty, which would be attained as a result of introducing additional moral and political principles to supplement the original conception.[47] Should justice be defined as "fairness" (Rawls), or as "from each according to his abilities to each according to his needs" (Marx)? To be able to argue for one or the other, we would need to introduce some further claims about scarcity, human needs and wants, the structure of the basic subject of justice, and the like to supplement our original concept of justice.

Applied to the question of how we move from general normative principles of human rights, as enshrined in the various covenants to specific formulations of them as enacted in various legal documents, this would mean the following: the core *concept* of human rights which would form part of any *conception* of the right to have rights would include minimally – so I would argue – the rights to life, liberty (including to freedom from slavery, serfdom, forced occupation, as well as protecting against sexual violence and sexual slavery);[48] the right to some form of personal property; equal freedom of thought (including religion), expression, association, representation, and the right to self-government. Furthermore, liberty requires provisions for the "equal value of liberty" (Rawls), through the guarantee of some bundle of socio-economic goods, including adequate provisions of basic nourishment, shelter, and education.

How is the legitimate range of rights to be determined across liberal democracies or how can we transition from general *concepts* of right to specific *conceptions* of them?[49] Even as fundamental a principle as "the moral equality of persons" assumes a justiciable meaning as a human right once it is posited and interpreted by a democratic lawgiver. And here a range of legitimate variations can always be the case. For example, while equality before the law is a fundamental principle for all societies observing the rule of law, in many societies such as Canada, Israel, and India, this is considered quite compatible with special immunities and entitlements which accrue to individuals in virtue of their belonging to different cultural, linguistic, and religious groups. For societies such as the United States and France, with their more universalistic understandings of citizenship, these multicultural arrangements would be completely unacceptable.[50] At the same time, in France and Germany, the norm of gender equality has led political parties to adopt various versions of the principle of "parité" – namely, that women ought to hold public offices on a 50–50 basis with men, and that, for electoral

127

office, their names ought to be placed on party tickets on an equal footing with male candidates. By contrast, within the United States, gender equality is protected by Title IX of the Education Amendments of 1972,[51] which applies only to major public institutions that receive federal funding. Political parties are excluded from this. There is, in other words, a legitimate range of variation even in the interpretation and implementation of such a basic right as that of "equality before the law." But the legitimacy of this range of variation and interpretation is crucially dependent upon the principle of self-government. *My thesis is that without the right to self-government, which is exercised through proper legal and political channels, we cannot justify the range of variation in the content of basic human rights as being legitimate.* Unless a people can exercise self-government through some form of democratic channels, the translation of human rights norms into justiciable legal claims in a polity is short-circuited. So, the right to self-government is the condition for the possibility of the realization of a democratic schedule of rights. Just as without the actualization of human rights themselves, self-government cannot be meaningfully exercised, so too, without the right to self-government, human rights cannot be contextualized as justiciable entitlements. They are coeval; that is, the *liberal* defense of human rights as limits on the publicly justifiable exercise of power needs to be complemented by the *civic-republican* vision of rights as constituents of a people's exercise of public autonomy. Without the basic rights of the person, republican sovereignty would be blind; and without the exercise of collective autonomy, rights of the person would be empty.[52]

Herein lies the distinctiveness of an approach based on communicative freedom. Freedom of expression and association are not merely citizens' political rights, the content of which can vary from polity to polity; they are necessary conditions for the recognition of individuals as beings who live in a political order of whose legitimacy they have been convinced with good reasons. They undergird the communicative exercise of freedom and, therefore, they are basic human rights as well. Only if the people are viewed not merely as subject to the law, but also as authors of the law, can the contextualization and interpretation of human rights be said to result from public and free processes of democratic opinion and will-formation. Such contextualization, in addition to being subject to various legal traditions in different countries, attains democratic legitimacy insofar as it is carried out through the interaction of legal and political institutions with free public spaces in civil society. When such rights principles are appropriated by people as their own, they lose their parochialism as well as the suspicion of Western paternalism often associated with them. I have called such processes of appropriation "democratic iterations."

By *democratic iterations* I mean complex processes of public argument, deliberation, and exchange through which universalist rights claims are contested and contextualized, invoked and revoked, posited and positioned throughout legal and political institutions, as well as in the associations of civil society. In the process of repeating a term or a concept, we never simply produce a replica of the first intended usage or its original meaning: rather, every repetition is a form of variation. Every iteration transforms meaning, adds to it, enriches it in ever so subtle ways. The iteration and interpretation of norms and of every aspect of the universe of value, however, is never merely an act of repetition.[53] Every act of iteration involves making sense of an authoritative original in a new and different context. The antecedent thereby is reposited and resignified via subsequent usages and references. Meaning is enhanced and transformed; conversely, when the creative appropriation of that authoritative original ceases or stops making sense, then the original loses its authority upon us as well.

If democratic iterations are necessary in order for us to judge the legitimacy of a range of variation in the interpretation of an individual right claim, how can we assess whether democratic iterations have taken place rather than demagogic processes of manipulation or authoritarian indoctrination? Do not democratic iterations themselves presuppose some standards of rights to be properly evaluated? I accept here Jürgen Habermas's insight that "the democratic principle states that only those statutes may claim legitimacy that can meet with the assent (*Zustimmung*) of all citizens in a discursive process of legislation which has been legally constituted."[54] The "legal constitution of a discursive procedure of legislation" is possible only in a society that institutionalizes a communicative framework through which individuals as citizens or residents can participate in opinion- and will-formation regarding the laws that are to regulate their lives in common. Through the public expression of opinion and action, the human person is viewed as a creature who is capable of self-interpreting rights claims. Having rights means having the capacity to initiate action and opinion to be shared by others through an interpretation of the individual right claim itself. Human rights and rights of self-government are intertwined. Though the two are not identical, through institutions of self-government alone can the

129

citizens and residents of a polity articulate justifiable distinctions between human rights and civil, political rights, and judge the range of their legitimate variation. I think that this is Habermas's meaning when he writes, "political rights ground the status of free and equal active citizens. This status is self-referential insofar as it enables citizens to change and expand their various rights and duties, or 'material legal status,' so as to interpret and develop their private and civic autonomy simultaneously."[55]

A lucid account of the dynamic interaction between politics and the law by Robert Post throws light on the interplay between rights claims and democratic iterations. Post writes:

> Politics and law are thus two distinct ways of managing the inevitable social facts of agreement and disagreement. As social practices, politics and law are both independent and interdependent. They are independent in the sense that they are incompatible. To submit a political controversy to legal resolution is to remove it from the political domain; to submit a legal controversy to political resolution is to undermine the law. Yet they are interdependent in the sense that law requires politics to produce the shared norms that law enforces, whereas politics requires law to stabilize and entrench the shared values the politics strives to achieve.[56]

But if "the boundary between law and politics is essentially contested, then judicial judgments engage but do not pre-empt politics."[57] It is this "engagement" between the juridical and the legal that democratic iterations also aim at.

Democratic legitimacy reaches back to principles of *normative justification*. Democratic iterations do not alter conditions of the normative validity of practical discourses that are established independently of them; rather, democratic iterations enable us to judge as *legitimate or illegitimate* processes of opinion and will-formation through which rights claims are contextualized and contested, expanded and revised through actual institutional practices in the light of such criteria.[58] Such criteria of judgment enable us to distinguish a *de facto consensus* from a *rationally motivated* one.

Human rights norms assume "flesh and blood" through democratic iterations. Such processes have also been called "saturation" and "vernacularization."[59] The democratic sovereigntists' fears, then, that cosmopolitan human rights norms must override democratic legislation are philosophically unfounded, because the very interpre-

130

tation and implementation of human rights norms are *radically dependent* upon the democratic will-formation of the *demos*, which is, of course, not to say that there can be no conflict either of interpretation or implementation – this is a question to which I return in the final section of this essay.

Cosmopolitan Norms and Legal Practice

What is the institutional interaction between cosmopolitan norms and legislative and non-legislative processes, and how can democratic iterations help us understand such processes better?[60] It is first necessary to distinguish between international and transnational law. By "international law," I understand public legal conventions pertaining to the world community at large, some of which may be formulated in written form, such as the Universal Declaration of Human Rights, and others of which, such as norms of *jus cogens*, are unwritten but pertain to customary international law. *Jus cogens* norms are peremptory; this means that any treaties or international agreements that engage in gross human rights violations by advocating genocide, ethnic cleansing, slavery, or mass murder are *eo ipso* invalid and command no obligation to be obeyed.

In defining "transnational law," I follow Harold Koh's focus on "transnational legal process." He writes:

> the theory and practice of how public and private actors including nation-states, international organizations, multinational enterprises, nongovernmental organizations, and private individuals, interact in a variety of public and private, domestic and international fora to make, interpret and enforce rules of transnational law . . . transnational law is both dynamic – mutating from public to private, from domestic to international and back again – and constitutive, in the sense of operating to reconstitute national interests.[61]

Duly executed foreign and international law is binding upon lawmakers, as the US Constitution itself states in Article VI on the status of treaties.[62] In this respect, there is no contradiction between the will of democratic legislatures and the force of international law and treaties. Entering into such agreements or declining to do so is a crucial aspect of sovereignty itself. Yet, unlike some jurisdictions in which foreign and international law automatically become part of domestic law, in the US treaties are not self-executing and require congressional ratification.

131

It is the jurisgenerative potential of transnational law in Harold Koh's sense which has interested me in this essay. Transnational norms are not opposed to democratic will-formation; they facilitate rather than limit the expansion of democratic legitimation. However, because the Universal Declaration is "only" a declaration of principles and does not detail mechanisms for enforcement, some argue that it does not function sufficiently *as* law,[63] while others see it as a different kind *of* law. In several articles, Judith Resnik has claimed that by ratifying treaties, domestic obligations are altered, and that, particularly in a federal system, judges duly regard valid treaties as binding law. Resnik calls such processes "law's migration."[64]

Another common method of implementation for UN provisions involves the establishment of "expert bodies" chartered to elaborate the meaning of conventions by promulgating "general comments" and by receiving reports from member-states, who in turn are obliged to detail how they are compliant with or failing to live up to their commitments as parties to conventions.[65] Further, in some jurisdictions (but not generally in the United States), international obligations can be a direct source of legally enforceable rights through litigation in national courts.[66] In addition to processes of law's migration and the establishment of expert bodies, cosmopolitan norms enshrined in multilateral covenants can create process of democratic iterations via the action of social movements and civil society actors.

Claiming Rights Across Borders: CEDAW and Women Living Under Muslim Law

In "Global Feminism, Citizenship and the State," the Iranian sociologist Valentine Moghadam analyzes the effects of an international human rights regime, of transnational civil society, and of a global public sphere on women's rights in Muslim countries.[67] Moghadam, who considers case studies from the Republic of Iran and the Kingdom of Morocco in addition to Egypt, Algeria, and Turkey, explores how "local communities or national borders" are affected by globalized norms. She asks: "What of the migration and mobility of feminist ideas and their practitioners? How do local struggles intersect with global discourses on women's rights? What role is played by feminists in the diaspora, and what is the impact of the state?" (Moghadam, "Global Feminisim: , Citizenship and the State": 255). By analyzing the formation of women's rights and feminist organizations, both

132

within specific countries and through transnational feminist networks, Moghadam shows that international conferences and treaties such as CEDAW have created tools that women can tailor to their own contexts.

Moghadam maps the "significant variations in women's legal status and social positions across the Muslim world" (ibid.: 260–1). Yet, in general, "similar patterns of women's second-class citizenship" (Moghadam: 260) can be identified in terms of family life and economic opportunity. Citizenship is transmitted through the father, and marriage laws give men rights that women do not have. In both Iran and Morocco, for example, the state, the family, and economic forms of dependency create what Moghadam calls the "patriarchal gender contract" (ibid.: 258).

Responding in the 1980s to efforts to strengthen application of gendered Muslim family law, various women's networks came into being. Nine women from Algeria, Sudan, Morocco, Pakistan, Bangladesh, Iran, Mauritius, and Tanzania, formed an action committee that resulted in Women Living Under Muslim Laws (WLUML), which serves as a clearing house for information about struggles and strategies. WLUML includes women with differing approaches to religion; some are anti-religious, while others, such as Malaysia's Sisters in Islam, are observant Muslims. Some women work to abandon religious strictures, while others challenge interpretations of religious laws and make arguments from within texts and traditions.

By reviewing recent conflicts in Iran and in Morocco on family rights, Moghadam argues that WLUML, along with the Women's Learning Partnership, had an impact through interactions between state-centered and transnational forms of action. She concludes that "The integration of North and South in the global circuits of capital and the construction of a transnational public sphere in opposition to the dark side of globalization has meant that feminism is not 'Western' but global" (Moghadam, "Global Feminisim, Citizenship and the State": 271). Her examples highlight ironies in global struggles: the struggle for women's equality requires revisiting the discourse of universalistic human rights just as the conditions of global migrations raise questions about whether to aspire to global citizenship, to particularized affiliations, or combinations thereof. Further, in an important confirmation of democratic iterations, Moghadam suggests that the more culturally embedded a group is within a nation-state, the more effective could be their efforts to incorporate universalist norms.

An extraordinarily interesting case of democratic iterations occurred when, in the course of a debate in Canada concerning whether or not religious arbitration courts ought to be legalized, Canadian Muslim women turned to WLUML to help them overturn Muslim arbitration courts. This case is worth considering in some detail, as follows.

Many countries now promote "alternative dispute resolution" fora to create state-enforced private settlements of conflicts in lieu of adjudication of rights.[68] As Audrey Macklin explains, in "Particularized Citizenship: Encultured Women and the Public Sphere," under the law of the Canadian Province of Ontario, women are rights holders when families dissolve and they can seek compensation for household labors that enabled their husbands to develop careers.[69] Ontario also permits resolutions through negotiations that result in "domestic contracts." In addition, when disputants use arbitration, those outcomes are enforceable in court. (In contrast, in Quebec, family law arbitrations are advisory rather than binding.)

In 2003, a then-new Islamic Institute for Civil Justice offered to arbitrate family and inheritance conflicts under Muslim law, prompting an inquiry about whether faith-based arbitration ought to be given legal force. Opposition came from the Canadian Council of Muslim Women, who worked with the transnational group, WLUML, discussed by Moghadam. Reliant on networks "as Canadians, as women, as immigrants, and as Muslims," the opponents built constituencies both locally and globally, just as they argued from national and transnational principles, including the UDHR's commitments to dignity and equality. Proponents of faith-based resolutions were similarly domestic and international – including "the Christian Legal Fellowship, the Salvation Army, B'nai Brith, the Sunni Masjid El Noor, and the Ismaili Muslims."[70] The denouement was Canadian legislation that does not prohibit parties from turning to faith-based tribunals but gives such judgments no legally enforceable effect.

As Macklin details, women played central roles in this case, expressing "political citizenship in the public sphere of law reform," and doing so through transnational and transcultural claims of equality. "Claiming their entitlement as legal citizens of Canada to participate in governance, they demanded equal citizenship as Canadian women. At the same time, they pointedly refused to renounce their cultural citizenship or to confine their gender critique to a specific cultural context" (Macklin, "Particularized Citizenship": 276).

Such practices not only render the meaning of citizenship more complex by revealing the interaction of the language of universal rights and culturally embedded identities; they also expand the vocabulary of public claim-making in democracies and aid them in evolving into "strong democracies." They reconstitute the meaning of local, national, and global citizenship through processes of democratic iterations in which cosmopolitan norms enable new vocabularies of claim-making to emerge, assume a concrete local and contextual coloration, and often migrate across borders and jurisdictions in increasingly complex and interconnected dialogues, confrontations, and iterations.

Conclusion

Transnational law creates wider and deeper interdependencies among nations, pushing them farther and farther towards structures of global governance. While the world system of states is not one of perfect cooperation with defined rules of justice, neither are relations among states "mere contractual obligations," as Thomas Nagel has argued. The current global system of interdependence is sufficiently thick enough to trigger significant relations of justice across borders, which are weaker than those within nation-states, but certainly stronger than those envisaged by the world picture of sovereigntistes. The demands for global coordination in response to the recent economic worldwide meltdown is but one indication, among many others, of this new phase of global interdependence.

The law's migrations and democratic iterations reveal that global human rights discourses move across increasingly porous borders to weaken and to render irrelevant the Rawlsian distinction between "liberal" and "decent-hierarchical" societies.[71] Some societies, particularly those in which the human rights of women, of ethnic, religious, linguistic, and other minorities were curtailed on grounds of faith and religion, must now contend with increasingly transnational movements and actors who network across borders in developing new strategies of claim-making such as to expand the human rights' agenda. These developments are all the more significant since they undermine the divide between "liberal tolerance" on the one hand and "liberal interventionism" on the other, by inducting citizens, social movements, churches, synagogues, mosques, cultural institutions, the global media, and so on, into a contentious dialogue about justice across borders. Recent movements mobilizing to end genocide in Darfur, to help AIDS victims in Africa, against the practice of female genital mutilation, for protecting the rights of undocumented migrants – *les sans-papiers* – and many others are illustrative of this new global activism enabled, in part, by the spread of cosmopolitan norms.

We have entered a new stage in the development of global civil society, in which the relationship between state sovereignty and various human rights regimes generates dangers of increasing interventionism, but also paradoxically creates spaces for cascading forms of democratic iteration across borders. I see no reason not to acknowledge the ambiguities of this moment. But, as a critical social theorist, I look for those moments of rupture and possible transformation when social actors reappropriate new norms such as to enable new subjectivities to enter the public sphere and to alter the very meaning of claims-making in the public sphere itself. This is the promise of democratic iterations and cosmopolitan norms in the present.

Despite these developments, or maybe because of them, there is also a multiplication of zones which seek to escape the force of law. From the *extra-ordinary renditions* of enemy combatants to unknown localities, with the cooperation of US and European governments, to the emergence of *maquiladoras* in Central and South America, and free-growth zones in China and Southeast Asia, not to mention the decline of the state everywhere in Africa, there is also a process of "dejuridification" afoot. The attempt is to resist the spread of global law and to create enclaves without democratic accountability and parliamentary supervision, and to deny the right to have rights altogether. In many free-trade and growth zones, the rights of workers to fair pay, to assemble, unionize, and organize are suspended and violently controlled. In the desperate straits that the current world economic crises will generate in many developing countries, it is likely that these norms will be further suspended in a Faustian bargain to keep foreign direct investment coming and the economies growing.

I don't have a good explanation for how or why these processes of *constitutionalization* and *dejuridification* continue to coexist in the world society at the present; but I want to insist on the significance of instruments of cosmopolitan norms to help combat them. These are not complicit in the legitimation of, but rather, they are enabling conditions of resistance to, the forces of a global capitalism run amok. Any defensible vision of global justice in the current world order will have to take these legal instruments and documents seriously and work with them rather than against them. We need to overcome not only the reductionist resistance of many on the left to the force of transnational law, but also the defensiveness of many on the right who see transnational law as undermining democratic sovereignty, when, in fact, it can enhance it. However, constitutionalization, without a people who can also claim the constitution as its own law, certainly as embedded in and as interactive with global cosmopolitan norms, is not an ideal that democrats can countenance without some concern. Call this loyalty to an old-fashioned Enlightenment ideal!

— 8 —

DEMOCRATIC EXCLUSIONS AND DEMOCRATIC ITERATIONS
Dilemmas of Just Membership and Prospects of Cosmopolitan Federalism

On Political Membership

At the dawn of the twenty-first century, the transnational movement of peoples has emerged as a major political and policy issue of our times. Whether they are caused by economic migrants from the poorer regions of the world trying to reach the shores of resource-rich democracies in the North and the West; whether they are undertaken by asylum and refuge seekers escaping persecution, civil wars, and natural disasters; or whether they are initiated by displaced persons, who are fleeing civil war, ethnic conflict, and state-inflicted violence in their own societies, such movements have presented the world state system with unprecedented challenges. Given the salience of these developments, it is surprising that the cross-border movements of peoples, and the philosophical as well as policy problems suggested by them, have been the object of such scant attention in contemporary political philosophy.[1]

In *The Rights of Others*, I intended to fill this lacuna in contemporary thought by focusing on *political membership*. By this term I meant the "principles and practices for incorporating aliens and strangers, immigrants and newcomers, refugees and asylum

---

This essay originally appeared as my response to critics, in *European Journal of Political Theory* 6 (October 2007): 445–62. Contributing to this Symposium were Alexander Aleinikoff, Rainer Bauböck, Angelia Means, and Saskia Sassen. It has been substantially revised. The postscript on "The Principle of Affected Interests" was not included in the original response.

seekers into existing polities" (*Rights of Others*: 1). The principal category through which membership has been regulated in the modern world, namely, national citizenship, has been disaggregated and unbundled into diverse elements, and state sovereignty has been frayed. "We are like travelers navigating an unknown terrain with the help of old maps, drawn at a different time and in response to different needs," I wrote. "While the terrain we are traveling on, the world society of states, has changed, our normative map has not" (*Rights of Others*: 2).

I approached political membership against the backdrop of the altered institutions of national citizenship and sovereignty and with the following conceptual scheme in mind:

- first, I highlighted the constitutive dilemma at the heart of liberal democracies between sovereign self-determination claims to control the quality and quantity of the movement of peoples across state boundaries versus adherence to universal human rights principles;
- second, I analyzed this constitutive dilemma in the light of a discourse ethic and asked whether a discourse-ethical approach could throw any light on conditions of just membership;
- third, I acknowledged a distinction between *the principle of rights* and the *schedule of rights* as being necessary to differentiate among the following: on the one hand, universalistic normative commitments that *ought* to bind the actions of the democratic legislature, versus the acceptable *scope* and the *variety* of civic, political, and socio-economic rights that can vary across historical, cultural, institutional, and jurisprudential traditions, on the other hand;
- fourth, I argued that "the human right to membership" follows from the application of discourse-ethical principles to practices of citizenship and naturalization. In my formulation, this right entails that no democratic polity *ought* to stipulate conditions of naturalization such that the "other(s)" would be permanently barred from membership. Reasons that barred you from membership because of the *kind* of being you were, your ascriptive and non-elective attributes such as your race, gender, religion, ethnicity, language community, or sexuality, would not be acceptable from a discourse-ethical point of view (ibid.: 138–9). Conditions such as length of residency in the host country, language competency, a certain proof of civic literacy, demonstration of material resources and marketable skills, surely, can all

be misused and abused in practice by governmental authorities; yet legislating some version of such conditions belongs within the scope of the differentiation between the principle of rights and the schedule of rights that can be enacted by different democracies in different ways. (For an explication of the distinction between the principle of rights and the schedule of rights, see pp. 74–5, 126–9 above.)

While finding this analytical frame on the whole plausible, my critics question how, if at all, I can justify democratic exclusions (Rainer Baubock and Angelia Means); they ask whether the right to membership, as I formulate it, is plausible in the light of the specific constitutional practices of various democracies (Alexander Aleinikoff); they challenge my distinction between normatively acceptable and normatively problematic restrictions on membership; they query whether the concept of democratic iterations is a normative or an empirical one (Baubock and Aleinikoff); and they take issue with the social theory behind the binarism of the national and the global, and push my vision of cosmopolitan federalism toward multiple configurations of rights, territoriality, and authority (Saskia Sassen).

Democratic Exclusions and the Paradox of Democratic Legitimacy

Means and Bauboeck each question the justification of principles of democratic closure in my account. Means notes, "While Benhabib is clear that certain reasons of excluding others are unjustifiable, the difference between her *principle of closure* and the principles of closure provided by political liberalism and communitarianism remains ambivalent. I think this ambivalence occurs because she is more comfortable detecting unjustifiable exclusion than justifying exclusion"[2] (*European Journal of Political Theory* 6: 410). Baubock reiterates this concern: "Under present conditions, porous borders are the best we can hope for. What remains unclear is whether Benhabib defends such moderate closure on principled grounds or as a constraint under non-ideal conditions."[3]

These are fair concerns, which go to the heart of my position.[4] In *The Rights of Others*, I distinguished the *cultural-communitarian*, the *civic-republican*, and the *cosmopolitan-federalist* approaches to democratic closure. The cultural communitarians – by which I meant

Michael Walzer's claims in *The Spheres of Justice* (1983) – argue that democracies are built on ethical communities who share ties of language, memory, and culture. The polity ought to reflect the self-understanding of these diverse ethno-cultural communities, each of which has its own distinct traditions, voices, and memories. To want to erase this diversity in some global mega-state would sap the roots of democratic freedoms which themselves can only grow upon the soil of such communal attachments. Just like the communitarians, civic republicans – and here I chose David Jacobson's work as being representative[5] – stress the shared character of ethical values and principles in constituting a democracy, but they add that the institution of *citizenship* would be devalued and lose meaning unless it included membership within bounded communities. Too much and too frequent immigration, they argue, not only strains the absorptive capacities of democracies, but devalues citizenship by making the political bonds increasingly thinner, until the polity is transformed into a community of strangers. Civic republicans defend bounded democracies not primarily because they want to protect the diversity of cultural communities, but because they want to protect the value of democratic citizenship itself.

In contrast to communitarians and civic republicans, I am concerned with the *logic of democratic representation* and see the necessity for closure to follow from this normative principle. Precisely because democracies enact laws that are binding on those who authorize them, the scope of democratic legitimacy needs to be circumscribed by the *demos* that has bounded itself as a people on a given territory (*Rights of Others*: 219). Following the insights of Montesquieu, Kant, and Arendt, each of whom rejected world government, I argue that an unbounded global polity cannot be a democratic one.

It belongs to the logic of representation, as noted by Thomas Hobbes in the *Leviathan* (1651), that there must be a unit that does the *authorizing* for another *to act in its name*.[6] *Representatives* are actors who impersonate the ones who authorize them. Representation entails demarcation. Whether this demarcation leads to national boundaries as they currently stand is certainly open to debate. As Rainer Bauböck notes, a territorial border serves to *demarcate* both a jurisdiction and to regulate the flow of peoples across it. While democratic self-governance involves the demarcation of jurisdiction, it ought not to prohibit the flow of peoples across borders in both directions. Porous borders, therefore, are not the second-best alternative under "non-ideal conditions" of imperfect

141

justice in a world-community; they are intrinsic to the logic of democratic representation and thus to the exercise of public and private
freedom.

Yet, unlike the communitarians and civic republicans, I do not
believe that the nation-state system alone, which has housed democracies since the late nineteenth century, is adequate to this task. Quite
to the contrary: I am fairly open to the suggestion that the peoples
of the world may one day decide to reconfigure themselves along
different boundaries and configurations from the ones by which they
do today. The 195-odd states represented in the United Nations may
be reduced or increased in number and non-state peoples may find
their own public agencies of representation. It is also possible that,
at some point in the future, in each unit representing the peoples of
the world two kinds of elections may be held: one for candidates
running for office in that specific nation-state, and the other for candidates to a Global Peoples' Assembly of cosmopolitan citizens. What
we cannot change, despite all institutional configurations, is the *logic
of representation* which forces delineation or demarcation from one
another of the units represented. Even world citizenship within a
federated structure cannot solve this riddle insofar as a federated
structure would still involve some units of jurisdiction, whether these
are separated from one another territorially, functionally, or along
some other criteria.

Frankly, this conclusion is not particularly troubling, since the
source of much global injustice in the world is not the necessity of
demarcating representative units from one another, but the fact that
the nation-state structures which have hitherto housed democracies
have become increasingly frayed in allocating membership and democratic voice fairly. Whether we think of the decisional units involved
in the first admittance of migrants, refugees, and asylum seekers as
today's nation-states or tomorrow's nested and decentered sovereignties that would reconfigure "rights, territory and authority" (Saskia
Sassen) along new lines, we would still face the normative question
which Means poses: "Once we are prepared to accept this human
right to membership, we must still ask how many new members (and
hence how much value pluralism) we can absorb before we overwhelm the iterative process of democratic nation-building" (*EJPT* 6:
410). I do not believe that the question as to "how many new
members" a nation – I would prefer to say a polity – can absorb,
permits a clear theoretical answer, because its addressee cannot be
the political philosopher but only the democratic citizens themselves.
That there are limits to democratic iterative processes – cultural,

economic, and legal ones – is clear; what is less clear is what *kind* of an answer one can give as a political philosopher to this question, if one is also normatively committed to the democratic self-reflexivity of polities in defining and refining themselves. From my point of view, there would be twofold normative constraints on any answer that may be given and once these constraints are met, a range of responses would be acceptable: respect for universal human rights and the institutionalization of just, fair, and open processes of democratic iteration such as would mediate between *all* those whose interests are affected and the democratic citizens themselves. Beyond that, I see no coherent answer to Means's challenging question.[7]

The Paradox of Democratic Legitimacy and Sovereignty

In *The Rights of Others*, I have circumscribed in general theoretical terms the paradox of democratic legitimacy. The paradox is that the republican sovereign ought to undertake to bind its will through a series of precommitments to a set of formal and substantive norms, usually referred to as "human rights." Rights protect the autonomy of citizens and residents as private persons, while also creating conditions of participation for them as public agents. While this paradox can never be fully resolved, its impact can be mitigated through the renegotiation and reiteration of the dual commitments to human rights and sovereign self-determination.

There are in effect two paradoxes: that of democratic precommitments and that of democratic closure.[8] In the context of this discussion, the paradox of democratic closure is more pertinent; I have tried to suggest a resolution to the second paradox in chapters 4 and 7 above. All democracies presuppose a principle of membership, according to which some are entitled to political voice while others are excluded. The decision as to who is entitled to have political voice and who is not can only be reached, however, if some who are already members decide who is to be excluded and who is not. This means that there can be no non-circular manner of determining democratic membership. Determining who is a member of the *demos* presupposes that some are already members with the privilege to exclude others; while others have no voice in their own exclusion. The boundaries of the *demos* remain, it seems, a matter of historical contingency and political domination. Before suggesting a solution to this paradox – albeit an imperfect one – let me restate the issue in terms of the logic of sovereignty.

143

Another way of stating the paradox of democratic closure is that *popular* sovereignty is not identical with *territorial* sovereignty, although the two are closely linked, both historically and normatively. Popular sovereignty means that all full members of the *demos* are entitled to have a voice in the articulation of the laws by which the *demos* governs itself. Democratic rule extends its jurisdiction to those who can view themselves as the authors of such rule. But there has never been a perfect overlap between the circle of those who stand under or are affected by the law's authority and those recognized as full members of the *demos*. Territorial sovereignty and democratic voice have never matched completely, because there have always been those resident upon a territory and affected by the laws enacted in the name of the sovereign, but who, nevertheless, have not enjoyed full membership, that is, national citizenship. The new politics of cosmopolitan membership is about negotiating this complex relationship between rights of full membership, democratic voice, and territorial residence. While the *demos*, as the popular sovereign, must assert control over a specific territorial domain, it can also engage in reflexive acts of self-constitution whereby the boundaries of the *demos* can be readjusted and democratic sovereignty itself can be disassembled or reaggregated.[9]

Such democratic iterations take place today not only within boundaries of the nation-state, but also in transnational public spheres of communication and action, in which migrants participate who are themselves often bi-nationals, ex-colonials and post-nationals, as well as being seasonal or temporary workers in their host countries. The immigration debate in the spring of 2010 in the USA, concerning the fate of undocumented aliens, illustrated the complexity of this new public sphere of democratic iterations very well. This debate about the status of the undocumented migrants, the majority of whom are of Hispanic, and particularly of Mexican origin, involved not only bilateral negotiations between the USA and Mexico, but negotiations and conversations among Mexican representatives and state and local leaders, particularly but not exclusively in those regions of the USA especially affected by migration, such as Arizona, Texas, California, and New Mexico.

On April 23, 2010, the Governor of the state of Arizona signed Arizona's immigration enforcement law that would permit local law enforcement officials to seek, identify, arrest, and detain, and even deport those immigrants unable to show "proper alien residency documents" when stopped and questioned by officials.[10] Not only did the law arouse legitimate concerns about "racial profiling," but there was the significant likelihood that officers would wrongfully arrest legal resident aliens.

In response to this measure, pro-immigrant activist groups engaged in militant actions throughout the cities of the USA. Human rights groups and groups defending the rights of migrants, such as MALDAF (the Mexican American Legal Defense Fund), undertook litigation in US courts. In a case filed in front of Judge Susan Bolton of the Federal District Court in Phoenix, one of the parties was the US Federal Government, who maintained that immigration policy was under the purview of the federal government and not of individual states. Surprisingly, the US government was supported by "The Mexican government, and was joined by seven other Latin American nations . . . the attorneys general of several states backed Arizona."[11]

The fact that Mexican and other Latin American governments can be parties to a lawsuit along with the US government in an American Federal Court, is indicative of the reality of transnational public spheres. Although this process of democratic iteration will reach some decisional closure at some future point, through the actions of the US Supreme Court or the adoption by the US Congress of an immigration Bill, this moment of decision, far from being one of finality, will lead to new and further democratic iterations. The political philosopher as discourse ethicist is committed to continue the democratic dialogue, such that the hiatus between the discursive community of all those whose interests are affected[12] by a legislation and the circle of formally recognized democratic citizens, while it can never be eliminated, can nonetheless be reduced through processes of ever-wider circles of public representation and participation. Millions of undocumented workers within the US have not yet acquired the status of legal residency, let alone of democratic citizenship; but they have become political agents by actively engaging in the public sphere through their strikes, petitions, and demonstrations.[13]

The Right to Membership: The Vicious or Virtuous Circle?

While acknowledging the paradox of democratic legitimacy, Alexander Aleinikoff is concerned to show that "no conversation can answer the prior question of who should participate in the conversation – or at least, it cannot do so without leaving itself open to the question of who should participate in the conversation about who should participate in the conversation about who should . . . you get the idea"[14] (*EJPT* 6: 427).

In *The Rights of Others*, I noted that, due to the open-endedness of discourses of moral justification, there would always be an inevitable and necessary tension between moral obligations and duties, resulting from our membership in bounded communities and the moral perspective that we must adopt as human beings *simpliciter*. From a universalist and cosmopolitan point of view, boundaries, including state borders and frontiers, require justification. Practices of inclusion and exclusion are always subject to questioning from the standpoint of the infinitely open moral conversation (14–15).

The dilemma is this: either a discourse theory is simply *irrelevant* to membership practices in that it cannot articulate *any* justifiable criteria of exclusion, or it simply *accepts* existing practices of exclusion as *morally neutral* and historically contingent arrangements that require no further validation. This would suggest that a discourse theory of democracy is itself chimerical insofar as democracy requires a morally justifiable closure, and this is a conclusion which discourse ethic cannot deliver.

In face of this, the discourse ethicist insists *upon the necessary disjunction, as well as the necessary mediation between the moral and the ethical, the moral and the political*. The task for her is one of mediations, not reductions. How can one mediate moral universalism and ethical particularism? How can one mediate legal and political norms with moral ones? Questions of membership confront one repeatedly with such challenges of mediation: if we do not differentiate between *the moral and the ethical*, we cannot criticize the exclusionary citizenship and membership practices of specific cultural, religious, and ethnic communities. If we do not differentiate between *morality and legality*, we cannot criticize the legally enacted norms of democratic majorities even when they refuse to admit refugees to their midst, turn away asylum seekers at the door, and shut off their borders to immigrants. If we do not differentiate between *morality and functionality*, we cannot challenge practices of immigration, naturalization, and border- control for violating our cherished moral, constitutional, and even ethical beliefs. The circularity in conversations of membership is thus not a vicious but a virtuous one: we are "always already" situated in some community of membership when we raise question about its boundaries; our being situated in this manner is the precondition for being able to raise the question of membership in the first place. This "hermeneutic circle" of membership presupposes some established understandings, practices, and institutions, and it also enables one to critically reflect upon them and to engage in the kinds of critical mediations outlined above.[15]

146

Does this mean, asks Aleinikoff, "whether anyone affected by the conversation should be able to participate?" From the moral point of view, my answer is a clear "yes." "But," objects Aleinikoff, "I don't think we structure our political institutions this way. Note that this would not limit membership to resident immigrants. Why under this theory, for example, ought not all Iraqis be members of the US conversation?" (*EJPT* 6: 428) Why not indeed?[16]

The moral point of view requires that all those who are affected by a norm, a law, a practice be included in the conversation of justification. Let us note that this discourse principle is necessarily indeterminate in that the circle of its addressees always needs to be adjusted according to which people can raise the claim of being affected by a norm and its potential consequences. Insofar as the US's declaration of war upon Iraq, without the approval of the UN Security Council, affected and destroyed the way of life of an entire nation, the Iraqis very much ought to be, and ought to have been, part of the moral as well as policy conversation in the US, though they are not part of the *decisional structure* of US institutions. Aleinikoff is concerned with how, where, and when there is a cut-off point such that nation-state centered institutions can reach legitimate decisions and closure can be attained. I am less interested in justifying the finality of closure, but rather more concerned with the *circulation of normative* issues and questions throughout the public spheres and civil societies of democracies, and beyond their borders, such as to enable the democratic conversation to continue despite such decisional closure.

Ascriptive versus Non-Ascriptive Criteria for Allocating Membership

Aleinikoff is equally troubled by the distinction between "ascriptive" and "non-ascriptive" grounds for denying access to membership. "Is it really true that denying one a place in the conversation on these grounds [i.e., skills, language and the like] is any less dehumanizing than denying a place on ascriptive grounds?" Aleinikoff is here voicing a concern that has been repeated by a number of critics of *The Rights of Others*.[17] Let me restate the assumptions that have guided me in making this distinction: I presupposed that moral beings are worthy of blame and praise for their actions, that is, for what they can help doing or omit doing, as opposed to what they cannot change or affect through their decisions and behavior. While one cannot alter at will one's sex, race, skin color, ethnicity, linguistic, and religious community one is born into, the latter three permit more negotiability and transformation over time than the first three (despite the presence of sex-change operations for a small group of people who can afford them). Thus, one can "pass" as a member of another ethnic group; one can "convert" to another religion; and one can learn to "speak the tongue of the other." Nevertheless, preventing an immigrant from becoming a member of a host country on the basis of such ascribed characteristics is to disrespect their moral agency in two ways: first, by blaming them for what they *cannot help* being, and, second, for rejecting them for the *kind* of being they are in virtue of their ethnicity, religion, and language group. This is discrimination and this contradicts the universal moral respect we owe each human being. The distinction between ascriptive and non-ascriptive characteristics is justified in the light of two moral principles: the first is the principle of attributing moral blame and merit to human beings on account of the exercise of their *free agency*; the second is respecting the principle of *non-discrimination*. Insofar as I did not distinguish clearly between these two principles as they led to denial of the right to membership on ascriptive grounds, I am grateful to my critics for having made me aware of the necessity of distinguishing them from one another.

What about poverty and dire economic conditions into which one is born? Aren't they also circumstances of birth for which one cannot be held accountable? Which human child is responsible for the condition of the society and the region of the world it is born into? Why should equitable life chances be influenced and determined by these arbitrary circumstances of birth? Furthermore, in reality isn't there a "color to poverty" so that discriminating against someone economically very often means discriminating against them racially or ethnically as well? In the minds of many, the distinction between ascriptive and non-ascriptive characteristics for allocating membership thus flows over into questions of global economic inequality in relation to migrations. Nonetheless, I will insist on keeping these issues separate while exploring their interconnectedness.

In defense of porous borders, I accept and very much emphasize the dynamic interconnectedness and interdependency of societies in a world economy. While from a social-scientific point of view, the connections between poverty and migrations are hard to establish, it is well accepted that it is not the world's poorest who migrate; nor is it the case that migration is always a solution to poverty.[18] Porous borders and flexible markets for economic migrants are beneficial not only for the receiving economies; they are also defensible in moral terms because the means to seek an adequate livelihood, wherever on the globe, is a fundamental human right.[19] However, we also have to accept the right of self-governing communities to determine *certain* conditions of first entry, as well as membership and to limit immigration. While it is unjust to deny eventual membership to anyone who has been absorbed into the civil society and market of a particular community for a certain period of time, it is simply incoherent to argue that communities everywhere and at all times have an obligation to admit *all* who claim first entry and who aspire to membership. Once first admittance occurs, membership ought to be open *in principle* to all those who aspire to it and who are willing to meet *certain* conditions to attain it – including the undocumented whose status can be legalized or regularized via amnesty, paying of fines, exiting a country to seek proper re-entry, and so on. But membership will involve satisfying some requirements such as language competence,[20] skills, and so on. It cannot be a status freely distributed to all. The hardest questions today in developing a just immigration and citizenship policy involve making these requirements compatible with general international human rights norms.[21]

In *The Rights of Others*, I certainly did not mean to suggest that an unemployed immigrant ought to be denied citizenship or thrown out of the country, as Corey Robin seems to imply.[22] If a person has been a member of a specific civil society and economy for a certain period of time and has become unemployed due to circumstances arising within that economy, these ought to be weighed in the same way that they would be weighed in determining the economic entitlements of a full citizen, rather than being considered justifiable for immediately deporting migrant, and often undocumented, workers. Nevertheless, *some* regulation of economic migration and the close supervision of the labor contracts and conditions of migrant workers are beneficial, not only for indigenous labor markets but principally for migrant workers themselves. Their labor is coveted precisely because they work for lower wages, have no entitlements to social and economic benefits; furthermore, their services can undermine the rights of domestic workers by offering a cheaper source of labor. Global capitalism richly benefits from these regional and inter-country discrepancies. It is foolish to believe that global capitalism will protect the cosmopolitan rights of workers; rather, they need to be fought for in transnational alliances with domestic workers, joining hands across borders as well as mobilizing the institutional means of transnational organizations such as

149

the International Labor Organization and even the World Trade Organization.

As Saskia Sassen points out, migrations occur under structured conditions of "pull" and "push" factors: certain migratory patterns get established over time because of the economic interdependencies of sending and receiving countries.[23] Not everyone in the world wishes to migrate to everywhere else in the world! Migrations are often due to historical causes, such as imperialism and colonialism and forceful acquisition of territories of indigenous peoples. To express this prosaically, "We are here," say the migrants, "because you were there"; or "We did not cross the border, the border crossed us."

These historical factors color every nation's immigration, citizenship, and naturalization laws and policies. Today's migrants are often ex-, neo- and post-colonials of the nations in which they reside or to which they seek admission. Such factors belong to the domain of the "ethical," that is, to those circumstances which have given rise to special obligations among peoples because of their shared histories, interactions, memories, and collective experiences. Nevertheless, such considerations alone cannot replace human rights principles that ought to govern just membership practices. Thus, many countries of the world grant privileged citizenship or permanent residency status to "co-ethnics," who wish to return to their countries of origin, or who wish to retain citizenship ties even while not residing in that said territory. The difficulties in such arrangements, as with Israel's Law of Return, for example – which grants Jewish people, defined in accordance with certain criteria, "a right of return" – is not that this privilege exists, but that it is denied to all others. Palestinian refugees, for instance, for whom the land of Israel is also a homeland, should have a right of return; likewise, those who are neither Jews nor Palestinians, but are either guest workers in Israel or children of migrants, ought to be granted regular naturalization options.[24]

The fact that migratory movements take place against the background of structured relations of interdependence in a world economy inevitably raises the question of global distributive justice and migrations. In *The Rights of Others*, I devoted chapter 3 to an analysis of global justice schemes developed by Thomas Pogge, Charles Beitz, and others (pp. 94 ff.). I remain more convinced than ever that what is required is not only a global redistribution of resources, but a restructuring of the institutions of the world economy, both at the institutional and non-institutional levels, such that poor countries of the world can be helped to develop sustainable economies and participate in the world economy under fair conditions of trade. Whether we give priority to a "global resource dividend," as Thomas Pogge has advocated,[25] or whether we prioritize sustainable development, as Amartya Sen pleads for, these economic reforms on a global scale cannot obviate the individual right to migration and crossing borders – whether those of economic migrants, refugees, or asylum seekers. These issues, although interrelated, operate along two different normative principles. I concur with Bauböck when he writes, "the primary value of open borders lies in increasing human liberty rather than in reducing human inequality" (*EJPT* 6: 401).

Democratic Iterations

All four critics are sympathetic to this concept and consider it a conceptual innovation in breaking through the deadlock of universalist rights claims and the prerogatives of popular self-determination. Bauböck and Aleinikoff rightly question whether the concept is empirical or normative. Another related concern is whether democratic iterations are only "jurisgenerative" or whether they can be "jurispathic" as well.[26]

Democratic iterations provide us with an idealized account of political legitimacy. This concept has both an empirical and a normative component – as all "legitimacy" concepts since Max Weber attest to.[27] The normative component derives from the constraints that a discourse ethic imposes on any deliberative process in order for it to be deemed justifiable, in the normative sense. Thus, if the conversations which contribute to democratic iterations are not carried out by the most *inclusive participation* of all those whose interests are affected; if these conversations and deliberations do not permit the *questioning* of the conversational agenda, do not guarantee *equality of participation*, then the iterative process is unfair, exclusionary, and illegitimate. In *The Rights of Others*, I built upon the premises of a discourse ethic which I had already articulated in *Situating the Self: Gender, Community and Postmodernism*.[28] Discourse ethics provides procedural constraints guiding the identity of the participants, the rules for agenda setting and the distribution of speech acts, and the like.

Democratic iterations take place in overlapping communities of conversation consisting of what can be named the "demotic community," that is, all those who are formal citizens and residents of a jurisdictional system, and other more fluid and unstructured "communities of conversation" that often involve international and transnational human rights organizations, such as Amnesty International, various UN representative and human rights monitoring bodies, and global activist groups such as Médecins Sans Frontières. Democratic iterations are not concerned with the question, "which norms are valid for human beings at all times and in all places?" but, rather, with questions such as: "In view of our moral, political and constitutional commitments as a people, our international obligations to human rights treaties and documents, what collective decisions can we reach which would be deemed both just and legitimate?" Democratic iterations aim at democratic justice.[29] They mediate between a collectivity's constitutional and institutional responsibilities, and the context-transcending universal claims of human rights and justice to which such a collectivity ought to be equally committed.

In developing the concept of democratic iterations, I relied upon Robert Cover's and Frank Michelman's analyses of "jurisgenerativity."[30] What interested me was the interplay between formal processes of lawmaking and informal processes of opinion- and will-formation. As Robert Cover points out, this interplay, even if uncontrollable by formal legislatures, can also become jurispathic, in that sources of meaning-generation may dry up and the law may stifle rather than stimulate contentious dialogue and the circulation of meaning.[31] Can democratic iterations likewise not be "jurispathic"? May they not hinder the circulation of meaning, cut processes of opinion-and-will-formation short, and restrict iterations to populist politics or formal lawmaking?

In *The Rights of Others*, I failed to clarify these more negative aspects and potential failures of democratic iterative processes. Although I wrote that "Democratic iterations can lead to processes of public self-reflection as well as generating public defensiveness" (198), I did not theorize the conditions under which such public defensiveness would ensue. Precisely because this concept has a normative as well as empirical component, it is situated between *justification* and *legitimation*; it is concerned to analyze how real processes of democratic discourse within and across state boundaries can create or fail to create *justification through legitimation*. I am indebted here to Thomas Franck's lucid statement: legitimacy is "a property of a rule or rule-making institution which itself *exerts a pull towards* compliance on those addressed normatively because those addressed believe that the rule or institution has come into being and operates in accordance with generally accepted principles of right process"[32] (my emphasis). Democratic iterations are also processes through which such "pull" emerges.

Toward New Configurations of Rights, Territory, and Authority

In her reflections on *The Rights of Others*, Sassen is less concerned with normative issues than with the social-theoretical presuppositions of my argument. Her central claim is that I still operate with the binarism of the national versus the global, and that consequently the project of cosmopolitan federalism, which Sassen endorses, remains limited in its normative vision as well as social scope. Sassen makes the following crucial observation:

> Thus the epochal transformation we call globalization is taking place inside the national to a far larger extent than is usually recognized. It is here that the most complex meanings of the global are being constituted, and the national is also often one of the key enablers and enactors of the emergent global scale. A good part of globalization consist of an enormous variety of micro-processes that begin to denationalize what had been constructed as national – whether policies, capital, political subjectivities, urban spaces, temporal frames, or any other of a variety of dynamics and domains.[33] (*EJPT* 6: 435)

Objecting to my phrase "the fraying of the national by the global," Sassen instead wishes to document the denationalization processes through which nation-states turn themselves inside out, so to speak, and enable the penetration of global processes into the national.

I find these observations unobjectionable and illuminating; what is less clear to me is how they can be brought to bear on my argument concerning just membership. Sassen sees the European Union as transcending the "familiar binary between the national and the universal" and as creating "denationalized" rights regimes for individuals. There is no disagreement here and my analysis of the "disaggregation of citizenship rights" supports this. I have documented the emergence of multiple, overlapping, and differentiated rights regimes among groups such as nationals of EU member-states, who may be long-term residents in EU countries other than those of their nationality; resident third-country immigrants who are citizens of states that are not among the 27 EU members, and refugees and asylees seeking entry to the European Union (*The Rights of Others*: 147–67). In

153

describing these processes as "disaggregation," I was also signaling the new configuration of rights, authority, and territoriality into "new jurisdictional geographies," to use Sassen's felicitous phrase.[34] It is, therefore, unclear to me whether our disagreement around this issue is merely terminological or more substantive.[35] In the vast majority of states in this world, whatever new configurations of "rights, authority and territoriality" may be taking place, the control of borders and of immigration policy still remains within the jurisdiction of centralized state authorities.

While Sassen is certainly right to delineate the emergence of the new within the old, it is hard for me to assess the extent to which overcoming the binarism of the national and the global really has altered the terms, practices, and conceptualization of national membership. Certainly, the example of the Mexican government emerging as a litigant in a federal court case, defending the rights of its own citizens against the state of Arizona, as discussed above, is an intriguing development whose consequences we do not yet know. But the increasing militarization and criminalization of the US–Mexican border has not been altered by this fact.

Although Sassen agrees that closure and "democratic attachments, including attachments that may not be directed toward existing nation-state structures," are important, she rejects my defense of nation-state centered forms of closure and "the mutual exclusivity of the national and the non-national." But, as I explicated above, I do *not* defend the "container theory" of the nation-state. Quite to the contrary; my arguments about closure and the need for boundaries are based on the logic of representation and not on the primacy of some attachment to the national.

Sassen conceives of citizenship as "an incompletely theorized contract between the state and its subjects" (*EJPT* 6: 439). Indeed, this is the meaning of democratic iterations which are processes through which the "contract," not only of citizenship but also of membership for short- and long-term residents, whether they be immigrants, refugees, or asylum seekers, is negotiated. Some of these processes lead to the denationalization of citizenship within the nation-state through the rise of disaggregated rights regimes; analytically, denationalization and post-nationalization, as Sassen notes, must accompany one another. If a person becomes a long-term resident of another country than that of his/her nationality, this individual becomes a post-national, straddling two jurisdictional regimes. Sassen emphasizes a point also noted by Bauböck, namely, the analytical, institutional, and normative interdependence of regimes of denationalized and post-national citizenship (*EJPT* 6: 402–3, 441). Since the focus of *The Rights of Others* was upon conditions of seeking membership into polities other than those of one's own, rather than upon the consequences of leaving one's country of origin and the nature of the ties that would follow from such a move, I did not pay sufficient attention to what Bauböck calls "external citizenship" (ibid.: 402), and what Sassen names "postnational citizenship" (ibid.: 438). I did note, though, the significance of similar developments throughout Southeast Asia and Central America, and referred to Aihwa Ong's category of "flexible citizenship" (ibid.: 215–16). Nevertheless, post-national citizenship is an important reality that needs to be explored in its own right.

Sassen concludes that the historically constitutive tension between self-determination claims and universal human rights may not be as decisive today, "as a result of multiple, often highly specialized, micro-transformations, both formal and informal" (ibid.: 442). I remain skeptical whether these micro-transformations, many of which are taking place under the leadership of, and for the sake of, multinationals and transnational economic and technological organizations, are also salutary from a normative point of view. It may indeed be that processes of denationalization are so far advanced that they herald not only a new configuration of democratic rule but post-democracy itself. Sassen is more sanguine about the prospects of such transformations than I am. Yet the irony of many of the developments we are witnessing through the emergence of "global law without a state" (Günther Teubner), with the rise of *maquiladoras* and Growth Triangles, and the shrinking of public institutions through denationalizations is that they have left the most vulnerable among citizens and residents, such as women, children, and the poor, even more vulnerable and more subject to the forces of global capitalism. The quest for just membership is not rendered irrelevant by these transformations; quite to the contrary, it is exacerbated by them. Nevertheless, I concur with Sassen that it is "an open question, empirically, operationally and theoretically," whether these developments will produce new forms of citizenship located outside the state, as can be observed with the transnational movement of undocumented workers or of *les sans-papiers* in many parts of the globe. Another alternative is that these same developments may lead to membership without citizenship, and that the movements of peoples worldwide may result in residents without a *civitas*. We may also be confronted simply with citizens for whom the *civitas* has become but another public corporation, membership in which they

155

can pick up and leave at will as if it were a soccer club or a golf association.

The migrant, the refugee, and the asylum seeker have become metaphors in the twenty-first century. This is not, as Giorgio Agamben[36] and others would have it, based on the fact that the liberal state rests on a foundation of unjustified violent exclusion. Rather, the worldwide movements of peoples reveals the fragility of private and public autonomy in a world in which states, while enabling the movement of capital, money, and commodities at ever-faster speeds across boundaries, catch, imprison, maim, and kill human beings who try to do the same. It is this unresolved paradox which haunts *The Rights of Others,* and I am grateful to my colleagues for having made me aware of how important and difficult these questions still remain.

Postscript on The Principle of "Affected Interests"

A lively discussion has erupted in recent years among theorists interested in addressing the "boundary problem of the demos" (Whelan) and in exploring its ramification for matters of migration and membership.[37] Since central questions of this debate are quite germane to my response to critics as well, let me briefly address this debate and elucidate continuities and discontinuities between these positions and mine.

Most contemporary authors (Abizadeh; Goodin; and Miller) accept that the boundary problem poses an irresolvable paradox for democratic theory. "The boundary problem," writes Whelan, "is one matter of collective decision that cannot be decided democratically . . . We would need to make a prior decision regarding who are entitled to participate in arriving at a solution . . . [Democracy] cannot be brought to bear on the logically prior matter of the constitution of the group itself, the existence of which it presupposes."[38] Prior to Whelan, Robert Dahl had already observed that the problem of how to legitimately make up the people had been neglected by all major democratic theorists.[39] Without a doubt, these issues remained invisible until very recently, in part because the Westphalian model of the sovereign state, dominating all that is living and dead within its boundaries, though it experienced its first massive crisis after the collapse of the European nation-state system, still guided our theory as well as practice (see chapter 1 above). In our days, it is the ubiquitous phenomenon of globalization and the intensified movement of peoples across borders that has finally placed the boundary problem on the agenda. Along with these socio-historical and economic trans-formations, the assumption that the democratic people is simply identical with the pre-given nation has also waned. Since the early nineteenth century, the nation had been assumed to constitute the pre-political identity of the people who were united as a *demos*. Nationalism served as a powerful principle of inclusion and exclusion in matters of citizenship as well as immigration. The *demos* rested on the *ethnos*.

The principle of democratic legitimacy is far more demanding normatively and cannot simply be based upon a nation that is con-sidered pre-politically constituted. Following Dahl, Goodin states the issue as follows: "In its most generic form, the 'all affected interests' principle simply says that 'everyone who is affected by the decisions of a government should have the right to participate in that govern-ment.' "[40] Goodin's argument, which I will not recapitulate here, then proceeds by a series of *reductio ad absurdum* claims to conclude as follows:

> If (as I believe to be the case) "the all affected interests" principle is the best principled basis upon which to constitute the demos, and if (as I have argued) the best interpretation of that principle is the expan-sive "possibilist" form, then it does indeed provide good grounds for thinking that (at least in principle) we should give virtually everyone a vote on virtually everything in the world.[41]

Since this seems "wildly impractical," according to Goodin, there are two options to bring the power of territorial states more in line with the principle of all affected interests. One would be to accept the necessity of "world government"; the second would be to subject territorial states' power to "international law." In any event, con-cludes Goodin, now bringing his argument to bear on matters of border control and immigration, "If people whose interests we affect are kept outside our demos, we are obliged – by principles of democ-racy, as well as ones of justice and humanity – to settle up."[42]

Goodin's argument shows quite convincingly that the current systems of territorial states are arbitrary from the standpoint of the demanding criterion of affected interests. But is the principle of "affected interests" the best way to state the principle of democratic legitimacy? I do not believe that it is. First, Goodin does not explore more precisely the *moral* as opposed to the *political* restatements of this principle. It is only because we hold morally that each individual is entitled to equal respect and concern that we can also argue that democratic rule must be justified to *all* those whose interests it affects. If we did not presuppose equal moral respect, why would we care if the interests of some were simply neglected by the majority or over-ruled by the majority? Democratic theorists, who wish to give the all affected principle a political reading alone and to detach it from any moral commitment to the equality of persons, thus have a hard time preventing democratic rule from sliding into simple majoritarianism.

In the second place, for Goodin, "interests" are exogenous and are not formed by processes of democratic deliberation. Since this concept is so undertheorized, interests can be construed under many possible descriptions and if such descriptions are simply exogenous to the theory, then indeed absurd consequences follow. For theorists of deliberative democracy, by contrast, this "thin" concept of interests, which seems to precede any argumentation or action-coordination in the polity in its articulation, is unacceptable. Yet, even if one is not committed to deliberative democratic theory, the idea that affected interests would stand independently of shared understandings of what constitutes individual autonomy and a good life in the polity, which themselves always are quite contested ideals, is wholly implausible.

What follows from these objections? Since, logically, many competing descriptions and constructions of interests are possible, it is easy to show that under some or another selected description, the decisions of one *demos* can be shown to affect the interests of the entirety of the world population. It is then possible to argue that all interests, actual or possible, affect each other and hence that any democratic decisional closure is impossible and unjustified. As Nancy Fraser has observed:

> The problem is that, given the so-called "butterfly effect," one can adduce empirical evidence that just about everyone is affected by just about everything. What is needed, therefore, is a way of distinguishing those levels and kind of effectivity that are deemed sufficient to confirm moral standing from those that are not.[43]

Another counterintuitive result which this principle leads to is the waxing and waning of the circle of all affected. Since every decision of the *demos* will affect the interests of a different group of individuals each time – say, the decision of the USA to regulate tuna fishing will affect Japanese fishermen who, in turn, will be distinct from the group affected by the anti-immigration Bill passed by the state of Arizona in 2010 – the constituency of *all* those affected can never be determined prior to and independently of each and every decision. This would make the functioning of democratic institutions impossible. The "all affected principle," then, as stated by Goodin, is subject to the conflation of the moral and political senses of this maxim; the indeterminacy of the concept of interests; and the "butterfly effect"; that is, the waxing and waning of the circle of all affected. Is something wrong here then?

As stated by Goodin, the all affected principle conflates two issues: the need to regulate our interactions on the basis of a principle that we can all find justifiable, as distinguished from the democratic constitution of the *demos*. Goodin cannot differentiate among these two, because proceeding from a frighteningly abstract concept of interests, he is unable to make distinctions between coercive power, undue influence, minimal consequence, and so on,[44] let alone formulate a criterion of democratic membership.[45]

This is one major difference between the discourse principle in Habermasian theory and the all affected principle. The basic premise of discourse ethics, D, states that only those norms can claim to be valid that meet (or could meet) with the approval of all concerned in their capacity as participants in a practical discourse.[46] The determination of "all concerned" is just as open in this formula as it is in Goodin's all affected interests principle. At any point in time, if an agent or group of agents can show that they have been arbitrarily excluded from participating in processes through which norms are formulated, if their points of view have been suppressed, if their rights to symmetrical participation in conversation have been violated, and the like, then the presumptive norm cannot be valid until subject to further deliberation. The discourse principle provides moral agents with a "veto power" (Rainer Forst); they can always demand that the conversation of justification resume and not be terminated unless their objections have been voiced, listened to, and resolved upon. This does not mean that politically valid or justifiable decisions can never be reached in timely fashion; it only means that all such decisions are subject to criticism if they have violated the right of those concerned to have their voices and views heard in the process. The first step in such a procedure of discursive validation is to show that one belongs among the circle of those concerned, and can act as a moral and political agent who has standing to "participate in practical discourses." Thus seen, the discourse principle in the first place is a principle of moral and political *justification*; it is not one for delineating the scope of democratic membership. Precisely for this reason, it does not lead to the absurdities that Goodin's formulation of the "all affected interests" does.

Let me be more precise: if an agent A exercises power over an agent B, from the standpoint of an egalitarian-universalist morality, A has a duty to justify to B why such constraint on B's action is legitimate. A owes B a duty of justification, because A has restricted B's communicative freedom. B has a moral right to seek an answer from A of the validity of which B could be convinced with good reasons. Although the all affected principle sounds deceptively similar to the principle of discursive validation, it is not. According to the latter, it is the obligation we owe to each other to justify the coercive use of force that is primary, and not the consideration of the affected interests of each. Of course, insofar as in coercing you in one form or other, I can always be said to affect your interests as well, then the principles of justification and that of all affected interests merge into one another; nevertheless, what is primary is the obligation I owe you to justify actions through which I exercise power over you. There may be many other practices, actions, and circumstances which affect your interest but which are neither the consequence of nor entailed by the coercive use of force.

In democratic theory, as opposed to moral philosophy at large, what we are concerned with is the *public justification of the coercive use of power*,[47] and not with any and all forms of human interaction in which human interests are interdependent or may be affected by each other. I agree with David Owen, who writes:

> while persons whose interests are affected by a decision made by a given polity do not thereby have an interest in membership of that first order polity or structure of governance, they do (in virtue of having an interest affected by that polity) have a common interest with all other persons affected by the decision (including those who are members of the first order polity) in membership of, or subjection to, a second order polity or structure of governance that has powers to regulate impartially the decisions made by the first order polity.[48]

What form such second-order structures of governance ought to take is a different question and one to which I suggested tentative answers at various points in the preceding chapters. Let me now consider another theory of the justification of democratic closure.

A Unilateral Right to Control Borders?

Arash Abizadeh accepts discourse theory and a deliberative model of democracy. He argues:

> that democratic theory either rejects the unilateral right to close borders, or would permit such a right only derivatively and only if it has been already successfully and democratically justified to foreigners. This is because the demos of democratic theory is in principle unbounded, and the regime of boundary control must consequently be democratically justified to foreigners as well as to citizens.[49]

For Abizadeh, in democratic theory, justification is "owed to all those over whom power is exercised." And he rightly notes that "all such persons must have the opportunity 1. actually to participate in the political processes that determine how power is exercised, on terms that 2. are consistent with their freedom and equality."[50] The crucial question is whether a regime of border control may exercise power not only over its members but also over all others; second, who are "all these others"? Abizadeh is quite clear on this issue:

> My argument appeals to a more restricted principle, which refers not to whom the political regime affects, but to whom it *subjects to coercion* . . . I take it that the argument's point of controversy lies in its tacit premise, which is reflected in the reference to "all" in the first premise – that is, a reference to all *persons* rather than *citizens* (members). This formulation of the democratic theory of popular sovereignty tacitly presupposes that the demos to whom democratic justification is owed is in principle unbounded. This is what I call the *unbounded demos thesis*.[51] (Emphasis in the text)

Can Abizadeh establish that a regime of unilateral border control "subjects to coercion" not just citizens and non-citizen neighbors whose territory abuts the *demos* in question, but *all persons?* All of humanity? Abizadeh writes:

> The upshot is this: Mexicans and Zambians who (1) are prevented from crossing the U.S. border by U.S. agents using physical force and those who (2) avoid crossing because of the coercive threat of U.S. legal sanctions share the honor of being subject to coercion with those who (3) illegally do cross the border and those who (4) never had any intention of entering.[52]

This conclusion, however, is wholly counterintuitive. Because the very presence of a regime of border control makes me change my desires and plans to visit a country or work in a country, this does mean that I have been subject to coercion. Suppose I am a member of Group X who wishes to enter and settle in country Z, but country Z is so overrun by my fellow country members that it has instituted a system of border controls in order to protect its native labor markets; therefore, I am permitted a visitor's visa but not the right to seek employment or stay longer term. This is a case that more or less accurately describes the current condition of Turkish citizens seeking entry into many EU member countries, and, even within the EU, entry controls have been instituted in order to prevent the inflow of nationals from the newly admitted East European countries, such as Poland, Hungary, Romania, the Czech Republic, and so on, into the more coveted labor markets in the UK, Germany, France, and other countries. Abizadeh would argue that in both cases members of group X are "subject to coercion" by country Z, because the actions of country Z negatively influence their autonomy, their valuable life options, and their independence:

> A *coercive threat*, by contrast, simply communicated the intention to undertake an action in the future whose (anticipated) effect is to prevent a person from choosing an option that she otherwise might choose. So beyond directly thwarting the pursuit of some options, states also threaten persons with sanctions should they carry out proscribed actions.[53]

I agree with Abizadeh's account of the democratic principle of justification and his rigorous analysis which shows that border controls are regimes of coercion which can and ought to be subject to discourses of justification. Insofar as his argument is that a *unilateral* system of border control cannot be normatively justifiable, I join him. Yet the argument greatly seems to overshoot its mark when the very *existence* of border controls among a system of states is said to subject not only *some* to coercion, but to pose coercive threats for *all others* – in fact for humanity – as such. Abizadeh might just as well conclude that the very existence of borders cannot be normatively justified at all – either from the standpoint of democratic theory or from the standpoint of moral philosophy. He might then conclude that only a world without borders is morally acceptable; this is a perfectly defensible moral position. But this conclusion cannot be reached on the premises of democratic theory, but rather only of moral theory as such.

This is not a solution which Abizadeh wishes to endorse. But can he avoid it? He writes:

> As a consequence, a state's regime of border control could only acquire legitimacy if there were cosmopolitan democratic institutions in which borders received actual justifications addressed to both citizens and foreigners . . . Democrats are required by their own account of political legitimacy to support the formation of cosmopolitan democratic institutions that have the jurisdiction either to determine entry policy or legitimately to delegate jurisdiction over entry policy to particular states (or other institutions).[54]

What would such cosmopolitan democratic institutions look like? Insofar as they would have the right to determine entry policy, they would in effect have sovereign authority over states that had hitherto considered themselves sole sovereigns. Some kind of "supra-sovereign" entity would emerge. Certainly, the model of the European Union shows that this is possible. As I have examined in this chapter, however, even in the case of the supra-sovereign model of the EU, contradictions regarding border control and immigration policies abound. There are always "insiders" and "outsiders" – however those insiders are constituted. Abizadeh also writes of the "delegation of jurisdiction." What is meant by this? Does he have in mind strengthening the International Organization for Migration, for example? Or the creation of other transnational organizations? Much, it seems to me, depends on whether by such "delegation of jurisdiction" we mean total delegation of control over borders to a supra-sovereign entity, or a partial delegation based on increased cooperation and coordination. I would think that the second is the only plausible model.

The complete delegation of jurisdiction over regimes of border control to a super-state authority is unlikely under current conditions, unless this were considered along the model of a world state; yet it is certainly possible to develop increasingly more coordinated international standards regarding migratory movements and to push for more justice in the treatment of migrants, refugees, and asylum seekers. Along with the heightened criminalization of migratory movements in recent years, the states of the rule of law has been transformed into securitized states. Often migrants are even more vulnerable than refugees whose status is at least covered by various international agreements.

So Abizadeh is right that current regimes of border coercion lack moral justification as well as full democratic legitimacy. But the first who need to be convinced of this democratic deficit are the peoples of the *demoi* themselves, who then must initiate processes of democratic iteration such as to subject existing systems to increased demands for justification and scrutiny. And, in most cases, since those who are not members of the *demos* are related to those who are, the lines between inside and outside are not as sharp as they may seem. Examples would be Turks currently living in Germany and Mexicans living in the United States. Regimes of border coercion that exclude their kin and relatives are coercive upon them first and foremost, and as members of the *demos*, they ought to – and in fact they do – mobilize on behalf of non-members. Such democratic iterations are processes through which the *demos* reconstitutes itself. This does not eliminate the initial arbitrariness in the constitution of the *demos*; in that sense, the paradox of democratic constitution remains unresolved. But there are more or less just, more or less inclusive, more or less democratic ways of handling the paradox.

I concur here with Nancy Fraser, who writes:

> Rather, we should try to envision ways to transform what looks like a vicious circle into a virtuous spiral. The idea is to begin by establishing, what could be called, with apologies to D. W. Winnicott, "good enough deliberation." Although such deliberation would fall considerably short of participatory parity, it would be good enough to legitimate some social reforms, however modest, which would in turn, once institutionalized, bring the next round of deliberation closer to participatory parity.[55]

What we should aspire to, then, are practices and institutions that meet criteria of "good enough deliberations."

Democratic iterations and "good enough deliberations" take place among transnational communities of discourse and action. Just as non-members have kin and relatives who are members of the *demos*, almost every *demos* has members who are themselves residents in other *demoi* and whose rights are regulated by the laws of these other countries, that is, who are themselves "post-national citizens." In a future worldwide system of republican federalism in which the markers of sovereignty would be repooled, the rights of residents and aliens as well as migrants and refugees would be increasingly harmonized in accordance with international law and human rights agreements.

Once we distinguish the principle of discursive justification – whether in its Habermasian version, in its "all affected interests" version, or in its form as a principle of democratic justification alone – from the matter of how to constitute membership in the *demos*, then the question as to who is entitled to be a member of a polity still remains unanswered. As I have argued above, although there is no *human right to first entry* into any country one may wish – and here I differ from Abizadeh – and one has to respect certain regimes of border control, all the while subjecting them to increasing forms of democratic justification, there is a *human right to membership*. This right to membership must be publicly and openly formulated, non-discriminatory, and compatible with international human rights agreements. Once such conditions are fulfilled, other conditions of membership such as language fluency may be plausibly stipulated. Membership in a *demos* is more than being either *affected by* or *subjected to* coercive power. It involves a commitment over time to cooperation with a specific human community, as well as a sense that one's own moral good and public-political voice are bound up with, although never exclusively, or even primarily, the fate of that human community.

This is a less radical conclusion than either Goodin or Abizadeh wish to embrace, but membership in the *demos*, no matter how arbitrary initially, can be self-reflexively adjusted only by the *demoi* themselves in ever-increasing and intersecting circles of transnational cooperation.

The next chapter discusses one of the most controversial examples of democratic iterations in their jurisgenerative as well as jurispathic forms in Europe and elsewhere – namely, the "scarf affair." It illustrates how public voice and membership can be attained by those who were initially subject to systems of coercion that excluded their voices. Migrants' long- and short-term residency in nation-states, which once considered themselves, or were considered, homogeneous brings forth constitutional, cultural, and political dilemmas, and calls attention once more to the question of how the "boundaries" of the *demos* are constituted. This is not merely a matter of the "inside/outside" distinction; it is also about the status of the so-called "others" within the *demos itself*.

— 9 —

THE RETURN OF POLITICAL THEOLOGY

The Scarf Affair in Comparative Constitutional
Perspective in France, Germany and Turkey

The End of the Secularization Hypothesis

Increasingly, in today's world, antagonisms around religious and ethno-cultural differences have intensified. Since September 11, 2001, the vocabulary of "the clash of civilizations" (Huntington) of the 1980s has given way to what is called a "global civil war" between the forces of political Islam and Western liberal democracies. The confrontation between political Islam and the so-called West has replaced the rhetoric of the Cold War against communism.

Unfortunately, this rhetoric is not only restricted to the destructive foreign policy of the administration of G. W. Bush and American neo-conservatives. Since the bombings in Madrid (2004) and London (2007), the Danish caricature controversy over the representations of the Prophet Mohammed (2005), the murder of Theo van Gogh in the Netherlands by a Moroccan militant (2004), and the French "scarf affair" (1989–2004), the confrontation between the forces of political Islam and Western liberal democracies has come to dominate European discourse and politics as well.[1] In view of these developments, we need to begin by reconsidering the "secularization" hypothesis.

Since Max Weber's essay, "Wissenschaft als Beruf" (1919), it has been axiomatic that modernity is characterized by *Entzauberung*, by

An earlier and briefer version of this essay was delivered as the inaugural lecture at the Reset Istanbul Seminars on June 2–8, 2008, in Istanbul. A short version appeared in S. Benhabib, "Turkey's Constitutional Zig-Zags," *Dissent* (winter 2009), pp. 29–32; and the fuller text was published as S. Benhabib, "The Return of Political Theology: The Scarf Affair in Comparative Constitutional Perspective in France, Germany and Turkey," *Philosophy and Social Criticism* 36/3–4) (2010): 451–71.

the loss of magic in the everyday world and the rationalized differentiation (*Ausdifferenzierung*) from one another of the spheres of
science, religion, law, aesthetics, and philosophy.[2] Max Weber was
giving expression thereby to a widely held view since the Enlightenment that the spread of knowledge and science would mean not only
"holding religion within the bounds of reason," as Kant had thought,
but dispensing with religion altogether in the name of modern reason
and an emancipated society, as Feuerbach, Marx, and Nietzsche had
postulated.

Yet this juxtaposition of modernity and religion was not as simple
as some would have us believe: already Karl Löwith and Hans Blumenberg had uncovered the theological sources of Enlightenment's
own faith in the secularization hypothesis by arguing that the idea of
a united mankind, capable of cumulative learning and progressing
toward a common Enlightenment, had its sources in religiously
inspired salvation myths.[3] The Enlightenment had not gone beyond
theology but was itself based on theological premises of a *Heilsge-
schichte* (salvific history). Early sociological students of modern
societies, such as Alexis de Tocqueville, also pointed out in the mid-
nineteenth century that the great modern experiment with democracy
required religious foundations. The most egalitarian modern society
of Tocqueville's time, the United States, he observed, remained deeply
religious. The secularization hypothesis always had its critics and
skeptics.

Today we are witnessing the worldwide growth of religious funda-
mentalisms and the intense challenges they pose to one crucial aspect
of the modernization process in particular: the separation between
religion and politics, between theological truths and political certitudes. The ever-fragile walls of demarcation between religion and the
public square have become increasingly porous. Certainly, this phenomenon is most strikingly observed with the rise of political Islam,
which rattles not only the separation of religion from politics but
which threatens the very boundaries of Islamic nation-states altogether in the name of the call to *Dar-ul-Islam* (the domain of Islam)
to prevail over *Dar-ul-Harb* (the domain of the infidels).

In this respect Turkey is unique: modern Turkey has been a republic
since 1923 and emerged as a nation-state after the collapse of the
Ottoman Empire and the abolishment of the Caliphate in 1924. Dis-
carding the theological trappings of the Ottoman state, where the
Sultan was also the Caliph (the religious leader of the Muslim world),
Turkey opted for the privatization of the Muslim faith, along
the model of liberal democracies, and for a version of republican

167

secularism, called *laiklik*. The revolutionary ideology of the founders of the modern Turkish republic, Kemalism, was also a dirigiste ideology, granting the state a great deal of control over religious affairs, and, for that matter, over the economy and civil society too. Religion became a matter of the private faith of individuals and the state abolished theological vocabulary from its own affairs, all the while acknowledging that the Muslim faith was the official religion of Turkish society. Through the influential Imam-Hatip Okullari, the Turkish state still educates the *hafiz* and *muezzins* (cantors of the Koran) and *imams* or *hocas* (Muslim clerics) who are responsible for the obligatory Friday prayers observed in millions of neighborhoods across the country.

Political theology is on the agenda in contemporary Turkey: in the last two decades the *cordon sanitaire* that tried to keep the Muslim faith out of public-political life has broken down, and Turkey, like the rest of Europe, is experiencing its own dilemmas of how to situate the Muslim religion in the public square.

Women's bodies in particular have become the site of symbolic confrontations between a re-essentialized understanding of religious and cultural difference and the forces of state power, whether in their civic-republican, liberal-democratic or multicultural form. A principal reason for the emergence of these public debates, with their constantly shifting terms, is a sociological one which I have characterized as "reverse globalization." The distinction between the cultural and the religious, as well as the identification of actions and customs as being one or the other, is occurring against the background of the history of colonialism and of the West's encounter with the "rest." Whereas at one time it was the historical experience of Western colonialism in facing its cultural and religious others that forced European political thought to clarify and solidify the line between the religious and the cultural, today it is mass migration from Africa, Asia, and the Middle East to the shores of resource-rich liberal democracies – the EU, the USA, Canada, and Australia – that is leading to the reframing of the distinction between the cultural, the religious, and the political.[4] Under conditions of immigration, a destabilization of identities and traditions is taking place, and tradition is being "reinvented" (Eric Hobsbawm). Certainly, among the best known of such contemporary controversies, one which continues to preoccupy public opinion throughout Europe and Turkey is the so-called "scarf affair," – *l'affaire du foulard* or *la voile* in French, *der Kopftuch Affaire* or *der Schleieraffaire* in German, and the *türban meselesi* in Turkish.

In this chapter, I argue that under conditions of globalization "political theology" is deployed as a complex term, capturing a space of instability between religion and the public square; between the private and the official; between individual rights to freedom of religion versus state considerations of security and public well-being.[5] The ensuing difficulties are pithily suggested by a question recently posed by Jürgen Habermas: "How should we see ourselves as members of a post-secular society and what must we reciprocally expect from one another in order to ensure that in firmly entrenched nation-states social relations remain civil despite the growth of a plurality of cultures and religious world views?"[6]

But what is political theology?

Carl Schmitt's Political Theology

In 1922, Carl Schmitt published *Political Theology: Four Chapters on the Concept of Sovereignty.*[7] Reissued in 1934 with a new Preface by Schmitt, this text, along with *The Concept of the Political* from 1932, and the earlier *The Crisis of Parliamentary Democracy* (*Zur geistesgeschichtliche Lage der heutigen Parlamentarismus*)[8] from 1923, established Schmitt as one of the most trenchant critics of the liberal democratic project. Schmitt documented not only the sociological transformation of liberal parliamentarianism into the rule of special interest groups and committees, which prevented parliaments from functioning as deliberative bodies; he also drove home the rationalistic fallacies of liberalism until its "limit concepts" – *die Grenzbegriffe* – were uncovered. These limit concepts, in Schmitt's view, constituted the secret and "unthought" foundations upon which the structure of the modern state rested. Sovereignty is one such limit concept; the principle of government by discussion, and the assumption that opinions will eventually converge through deliberation, are others.

Schmitt's sociological and philosophical critiques have proven formidable and have inspired thinkers on the right as well as the left. From Otto Kirchheimer and Walter Benjamin to Hans Morgenthau and Leo Strauss, to Chantal Mouffe, Ernesto Laclau,[9] and many others in our times, Schmitt is the *éminence grise* to whom one turns when the liberal-democratic project is in deep crisis. There is no need here to document the extensive Schmitt renaissance which has flourished in Europe as well as the United States. Instead, I would like to briefly recall some theses of Schmitt's *Political Theology* in order to

169

demarcate the continuities as well as discontinuities between contemporary concerns that may be gathered under the term "political theology" and Schmitt's own preoccupations.

There are at least three interrelated, and not always clearly distinguished, theses in Schmit's *Political Theology*. First is a thesis in the history of ideas, sometimes referred to by Schmitt as the "sociology of concepts" as well (45), and best expressed through the following claim: "All significant concepts of the modern theory of the state are secularized theological concepts not only because of their historical development – in which they were transferred from theology to the theory of the state, whereby, for example, the omnipotent God became the omnipotent lawgiver" (36). In the second place, Schmitt explores *legal hermeneutics*, that is, the dialectic of the general and the particular, the law and the instances to which it applies. In the third place, Schmitt develops a thesis about the *construction and prerogatives of sovereignty* as the seat of legitimacy in the modern state. What resonates most in contemporary debates are neither the first nor the second of Schmitt's theses, but rather the third – his theory of the exception. It is as if the political zeitgeist has given new life to the famous opening lines of Schmitt's *Political Theology*, "Sovereign is he who decides on the exception" (5).

The "exception," this most notorious concept, which has now become a *bon mot* for our time, ranges in meaning from what defies a norm, or lies outside the norm, to the more technical sense in constitutional law of a situation in which martial law is declared, and some, if not all liberties, are suspended, namely, an "emergency situation" – a *Notstand*. But the state of exception, which is at times hard to distinguish from the state of emergency, is not just about the constitutional suspension of liberties and the assuming by the state of extraordinary powers; the state of exception is a moment of utmost crises when the very foundations of the order of the political as such are challenged. In Giorgio Agamben's *State of Exception*,[10] this wide-ranging ambivalence of "the exception," vacillating between a theory of the particular and the unique in the context of legal hermeneutics, and a condition in constitutional law when some laws and liberties are suspended, is retained and well articulated.[11]

Although the concept of political theology is widely used in contemporary debates, when uncoupled from Schmitt's doctrine of sovereignty and the exception, the phrase refers to quite a different set of issues than it did for Schmitt. In fact, in addressing *our* politico-theological predicament, I want to argue, Carl Schmitt is of little use.

Political Theology Beyond Schmitt

In his Introduction to *Political Theologies. Public Religions in a Post-Secular World*, Hent de Vries asks:

> what *pre-*, *para-* and *post*-political forms do religion and its functional equivalents and successor beliefs or rituals assume in a world where the global extension of economic markets, technological media, and informational networks have contributed to loosening or largely suspending the link that once tied theologico-political authority to a social body determined by a certain geographic territory and national sovereignty? Is a disembodied – virtual, call it transcendental – substitute for the theologico-political body politic thinkable, possible, viable, or even desirable?[12]

By situating political theology within a global economic, technological, and mediatic context, which loosens the ties that once moored theologico-political authority "within a certain social body determined by geographic territory and national sovereignty," de Vries draws an important contrast. The historical model of the theologico-political sphere confined to the nation-state and today's deterritorialized, transnational, televisually mediated, and sometimes electronically transmitted, contemporary religions and religious movements are radically different. Ironically, in this respect, there is very little difference between the communicational forms of evangelical Churches in North and South America, Jehovah's Witnesses in Russia, Wah'habism in Saudi Arabia, and al-Qaeda's sophisticated use of the Internet and other contemporary media, enhanced through the powerful new voices of itinerant Islamic interpreters such as Al-Madoodi. In the global age, deterritorialized religions challenge not only the authority of the nation-state but dislodge national senses of collective identity too. Particularly in societies of the Middle East such as Turkey, Egypt, Jordan, and Iraq, which were created after the abolition of the Caliphate, the collapse of the Ottoman Empire, and the retreat of British and French imperialisms from this region, the replacement of the spiritual authority of the Islamic *umma* by the authority of the nation-state as the principal site of solidarity, identity, and self-definition was always fragile. The principle, *cius regio, eius religio* (whose rule, whose religion), and the "territorialization of ecclesiastical authority" were always contested experiences in Islamic societies, which did not experience the Westphalian demarcation process between religion and the state as it unfolded in Western Europe.

171

Paradoxically, by undermining the authority of the nation-state, the deterritorialization of religion under conditions of globalization evokes memories of pre-modernity, and enflames the power of the tribes which are now busy renewing themselves with the means provided by decentralized instruments of post-modern communication, exchange, commerce, and information. Hans Jonas observes that "'Post-Secular' doesn't mean, then, an increase in the meaningfulness of religion or a renewed attention to it, but a changed attitude by the secular state or in the public domain with respect to the continued existence of religious communities and the impulses that emerge from them."[13]

I would like to examine the challenges posed by the deterritorialization of religious faith to the formation of complex democratic identities in liberal democracies, by focusing on the so-called "scarf affair." The politics of the scarf has become a transnational struggle, revealing complex moves and counter-moves among ethno-cultural and religious groups who mobilize around the symbolic markings of the female body, challenging the sovereignty of the secular state, and leading to difficult legal, and, in some cases, constitutional negotiations.

For all three countries which will be considered below, the Universal Declaration of Human Rights, the International Covenant on Civil and Political Rights, and the European Convention on Human Rights, to which France, Germany, and also Turkey are party, provide the discursive frame of legal reference. Both ICCP and ECHR use Article 18 of the UDHR as a template. It reads: "Everyone has the right to freedom of thought, conscience and religion; this right includes freedom to change his religion or belief, and the freedom, either alone or in community with others and in public or private, to manifest his religion or belief in teaching, practice, worship and observance."[14]

L'Affaire du Foulard (the Scarf Affair)[15]

L'affaire du foulard[16] refers to long public confrontations which began in France in 1989 with the expulsion from their school in Creil (Oise) of three scarf-wearing Muslim girls, and continued to the mass exclusion of 23 Muslim girls from their schools in November 1996, upon the decision of the Conseil d'Etat.[17] Finally, after nearly a decade of confrontations, the French National Assembly passed a law in March 2004 with a great majority, banning not only the wearing of the

172

"scarf" – now interestingly referred to as *la voile* (the veil) – but the bearing of all "ostentatious signs of religious belonging in the public sphere." The Commission, headed by Bernard Stasi and presented to the President of the Republic, considered the wearing of the scarf as part of a growing political threat of Islam to the values of *laïcité*.

The affair, referred to as a "national drama"[18] or even a "national trauma," occurred in the wake of France's celebration of the second centennial of the French Revolution and seemed to question the foundations of the French educational system and its philosophical principle, *laïcité*. This concept is hard to translate in terms like the separation of Church and State or even secularization: at its best, it can be understood as the public and manifest neutrality of the state toward all kinds of religious practices, institutionalized through a vigilant removal of sectarian religious symbols, signs, icons, and items of clothing from official public spheres. Yet within the French Republic the balance between respecting the individual's rights to freedom of conscience and religion, on the one hand, and maintaining a public sphere devoid of all religious symbolisms, on the other, was so fragile that it only took the actions of a handful of teenagers to expose this fragility. The ensuing debate went far beyond the original dispute and touched upon the self-understanding of French republicanism for the left as well as the right, on the meaning of social and sexual equality, and liberalism vs republicanism vs multiculturalism in French life.

The French sociologists Gaspard and Khosrokhavar capture this set of complex symbolic negotiations as follows:

> [The veil] mirrors in the eyes of the parents and the grandparents the illusions of continuity whereas it is a factor of discontinuity; it makes possible the transition to otherness (modernity), under the pretext of identity (tradition); it creates the sentiment of identity with the society of origin whereas its meaning is inscribed within the dynamic of relations with the receiving society . . . it is the vehicle of the passage to modernity within a promiscuity which confounds traditional distinctions, of an access to the public sphere which was forbidden to traditional women as a space of action and the constitution of individual autonomy.[19]

L'affaire du foulard eventually came to stand for all dilemmas of French national identity in the age of globalization and multiculturalism: how to retain French traditions of *laïcité*, republican equality, and democratic citizenship in view of France's integration into the European Union, on the one hand, and the pressures of multiculturalism generated through the presence of second- and third-generation immigrants from Muslim countries on French soil, on the other hand? Would the practices and institutions of French citizenship be flexible and generous enough to encompass multicultural differences within an ideal of republican equality?

What exactly was the meaning of the girls' actions? Was this an act of religious observance and subversion, one of cultural defiance, or of adolescents acting to gain attention and prominence? Were the girls acting out of fear, out of conviction, or out of narcissism? It is not hard to imagine that their actions involved all these elements and motives. The girls' voices were not heard much in this heated debate; although there was a genuine public discourse in the French public sphere and some soul-searching on questions of democracy and difference in a multicultural society. As the sociologists Gaspard and Khosrokhavar pointed out, until they carried out their interviews the girls' own perspectives were hardly listened to. Even if the girls involved were not adults in the eyes of the law and were still under the tutelage of their families, it is reasonable to assume that, at the ages of 15 and 16, they could account for themselves and their actions. Had their voices been heard and listened to, it would have become clear that the meaning of wearing the scarf itself was changing from being a religious act to one of cultural defiance and increasing politicization. Ironically, it was the very egalitarian norms of the French public educational system which brought these girls out of the patriarchal structures of the home and into the French public sphere, and gave them the confidence and the ability to *resignify the wearing of the scarf.*

There is sufficient evidence in the sociological literature that in many other parts of the world too Muslim women are using the veil as well as the *chaddor* to cover up the paradoxes of their own emancipation from tradition.[20] To assume that the meaning of their actions is purely one of religious defiance of the secular state denigrates these women's own capacity to define the meaning of their own actions, and, ironically, reimprisons them within the walls of patriarchal meaning from which they are trying to escape.

The women's movements and organizations were split in their assessment of the ban against the wearing of the scarf: while the members of the organization Ni Putes, Ni Soumises (Neither Whores nor Downtrodden) celebrated the ban, organizations such as the Parent-Teacher Federation, SOS Racisme, Une École pour Toutes et Tous (A School for All) argued that the girls' human rights to freedom of religion, to education, and to freedom from discrimination were violated. Outside observers, including Human Rights Watch, the

Islamic Human Rights Commission, and the US-based KARAMAH, Muslim Women Lawyers for Human Rights, agreed.[21]

Likewise, the interpretation of these events remains controversial in the scholarly literature: while Joan Scott considers the headscarf ban as manifesting a sexist and Eurocentric repressive French republican tradition, Christian Joppke, in *Veil: Mirror of Identity*, argues differently. According to Joppke, "At the critical moment, when the national allegiance of French Muslims was tested, they passed the test with flying colors, advancing from 'victims' to 'heroes' of the republic."[22] Joppke is referring to the spectacular kidnapping of two French journalists by radical Islamists in Iraq, who then demanded a repeal of the headscarf ban, thereby provoking an unprecedented closing of ranks behind the French state. In a demonstration which brought hundreds of thousands to the streets of Paris, ironically, many who wanted the ban on the veil lifted also rejected the unwelcome meddling of radical Islamists in their struggles.[23]

Joppke also provides some sobering numbers: in September 2004, after the law was passed, only 639 pupils showed up with the headscarf and 100 refused to take it off; one year later there were only 12 at the start of the school year. When compared to 1,123 cases out of 9 million students in 1994, and 1,256 in 2003, we see that the law has accomplished its goals. But, unlike Joppke, I am not convinced that the successful integration of Muslim youth into French society has been achieved. The riots of spring 2005 in the predominantly migrant neighborhoods of Paris show that the flames of resentment, alienation, and defiance against the French state can easily be stoked and can explode, as they did during the riots. As debates about the Belgian and French banning of the wearing of the *burka*[24] swirl in the European public sphere, we need to conclude that the symbolic politics of the scarf affair are far from over.

The German "Scarf Affair": The Case of Fereshta Ludin[25]

In recent years, the German courts have dealt with a challenge quite akin to the scarf affair in France. An elementary school teacher in Baden-Württemberg, Fereshta Ludin, of Afghani origin and a German citizen, insisted on being able to teach her classes with her head covered. The school authorities refused to permit her to do so. The case ascended all the way to the German Supreme Court and on September 30, 2003, the court decided as follows. Wearing a headscarf, in the context presented to the court, expresses that the claimant belongs to the "Muslim community of faith" (*die islamische Religionsgemeinschaft*). The court concluded that to describe such behavior as lack of qualification (*Eignungsmangel)* for the position of a teacher in elementary and middle schools clashed with the right of the claimant to equal access to all public offices, in accordance with Article 33, paragraph 2 of the Basic Law *(Grundgesetz)*, and also clashed with her right to freedom of conscience, as protected by Article 4, paragraphs 1 and 2 of the Basic Law, without, however, providing the required and sufficient lawful reasons for doing so (BVerfGe, 2BvR, 1436/02, IVB 1 and 2; my translation). While acknowledging the fundamental rights of Ms Fereshta Ludin, the court nevertheless ruled against the claimant and transferred the final say on the matter to the democratic legislatures (BVerfGe, 2BvR, 1436/02, 6).

The German Constitutional Court, much like the French Conseil d'Etat, while acknowledging the fundamental nature of the rights involved – freedom of conscience and equal access of all to public offices – refused to shield these rights from the will of the democratic legislatures. But note that in the German case the headscarf ban applies to teachers only and not to students, since it has never been questioned that the pupils' wearing of the headscarf is protected by their religious liberty rights, according to Articles 4 and 2 of the German Basic Law. By not handing the matter over to the exclusive jurisdiction of the school authorities, and by stressing the necessity for the state to maintain religious and worldview neutrality, the court also signaled to democratic lawmakers the importance of respecting legitimate pluralism of worldviews in a liberal democracy. Still, the court did not see itself justified in positively intervening to shield such pluralism, but considered this to be the jurisdiction of the Länder.[26] Undoubtedly, the fact that teachers in Germany are also *Beamten*, that is, civil servants of the state, who stand under the special jurisdiction of various civil service Acts, may have played a role. Nevertheless, it is hard to avoid the impression that the real worry of the court was the more substantive rather than the procedural question as to whether a woman who ostensibly wore an object representing her as belonging to the traditions of her community of origin could carry out the duties of a functionary of the German state. As the Baden-Württemberg's Minister of Education, Annete Schavan, argued in the opening salvo of the German headscarf controversy, "The headscarf . . . also stands for cultural segregation (*Abgrenzung*), and thus it is a political symbol [which puts at risk] social peace."[27]

Despite the fact that Ms Ludin was a German citizen of Afghani origin who had successfully completed the requisite qualifications to become a teacher, the two dimensions of her citizenship rights – the entitlement to the full and equal protection of the law and her cultural identity as an observant Muslim woman – seemed in contradiction with one another.

Again, the German Court's decision had some paradoxical implications: on the one hand, all existing regulations protecting or banning religious symbols in public schools were immediately nullified, and state governments "intent on prohibiting the headscarf for teachers were required to pass legislation to that effect in that respect instantly" (Joppke, *Veil*: 70). President Johannes Rau as well as the then Cardinal Ratzinger, now Pope Benedict XVI, argued that the legislation had the effect of prohibiting *all* religious symbols from public schools, and, unless otherwise decided by the legislatures, this would set Germany on the road toward *laïcité*. Since Germany is not a *laïque* state but one deeply wedded to the *christlich-abendländische* (Christian-Western) tradition, in which the three recognized denominations – Protestant, Catholic, and Jewish – are financed by a tax known as *Kirchensteuer*, directly levied on the believers, the only way to prevent French-style *laïcité* was to pass legislation singling out Islamic symbols as inherently political and provocative. As Joppke observes, "with the exception of Berlin, the anti-head scarf legislation passed in seven other *Länder* (Baden-Württemberg, Bavaria, Hesse, Lower Saxony, Saarland, and more recently Bremen and North Rhine-Westphalia) more or less exempted Christian and Jewish symbols from its reach" (Joppke, *Veil*: 71).

Baden-Württemberg's anti-headscarf legislation, which is contained in three new sentences introduced into paragraph 38 of the state's educational law, is blatant in its discriminatory treatment of Islam: "The representation of Christian and occidental values and traditions corresponds to the educational mandate of the [regional] constitution and does not contradict the behavior required according to sentence 1." Sentence 1 in turn states that "Teachers are not allowed . . . to give external statements of a political, religious [or] ideological nature." which could endanger or disturb neutrality toward pupils and parents (Joppke, *Veil*: 72–3). There seems to be no question at all that the headscarf, much like a corporate logo, has an intrinsic meaning, which permits a univocal interpretation, and it does not matter what the one wearing the headscarf intends thereby.

The German Constitutional Court failed to present a robust constitutional defense of pluralism. By turning the regulation of the wearing of the headscarf to the legislators' discretion to ban it via statutory law, it failed to protect a fundamental human right and furthermore gave the green light to a series of highly discriminatory and punitive legislation singling out Islam in particular. [28]

The Turkish "Turban Affair"

In February of 2008, the ruling Turkish party, the AKP (Adalet ve Kalkinma Partisi) decided to reform the law that banned the wearing of headscarves and turbans in institutions of higher learning in Turkey. In June of 2008, the Turkish Constitutional Court overturned the new legislation, arguing that it was subversive of the secular nature of the Turkish state.[29] Opponents of the AKP tried to have the party itself banned for seeking to subvert Turkey's *laik* (secular) constitution altogether. Contrary to many fears and expectations, the court declared in August 2008 that the AKP would not be shut down; rather, it would be fined for actions contrary to the *laik* (secular) constitutional order.[30]

Initially, the decision to reform Articles 10 and 42 of Turkey's Basic Law (*Anayasa*) included another motion to reform the notorious Article 301, which prohibits "insulting Turkishness," and which was used by many nationalist and ultra-nationalist prosecutors to bring charges against liberal writers and intellectuals such as Orhan Pamuk. This proposal was dropped and one of the most anti-democratic and anti-liberal articles of the Turkish Constitution remained in place.

Article 10 concerns "Equality Before the Law," and proclaims that "Everyone, regardless of distinctions of language, race, color, gender, political belief, philosophical conviction, religion, ethnicity and like grounds, is equal in the eyes of the law." In addition, it is stated that "Women and men possess equal rights. The state is responsible to ensure that this equality becomes effective." The changes come in the fourth paragraph of the Article, which in its older version read: "Organs of the state and administrative authorities are obliged to act according to the principles of equality before the law in all their transactions." The new version reads: "Organs of the state and administrative authorities are obliged to act according to the principle of equality before the law in all their transactions and *in all activities pertaining to the provision of public services*" (my emphasis). The Turkish Parliament thus upheld the principle of non-discrimination, reaffirming that gender discrimination was against the law and also that discrimination on the basis of language and ethnicity was illegal.

Within the Turkish context, where approximately 15 million Kurds live in the country and speak their own language as well as Turkish, this parliamentary reaffirmation of the non-discrimination principle had multiple meanings. If some deputies of the AKP party and others entertained the hope that Turkey one day would adopt *Shari'a* law, introducing the inequality of the sexes, they would now have their own legislative actions to contend with. Ironically, the egalitarian and civic-republican legacies of the Turkish Kemalist tradition led the Parliament, with its Islamicist majority, nevertheless to formulate a resounding restatement of the principle of non-discrimination for all Turkish citizens in their procurement of public services.

Yet it was left ambiguous whether the *providers* as well as the *receivers* of public services would benefit from non-discrimination. Did the law intend to protect only religious women against discrimination in receiving educational, medical, and other services, or did it also intend to protect those who provided such services from discrimination? The difference between the two is enormous. If the law protects not only the *recipients* but also the *providers* of public services, then teachers, government officials, doctors, attorneys, and, indeed, the President's own wife, would be able to wear the headscarf in their official capacity and in the performance of official functions.

From a moral standpoint, one could argue that any distinction between the *receivers and providers* of public services is indefensible. What matters is that the state protects the individuals' freedom of conscience and rightful claim not to be discriminated against on account of their faith. These considerations are directly analogous to the Fereshta Ludin story. In the Turkish case, too, it is often asserted that in the public sphere *laïcité,* understood as the strict banning of sectarian religious symbols in the provision of *state services*, such as education, health care, and transportation, must be upheld.

The legislative revision of Article 42 of the Turkish Basic Law, which pertains to "The Right of Education and Instruction," was more straightforward, although this Article is riven by many clauses of ambivalent, and even repressive, political import. It reads: "No language other than Turkish can be taught . . . in any institutions of learning and instruction as a mother tongue." This is a militant assertion of the supposed "homogeneity" of the *ethnos* upon which the *demos*, the political nation, is based. It reveals the tension between the *demos* of the Turkish republic which consists of Turkish citizens, regardless of their religion, ethnicity, creed, and color, on the one hand, and the imaginary unity and supposed homogeneity of the

Demos
vs Ethnos

ethnos, a nation which is supposed to have no other mother language than Turkish, on the other hand. The reforms of February 10, 2008, left the gist of this Article untouched. There was simply an addition that "No one can be denied their right to attain higher learning on the basis of reasons not clearly formulated in writing by law. The limits of the exercise of this right are determined by law." This clause aimed to censure those instructors, professors, as well as administrators, who took it upon themselves to ban by administrative fiat alone women and girls wearing the headscarf from entering these institutions or sitting for their exams with their heads covered. But even after the legislation was passed such incidents did not stop. Even local officials in public health-care clinics were reported to have refused to serve women wearing the scarf.

One may object that all this is now ancient history since both amendments were rescinded and the *status quo ante* re-established by the Turkish Constitutional Court. But it is important to note that between February 2008 when the new legislation was passed and June 2008 when it was overturned, Turkey missed the chance to embark on the long process of creating a new *demos* and a new political identity for a truly pluralistic society. It missed the chance to recognize the cleavage between observant and non-observant Muslims as only *one,* and by no means the principal one, among the many differences and divisions currently surfacing in Turkish society.

Civil society in Turkey today is showing unprecedented effervescence and self-examination. Atrocities committed against the Ottoman Armenians in 1915; repressive measures directed at the non-Muslims with the passing of the so-called "Varlik Vergisi," which redistributed the wealth of Jews, Greeks, and Armenians primarily to the nascent Turkish bourgeoisie; the repressive Kemalist ideology of the ruling elites; and the origins of the Kurdish problem, which go back to the compromises reached between these very Kemalist elites and Kurdish feudal landlords, are all topics being examined by the media, by newspapers, by works of art and theater, and in contemporary scholarship.[31] Seen against this background, the headscarf debate essentially centers around the pluralization of identities in a post-nationalist and democratic society. It is not about regression to an Islamist republic, as many secularists claim. The Kemalist elites – the army, the civil bureaucracy, teachers, lawyers, engineers, and doctors – look upon these developments as *failures* of the republican experiment. On the contrary, they may be seen as manifestations of its success. Whereas Kemalist republican ideology, despite its Enlightenment pretensions, equates citizenship with ethnic Turkish and reli-

180

gious Muslim identity, today we see not only the proliferation of ethnicities but also the reclaiming of different ways of being Muslim. It is not only the right *to* wear the headscarf which must be defended but also the right of girls and women *not* to wear the headscarf, and not to observe mandatory fasting during Ramadan, and so on, that must be asserted. But neither the ruling AK Party nor the oppositional CHP (Republican People's Party) are deep democrats in this sense. It is altogether possible that had the Turkish Constitutional Court decided to accept the new legislation as constitutional, the AKP would have seen a green light to ban the public drinking of alcohol, to impose further restrictions on the dress habits of non-observant Turkish girls, and to demand that everyone fast during Ramadan. In other words, the public face of Turkish civil society could have come to resemble that of Saudi Arabia and Malaysia[32] rather than that of Israel or Canada, countries in which religious groups enjoy great freedoms and some degree of self-government in many areas of civil and political life.

In the weeks following the reform of the headscarf ban, a group of nearly 800 women wearing the headscarf signed a petition stating that "If freedom of expression is at stake, nothing can be considered a detail. We are not yet free." These women took aim at what they call "repressive governmentality" – they demanded the abolition of the Turkish Council on Higher Education (YÖK), they wanted assurances that the rights of Alevis (a dissident Muslim sect) would be protected, that there would be a solution to the Kurdish problem, and that Article 301 would be abolished. The right to wear the headscarf was seen in the context of broadening civil rights for other groups.

Conclusion

What can we conclude from our brief review of this legal landscape – a landscape which shows convergences as well as divergences? Clearly, in all three countries, and now increasingly in the UK too, the headscarf is not seen simply as a religious item of clothing, expressing a subjective choice and attitude toward their faith on the part of those who wear it, but as a political symbol requiring careful state regulation and monitoring.[33] All three states construe the wearing of the headscarf not as an act of religious conscience but as a potential political threat, and regulate it at that level.

In this process of confrontation between state power and girls and women with the headscarf, the meaning of the symbol itself is undergoing changes: for the girls and women involved, the headscarf and turban are no longer simply expressions of Muslim humility but symbols of an embattled identity and signs of public defiance. The wearing of the headscarf itself has politicized them in all three countries and has transformed some of them from being "docile objects" into increasingly confrontational subjects. I am personally convinced that such confrontations will not end: newer modes of symbolizing ethno-religious identity will appear and courts will be confronted with ever more cases concerning the integration of Islamic religious and cultural differences into modern liberal democracies. Contemporary controversies about whether Muslim girls can be forced to attend co-educational gym classes, and about wearing "burkinis" (combining burkas and bikinis) in public swimming pools and the like, indicate that these symbolic and political controversies are far from over. With the banning of the building of minarets in Switzerland in early 2010, and the outcry in the summer of 2010 around the building of a mosque near the site of the old World Trade Center in New York, it is clear that the very public presence of Islam still poses an unresolved challenge in Western liberal constitutional democracies.

Through such controversies, the dialectic of rights and identities are mobilized in processes of democratic iterations. Rights, and other principles of the liberal democratic state, need to be periodically challenged and rearticulated in the public sphere in order to retain and enrich their original meaning. It is only when new groups claim that they belong within the circles of addressees of a right from which they have been excluded in its initial articulation that we come to understand the fundamental limitedness of every individual right claim within a specific constitutional tradition, as well as the context-transcending validity of such claims. The democratic dialogue, and also the legal hermeneutic one, are enhanced through the repositioning and rearticulation of rights in the public spheres of liberal democracies.[34] The law sometimes can guide this process, in that legal reform may run ahead of popular consciousness and may raise popular consciousness to the level of the constitution; the law may also lag behind popular consciousness and may need to be prodded along to adjust itself to it. In a vibrant liberal multicultural democracy, cultural-political conflict and learning through conflict should not be stifled through legal maneuvers. The democratic citizens themselves have to learn the art of separation by testing the limits of their overlapping consensus.

Sterile, legalistic, or populistic jurispathic processes may also occur.[35] In some cases, no normative learning may take place at all, but only a strategic bargaining among the parties may result; in other cases, the political process may simply run into the sandbanks of legalism or the majority of the *demos* may trample upon the rights of the minority in the name of some totalizing discourse of fear and war. Violence may ensue. Jurisgenerative politics is not a politics of teleology or theodicy. Rather, it permits us to conceptualize those moments when a space emerges in the public sphere, when principles and norms which undergird democratic will-formation become permeable and fluid enough to absorb new semantic contexts, which, in turn, enable the augmentation of the meaning of rights. I have suggested that we are traversing such a moment in history when *jurisgenerative* and *jurispathic* politics face each other around the controversies over religio-cultural differences. We are far from having achieved that "civility in social relations," of which Habermas speaks, and which is very much required precisely because and not "despite the growth of a plurality of cultures and religious world views."[36]

—— 10 ——

UTOPIA AND DYSTOPIA IN
OUR TIMES

Natural Rights and Social Utopias

The award of a prize in the name of a great thinker places the recipient in the position of seeking affinities and influences between herself and the one whom she has been chosen to honor. In my case, this was not hard: my first book, *Critique, Norm and Utopia: A Study of the Foundations of Critical Theory*, published in English in 1986 and translated into German in 1992 (Fischer Verlag), ended with these words of Ernst Bloch's:

> It is just as urgent *suo modo* to raise the problem of a heritage of classical natural law as it was to speak of the heritage of social utopias. Social utopias and natural law had mutually complementary concerns within the same human space; they marched separately but, sadly, did not strike together . . . Social utopian thought directed its efforts toward human happiness, natural law was directed toward human dignity. Social utopias depicted relations in which *toil* and *burden* ceased, natural law constructed relations in which *degradation* and *insult* ceased.[1]

What seemed to me especially important in this insight was the insistence on the concept of utopia despite the demise of "the phi-

This chapter was delivered as my Ernst Bloch Prize Acceptance Speech at the Ernst Bloch Zentrum in Ludwigshafen, Germany on September 25, 2009. It is being published in revised English version for the first time. It has appeared in German as "Zur Utopie und Anti-Utopie in unseren Zeiten. Rede anlässlich der Verleihung des Ernst-Bloch Preises 2009," in: *Bloch-Almanach* 28/2009, ed. Klaus Kufeld (Talheimer: Mosseingen-Talheim, 2009), pp. 11–27.

losophy of the subject." Let me elaborate. Classical Marxism presupposed the model of a demiurge-like humanity externalizing itself through its own activity in history and yet facing its own externalized capacities as "capital," as the sum total of those alienated forces that came to oppress individuals. Emancipation would then mean the reappropriation of this alienated potential by individuals themselves.[2] With this claim, Marx's critique of Hegel initiated the transition turn from the *subject of reflection* to the *subject of production*. The essential constituents of our humanity would no longer be defined as that of an *animal rationale* but as an *animal laborans*. The act that raised us out of nature was not reflection but production, understood as "material, world-constitutive praxis." Nature was not an emanation of Spirit, as Hegel would have it; rather, nature signified the totality of those objective conditions, shaped and altered by the activity of human subjects. Nevertheless, this Marxist inversion of Hegel continued the presuppositions of what I name "the philosophy of the subject" (*Critique, Norm and Utopia*: 133–43).

The philosophy of the subject has its roots in the model of Hegel's *Phenomenology of Spirit*, namely, that of a collective singular subject called *Geist*, externalizing itself in history and returning to itself by reappropriating this "second nature" facing it. Whereas Hegel posited a reconciliation (*Versöhnung*) that would follow upon *Geist*'s reflection upon the conditions of its own becoming, Marx, then Lukács, and the early Bloch, as well as members of the Frankfurt School, envisaged such reappropriation to proceed along two dimensions: first, world-constitutive activity, understood as the material practice of social production; and, second, transformative, revolutionary practice. In this tradition, the activity of world constitution called *praxis* thus referred to two processes: material production on the one hand and revolutionary activity on the other. Collapsing the Aristotelian distinctions between *poeisis* and *praxis*, between making and doing, the Marxist-Hegelian tradition to which the young Bloch belonged was unable to elaborate the different logics, structures, and developments of these activities, with objectionable consequences for theory and practice.

Bloch and the Philosophy of the Subject

Since Jürgen Habermas's famous early essay on "Labor and Interaction: Remarks on Hegel's Jena *Philosophy of Mind*,"[3] contemporary critical theory has distinguished among the logics of these different human activities that were mistakenly conflated into one under the concept of *praxis* as "world-constitutive activity." The conceptual pair of "redistribution" and "recognition," used in our days by Axel Honneth and also Nancy Fraser, is an attempt to differentiate these two dimensions from one another and is indebted to this distinction between labor and interaction.[4]

The young Bloch, it seems to me, on the one hand is indebted to the philosophy of the subject, and, on the other hand, is deeply struggling against it. In the *The Spirit of Utopia* ([1923] 2000), we read:

> And precisely to this class, to its *a priori* economically revolutionary class struggle, Marx, in a magnificently paradoxical conjunction, gives over the legacy of all freedom, the beginning of world history after prehistory, the very first true total revolution, the end of every class struggle, liberation from the materialism of class interests as such.[5]

As we can infer from this passage, the most important consequence of the unitary concept of *praxis* that dominated the philosophy of the subject was not only analytical, but also normative. In classical Marxism, whether orthodox or critical, the emphasis on the economy went hand in hand with a political commitment to the interests of that privileged class, namely, the industrial proletariat, now considered to be representative of humanity as such. Not only could this view not explain the pluralization of forms of political conflicts and the emergence of new emancipatory actors in late-capitalist societies, but in the historical *praxis* of Marxist movements it also led to a *politics of collective singularity*.[6] By this, I mean a mode of politics where one group or organization acts in the name of the whole. It is evident that this usurpation of universality by a single group, which is then said to be represented by the Party, which is then said to be represented by the Executive Committee, which is then said to be represented by the Leader, and so on, can only lead to a repressive and anti-democratic politics. While distancing themselves from orthodox Marxism and Stalinist politics, critical Marxists did not radically revise the "universality" claims of the proletariat until the very late 1930s, when European reality and the rise of fascism left them with no other alternative. Ernst Bloch, too, has been charged with not having distanced himself sufficiently from Stalinism.[7]

However, already the young Bloch criticizes the "theory of the cunning of reason taken over from Hegel" (*Spirit of Utopia*: 241). Marx, claims Bloch, despite exposing the fetishized character of the process of production, by "exorcizing" all dreams, all active utopia, and all religiously inspired end-goals from history, came to confirm this very "cunning of reason." Marx, "with his 'forces of production,' with the calculus of the 'process of production'," comes to uphold, observes Bloch very shrewdly, "the same all too constitutive game, the same pantheism, mythicism . . . the same guiding power which Hegel upheld for the 'Idea'" (ibid.: 241). This is a clear repudiation of the philosophy of the subject. In other passages too, despite his rather naive subscription to the Marxist-Leninist doctrine of the "withering away of the state" (ibid.: 241), Bloch of the *Spirit of Utopia* already evokes "a communitarian society" (ibid.: 246), praising Marx for having "purified Socialist planning . . . of mere Jacobism" (ibid.: 236), and for having "restored the spirit of Kant and Baader" (ibid.).

The young Bloch, then, in many respects, has more in common with the anarchist and cooperativist traditions of the early utopian socialists than with Marxist-Leninist attempts to overtake the state via the dictatorship of the proletariat. The well-known section on "The Socialist Idea" ends with this apocalyptic vision: "It is as the Baal Shem says: the Messiah can only come when all the guests have sat down at the table; this table is first of all the table of labor, beyond labor, but then at the same time the table of the Lord," and concludes this passage with one wholly ambivalent in its meaning: "in the philadelphian Kingdom the organization of the earth finds its ultimately coordinative metaphysics" (ibid.: 246). Whom could Bloch be referring to? Does Bloch have in mind the "city of brotherly love" of the Quakers, or the signing of the American Declaration of Independence in 1776? We don't know. Most likely, both. And is this welcome or to be rejected?

By contrast to the apocalyptic messianism of the *Spirit of Utopia*, which sometimes endorses and sometimes departs from the philosophy of the subject, Bloch's later work, *Natural Law and Human Dignity* ([1961] 1985), is a more sober reckoning with law and with the doctrine of rights, or with what we would today call the tradition of "political liberalism." In a radio address of 1961 with the title "Naturrecht und menschliche Würde" ("Natural Law and Human Dignity"), intended to introduce the book to a larger audience, Bloch writes:

> To the extent that there is no possible human dignity – the kind essentially intended by natural law – without economic liberation, likewise there can come to pass no economic liberation without the issue of human rights in it . . . And so no real achievement of human rights

187

without the end of exploitation, but also no real end of exploitation without the achievement of human rights.

And, further:

> Granted that human dignity (which is the fundamental intention of all natural right theories) is not at all possible without economic emancipation, economic emancipation, however, cannot take place without human rights being realized in it either . . . No real establishment of human rights without an end to exploitation, but neither a true end to economic exploitation without the establishment of human rights.[8]

How can we think of the end of exploitation and the realization of human rights? Are we not in danger of falling back upon *das abstrakte Sollen* (the abstract ought), as Hegel's famous critique of Kant so trenchantly formulated? [9] Bloch himself spoke of "concrete utopia," or "reflective utopia."[10] Social utopias did not exhaust themselves in the social engineering dreams of early bourgeois thinkers, but aimed at the *noch-nicht*, the not-yet. When and how does the "not-yet" manifest itself?

Utopia and New Social Movements

The end of the philosophy of the subject and the turn from the "critique of instrumental reason" to that of communicative rationality changes the meaning of utopia in our societies. For over two decades now I have accepted the broad outlines of this paradigm shift, which allows us to rethink utopia in new terms, which nonetheless, I believe, bear remarkable closeness to the thought of Ernst Bloch. We can no longer assume there is a privileged standpoint in the social structure that bestows upon its occupiers a special vision of the totality. Nor can it be presupposed that the utopian sources of objective spirit have dried up. The new social movements of our times – from the women's movement of the last six decades to the ecology movement, from the movement of *les sans-papiers*, the undocumented immigrants and refugees, to the activists of the world social forum who aim at empowering the "global South" – do not share the hubris of the late nineteenth and early twentieth centuries; they do not insist that one particularity can represent universality as such. They are aware of "difference," "otherness," and the "heterologics" of their differently situated experiences; they struggle to recognize this heterologic of plurality as a moment of strength rather than weakness.

188

These movements continue in the spirit of natural right and social utopia insofar as they aim at creating a "polity" of rights and entitlements *and* an "association of needs and solidarity."[11] By a *polity*, I understand a democratic, pluralistic unity, composed of many communities, and held together by a common democratic legal, political, and administrative apparatus. By contrast, an *association of needs and solidarity* is a community in action, formed by a set of shared values and ideals which uphold the concreteness of the other on the basis of acknowledging her dignity as a generalized other. Such communities are not pre-given; they emerge through the struggles of the oppressed, the exploited, and the humiliated. The community of needs and solidarity is created in the interstices of societies by those new social movements, which on the one hand fight to extend the universalizing promises of objective spirit – justice, social, and political rights – and on the other hand seek to combine the logic of justice with that of friendship and solidarity. The perspective of the "generalized other," represents the legacy of natural right, while that of the "concrete other" continues the aspiration of social utopias.

I developed the contrast and complementarity between the perspectives of the "generalized" and the "concrete other," in the early 1990s as a result of my engagement with feminist theory and feminist ethics.[12] Still, Bloch's phrase that "Social utopias and natural law had mutually complementary concerns within the same human space; they marched separately but, sadly, did not strike together" (*Natural Law and Human Dignity*: xxix), which I cited in the Conclusion to *Critique, Norm and Utopia* (353), was inspirational in this regard.

The Reframing of State and Society under Globalization

How can we think of the complementarity of natural right and social utopias, or in ethical terms, or of the interdependence of the generalized and concrete other more specifically? Today we face a challenge which has shaken up the framework not only of Marxian critical social thought, but of classical sociology in general. The classics of social theory – Tönnies, Marx, Weber, Durkheim, Simmel, and the theorists of the Frankfurt School – assumed that the unit of social analysis was civil society organized as the nation-state. Many of the dualisms around which these models centered – society versus community; organic versus mechanical solidarity; instrumental rationality versus value rationality; money versus love; the stranger versus the neighbor; instrumental versus substantive reason – reflected the contradictions of modern capitalist society in the process of developing its institutions of social integration. The question was whether such societies could accomplish the integration of their members into a coherent socio-cultural whole or whether they would collapse under the weight of their own contradictions, generated by the dysfunctionalities of the marketplace and the demands of capitalist civil society. The state was at times considered a mere epiphenomenon to these larger forces; at other times, the state was viewed as an independent power, prevailing over civil society and entrusted with the tasks of education, military defense, and regulation of the economy such as to protect society from imploding from within.

Today, as we move toward the formation of world society, we face the question whether we should speak of "society" at all. We may be facing a "desocialization of society." As society becomes world society, many functions of politico-economic steering and socio-symbolic integration are entrusted to other agents: in the USA, in particular, we see the increasing privatization of the educational system through vouchers and charter schools, as well as the privatization of prisons and even of military functions, through the emergence of organizations such as Blackwater, active in the Iraq War, and now called by a science-fiction name, "Xe." Chip by chip, the public functions of the nation-state are being transferred to private organizations, which themselves are undermining the power of the rule of law by avoiding parliamentary and juridical oversight. In fact, transferring state functions such as surveillance, incarceration, and military defense to these organizations is a way of avoiding parliamentary and democratic controls which are seen as politically noxious forms of interference with the judgment of so-called "professional military cadres," and their paramilitary companions. Certainly, these trends are most visible in the USA. Countries of Europe have been able to withstand some of the onslaught of these global forces only by abdicating classical Westphalian sovereignty, and consequently by increasing the steering capacity of the state in some areas, such as border control, and losing it in others, such as economic and fiscal policy. Bit by bit, though, both the steering and integration functions of the nation-state are devolving toward other structures: either toward subnational structures as in the case of "outsourcing" or toward supra-national structures of economic, military steering, and socio-economic integration as in the case of the European Union. The World Wide Web and the world entertainment system today have stronger hold on the imaginations of the generation between 15 and 25 than do schools, parents, or other civil society associations.

190

In the face of the greatest economic crisis since the Great Depression of the 1930s, however, our political systems are still floundering within the old regulatory frameworks of the world economy. On the one hand, we face societies which are losing their socio-cultural and symbolic capacities of integrating increasing numbers of individuals; on the other hand, we face a world economy which has rattled almost every country on all continents but, in the face of this crisis, only tired, old slogans of regulating offshore profits and better cooperation are repeated. Let us recall Bloch once more: "no real achievement of human rights without the end of exploitation, but also no real end of exploitation without the achievement of human rights." Today, the framework for raising claims of justice and of demanding socio-economic rights has been transformed. In the era of global socio-economic interdependence nation-states alone cannot be the exclusive addressees of redistributive claims, although they do bear the primary responsibility for meeting the demands of their citizens and residents with all the means in their power.

But in the early twenty-first century, global socio-economic interdependence is experienced less as if we were members in a "world republic," in the Kantian sense, and more in the form of the increasing cruelty of "haves" against "have-nots." The European Union's recent policies of migration and asylum are an example in point: the shores of the Mediterranean are becoming graveyards, strewn with the bodies of African, Chinese, and Middle Eastern peoples fleeing poverty in their own countries, then meeting death at the hands of deceitful guides and captains. Those who are lucky enough not to die en route instead face "collection camps" or "transit-processing camps," in which they are placed for an indefinite future before being deported to countries from which they originally fled because of fear of persecution. The distinction between the economic migrant and the political refugee, which may have served the world-state system well as a guideline in the immediate aftermath of World War II and during the Cold War, is no longer useful. Political persecution and economic marginalization and discrimination are interdependent. Nevertheless, migratory movements the world over are becoming criminalized without a clear sense of the world economic forces that give rise to them.

There is an example that I use to explain to my students why migrations occur as a result of the "pull-and-push" forces in a world economy. The migrants say "We are here, because you were there"; "we did not cross the border; the border crossed us." What does this mean? For example, through the NAFTA agreement in the 1990s, the

USA started exporting corn into the Mexican market. These corn strains were more resistant to disease and infestation than local strains, and soon American corn exports drove Mexican farmers out of the market. These farmers in turn became destitute and unemployed migrants, trying to cross the desert to reach the United States, where ironically they would become – if lucky, that is – undocumented migrant workers on the agricultural fields of California, or day laborers in Arizona and New Mexico.

What is the response to this human tragedy? Criminalization of the migrant, militarization of the border, and the hypocrisy of governmental officials and political leaders who are too scared to face the retribution of agro-business by curbing its destructive effects on the Mexican economy. Similar scenarios are repeated within the European Union, too, which protects its own farmers with lucrative subsidies, while devastating African ones by refusing to open domestic markets to their products.

A Blochian Legacy

What shape, then, can a concrete and reflective utopia take under these circumstances? First, we need to expand the legacy of natural rights to include the struggles of the women's movement and the movement of *les sans-papiers* and "undocumented migrants." We have to fight against the criminalization of the migrant and the foreigner; we have to fight for the recognition of the civil and socio-economics rights of others; and for eliminating the obstacles to acquiring citizenship that are placed on the path of long-term residents. These demands extend natural rights beyond state borders, and, maybe for the first time in human history, they extend the cosmopolitan kernel of all natural rights thinking which has been present since the Stoics to all of humanity. This means the treatment of the migrant, the refugee, and the foreigner as the "generalized other," with whom we are willing to share equal rights. I find a beautiful passage in Bloch's writing that confirms this vision. He writes:

> The contents of this law of humanity, of this nomos anthropos as it resurfaced in Stoic natural law, were the innate *equality* of all people (the abolition of difference in worth between slaves and masters, barbarians and Greeks), and the *unity* of all people as members of an international community, that is, the rational empire of love. (Bloch, *Natural Law and Human Dignity*: 13; emphasis in text)

192

But over and beyond extending the perspective of the generalized other, we also need to exercise the powers of "enlarged thought" through our moral imagination, in order to understand the perspective of the concrete other. Can we see the world through the eyes of that mother of four from Ecuador or Ghana, whose husband has been murdered or gone missing in some gang violence, and who leaves her children to be watched over by an aging mother and aunt, while she risks crossing the border to Arizona or goes afloat a dinghy from Tangiers in order to reach Italy? Can we understand that this woman is not a criminal but one who has a concrete history, concrete needs, desires, and wishes, like you and me? Can we find the solidarity in our selves not to criminalize her but to help her with a decent job? Can we find the decency to invest in her country in various programs so that she can learn to help herself and her children? These ideas of solidaristic development and cooperative investment in the global South are not new, but they have receded from our consciousness. The social utopia of the concrete other demands that we treat the stranger not only with respect, but also with compassion; in the face of the interdependence of our needs, we ought to move toward interdependent solutions by exercising social imagination. Cosmopolitanism does not mean eliminating local differences or dismissing attachments to those nearest to us; it means enlarging the compass of our moral sympathy ever wider so that more and more human beings appear to us as "concrete others" for whose rights as "generalized others" we are willing to speak up and fight.

This utopia of cosmopolitanism has become much more concrete in our times than when it was articulated by thinkers like Kant in the eighteenth century. Kant saw the expansion of Western maritime and commercial capitalism toward India and China in particular with ambivalence: on the one hand, insofar as this spirit of capitalism brought the human race together through trade, he welcomed it; on the other hand, he had no illusions that trade often was unequal exchange which could bring misery to the non-European peoples.[13] Today we live in a global world society. News and germs, commodities and stocks, fashion and entertainment circulate in a world public sphere; but this world public sphere is not yet a global public space of action and decision. We become aware that the consequences of our actions inalterably affect those in remote parts of the world through global calamities such as climate change, droughts, typhoons, financial catastrophes, and spread of diseases. We need to develop both a *planetary ethics* to guide us in the face of the devastation we are causing to the earth as a species, and a global public sphere, as a sphere of action and deliberation, in which we interlock through ever more interdependent formal and informal spheres and institutions toward republican federalism. These would be the concrete utopia of our times.

The Threat of Dsytopias

Let us not forget the potential dystopias of our times, lest these hopes may appear as none other than pious wishes or as abstract utopias. Among the dystopias of our time, one that seems plausible to many, is that of an increasingly militarized empire, a world hegemon, subjecting every country in the world to increasing criminalization and surveillance; punishing the poor by incarcerating them and letting the needy and the destitute fall through the social net into criminality, madness, and drug abuse. The United States came very close to such a dystopia in the eight years of the administration of George W. Bush and this is the reason why the shock of Hurricane Katrina in 2005 has remained in the American psyche. It seemed as if a mirror was held to one's worst fears about the dystopic possibilities in the United States.

If the dystopia for the United States is that of a militarized post-democratic polity, for Europe it is the growth of regional egotism, and increasing conflict between North and South, East and West. These fissures in the European fabric manifested themselves with the so-called Greek crisis in the summer of 2010. It seemed as if the European project was and continues to be in tatters. The damage done to the European sense of solidarity is intense and will not be so easily and so quickly healed. European dystopia also manifests itself in hatred toward foreigners, and particularly Islam; in the increasing marginalization of those who cannot re-enter the job market; in the turn inwards toward a form of great civilizational chauvinism, already evident in the many pronouncements of French President Sarkozy; in the withering away of political culture through the weakness of an increasingly boring social democracy which is too squeamish to embrace internationalism, or implement the tough and innovative solutions that could curb global capitalism.

Dystopic possibilites also exist for nations such as China, Brazil, and India, who are now facing all the turmoils of integration into the global world market. In these countries and in many others, a globally networked elite is removed from – in fact protected from – the miserable masses of the population by bodyguards, and by special security forces guarding gated communities. Brazil's elite fly with helicopters from rooftop to rooftop in order to escape the misery and danger of driving through the *favelas*. In the meantime, the working masses in China face factory shutdowns, and are served baby food laced with chemical substances, young boys and girls in Thailand and other places sell themselves as prostitutes to willing Western tourists, and poor peasants struggle with ever more intense droughts, as well as floods, throughout Southeast Asia.

It is the obligation of concrete utopian thinking, or reflective utopian thinking, to countenance these dystopias as well. The framework for realizing both natural rights and social utopias today requires a cosmopolitan imagination. Only then, and maybe only then, can we approach the future in the spirit of an *experimentum mundi*, in Bloch's words – an experiment with, and of, the world, in which we strive toward a planetary ethic and a global public sphere.

NOTES AND REFERENCES

PREFACE

1   See Esther Benbassa and Aron Rodrigue, *Sephardi Jewry: A History of the Judeo-Spanish Community, 14th–20th Centuries* (Berkeley, CA: University of California Press, 2000).

CHAPTER 1   INTRODUCTION: COSMOPOLITANISM WITHOUT ILLUSIONS

1   Samuel P. Huntington, "Dead Souls: The Denationalization of the American Elite," *The National Interest* (March 1, 2004): 5–18.
2   Quoted by Huntington, ibid., p. 5.
3   David. J. Depew, "Narrativism, Cosmopolitanism, and Historical Epistemology," *CLIO* 14/4 (1985): 357–78; here 375.
4   For classical studies in the history of ideas, see Friedrich Meinecke, *Cosmopolitanism and the National State*, trans. Robert B. Kimber. (Princeton, NJ: Princeton University Press, 1970), and Thomas Schereth, *The Cosmopolitan Ideal in Enlightenment Thought* (Notre Dame, IN: University of Notre Dame Press, 1977).
5   Cf. Pheng Cheah and Bruce Robbins, eds, *Cosmopolitics: Thinking and Feeling Beyond the Nation* (Minneapolis, MN: University of Minnesota Press, 1998); Pheng Cheah, *Inhuman Conditions: On Cosmopolitanism and Human Rights* (Cambridge, MA: Harvard University Press, 2006); for philosophy, see the debate started by the volume of Joshua Cohen and Martha Nussbaum, eds, *For Love of Country? Debating the*

Limits of Patriotism (Boston, MA: Beacon Press, 1996), and Nussbaum's well-known essay in this volume, "Patriotism and Cosmopolitanism": 3–17; but see Nussbaum's later retractions, in "Toward a Globally Sensitive Patriotism," *Daedalus* 137/3 (summer 2008). Cf. Anthony Appiah, *Cosmopolitanism: Ethics in a World of Strangers* (New York: W.W. Norton and Company, 2006); Thomas Pogge, "Cosmopolitanism and Sovereignty," *Ethics* 103/1 (October 1992): 48–75; Thomas Pogge, *World Poverty and Human Rights: Cosmopolitan Responsibilities and Reforms* (Cambridge: Polity, 2002); Stan van Hooft, *Cosmopolitanism: A Philosophy for Global Ethics* (Montreal and Kingston: McGill-Queen's University Press, 2009). For the pioneering work in political theory and international relations, cf. Daniel Archibugi, David Held, and Martin Kohler, *Re-Imagining Political Community: Studies in Cosmopolitan Democracy* (Stanford, CA: Stanford University Press, 1998); David Held, *Democracy and the Global Order* (Stanford, CA: Stanford University Press, 1994); David Held, *Cosmopolitanism: Ideas and Realities* (Cambridge: Polity, 2010); Daniel Archibugi, *The Global Commonwealth of Citizens: Toward Cosmopolitan Democracy* (Princeton, NJ: Princeton University Press, 2008); for sociology, see the tireless efforts of Ulrich Beck, *Power in the Global Age: A New Global Political Economy* (London: Sage, 2006); Ulrich Beck, *Cosmopolitan Vision*, trans. Ciaran Cronin (Cambridge: Polity, 2006); Ulrich Beck and Edgar Grande, *Cosmopolitan Europe* (Cambridge: Polity, 2007); for urban studies, Leonie Sandercock, *Cosmopolis II. Mongrel, Cities in the 21st Century* (London: Continuum, 2003).

6   For a recent lucid statement of the end of the "Westphalian-Keynesian-Fordist" paradigm, see Nancy Fraser, *Scales of Justice: Reimagining Political Space in a Globalizing World* (New York: Columbia University Press, 2009), pp. 1–30.

7   Pheng Cheah, *Inhuman Conditions: On Cosmopolitanism and Human Rights*, p. 18.

8   See Cheah, *Inhuman Conditions*, pp. 45–73.

9   See Craig Calhoun for a complaint similar to Huntington's, "The Class Consciousness of Frequent Travelers: Toward a Critique of Actually Existing Cosmopolitanism," *South Atlantic Quarterly* 101/4 (2002): 869–97.

10   For an influential statement, see Costas Douzinas, *Human Rights and Empire: The Political Philosophy of Cosmopolitanism* (New York and Abingdon, Oxford: Routledge-Cavendish, 2007).

Douzinas's learned account best exemplifies postmodernist skepticism as well as left suspicions toward the cosmopolitan project, considering it deeply implicated not only in neo-liberal globalization but in the deluded foreign policy of the George W. Bush administration too.

11 Darrin M. McMahon, "Fear and Trembling: Strangers and Strange Lands," *Daedalus* 137/3 (summer 2008): 5–17; A. A. Long, "The Concept of the Cosmopolitan in Greek and Roman Thought," *Daedalus* 137/3 (summer 2008): 50–8.

12 Michel de Montaigne, "Education of Children," *The Complete Essays of Montaigne*, trans. Donald M. Frame (Stanford, CA: Stanford University Press, 1965), p. 116.

13 Cited by de Montaigne, p. 7.

14 As quoted in McMahon, "Fear and Trembling: Strangers and Strange Lands," p. 9.

15 Kwame Anthony Appiah observes that Marcus Aurelius, who as emperor of Rome persecuted the Christian sect, nonetheless found millions of Christian readers through his *Meditations*. See Kwame Anthony Appiah, *Cosmopolitanism: Ethics in a World of Strangers* (New York and London: W.W. Norton, 2006), p. xiv.

16 Immanuel Kant [1795], "Zum Ewigen Frieden. Ein philosophischer Entwurf," in *Immanuel Kants Werke*, ed. A. Buchenau, E. Cassirer, and B. Kellermann (Berlin: Verlag Bruno Cassirer, 1923); English edition, Immanuel Kant, "Toward Perpetual Peace: A Philosophical Sketch," in *Toward Perpetual Peace and Other Writings on Politics, Peace, and History*, ed. and with an introduction by Pauline Kleingeld; trans. David Colclasure; with contributions by Jeremy Waldron, Michael W. Doyle, and Allen W. Wood (New Haven, CT, and London: Yale University Press, 2006), pp. 67–110. All references in the text are to these two editions: the first page number refers to the German; the second to the English editions. I have used my own translations in consultation with this edition; for further discussions of Kant's contribution to cosmopolitan theory, see Seyla Benhabib, *The Rights of Others: Aliens, Citizens and Residents* (Cambridge: Cambridge University Press, 2004), pp. 25–48.

17 Seyla Benhabib, *The Rights of Others: Aliens, Residents and Citizens*, pp. 25–43.

18 Jacques Derrida, *On Cosmopolitanism and Forgiveness*, trans. Mark Dooley and Michael Hughes (New York: Routledge, 2001), p. xx.

19 Sankar Muthu gives a compelling account of the broader context of Kant's text, in *Enlightenment and Empire* (Princeton, NJ: Princeton University Press, 2003). For a more extensive discussion of this problem, see Benhabib, *The Rights of Others*, pp. 26–31. While the distinction between *Gastrecht*, "the right of permanent visitation," and *Besuchsrecht*, "the right of temporary sojourn," in the context of eighteenth-century developments of European maritime imperialism was a progressive one, and established the philosophical–discursive space for condoning those nations such as the Chinese Empire that wanted to resist contact with the West to do so, it no longer is. The claim of the foreigner to citizenship rights must be guaranteed by democratic constitutions, and it can no longer be considered a *wohltätiger Vertrag*, a "contract of beneficence" granted by the sovereign, as Kant thought. The entitlement to citizenship itself will of course depend upon the fulfillment of certain conditions, as defined by each democratic sovereign more or less narrowly. Both the "right to emigration" and the "right to nationality" are human rights guaranteed by Articles 13 and 15 of the Universal Declaration of Human Rights respectively.

In a provocative new reading of Kant's essay, David Harvey engages at multiple levels with the anthropological, geographical, and cultural assumptions of Kant. Harvey believes that Kant is more poisoned by a Eurocentric proto-nationalist anthropology than many of us, myself included, admit. See David Harvey, *Cosmopolitanism and the Geographies of Freedom* (New York: Columbia University Press, 2009), pp. 17–37. I find Harvey's theses provocative but not accurate. Kant is a difficult thinker and fitting together the pieces of his system on moral and political philosophy, anthropology, and geography is not always easy. For a more careful reconstruction of Kant's position than Harvey's, see Thomas A. McCarthy, *Race, Empire, and the Idea of Human Development* (Cambridge: Cambridge University Press, 2009), pp. 42–69.

20 See Peter Niesen's observation: "Cosmopolitan rights holds among individuals, and between individuals and peoples, and between peoples, whether or not these peoples have set up a

state. The default presumption seems to be that between any two actors x and y, x has a right to attempt or offer communication and association with y. If x has a right to attempt communication with y, nobody may hinder her performance of this attempt." In "Colonialism and Hospitality," *Politics and Ethics Review* 3/1 (2007): 90–108; here 98. Niesen disagrees with my justification of cosmopolitan right in *The Rights of Others* (pp. 34–35) with reference to Kant's doctrine of "external freedom" (Niesen, pp.100 ff.). I cannot discuss his criticism at length here but suffice it to say that Niesen's own alternative justification of cosmopolitan rights, through the "unintended dynamic of acquired rights," presupposes an economic doctrine of interdependence which is quite advanced as an economic doctrine for Kant's times; cf. Niesen, pp. 102 ff.

21   But let us not forget or ignore that despite this tremendous achievement Kant's liberalism is much less robust than we would wish it to be: in Kant's republic women, domestic servants, and propertyless apprentices are named "auxiliaries to the commonwealth" and their legal status is made dependent upon the male head of household. Nor will I discuss in this context the continuing controversy about Kant's views of Jews and Judaism in his writings on anthropology and religion: it is still debated whether Kant believed that Jews could only be citizens in a republic by giving up their proper laws and traditions, or whether Kant advocated for the Jews of Germany that Judaism could be considered a "religion within the limits of reason" as well, which would be acceptable with its own rules of prayer, dietary rules, and so on. Cf. Hermann Cohen, *Innere Beziehungen der Kantischen Philosophie zum Judentum*, in *Jüdishe Schriften*. (Berlin: Hrsg. Von Bruno Strauss, 1924); Julius Guttmann, *Kant und das Judentum: Ein philosophiegeschichtlicher Exkurs*, in Nathan Porges and Joseph Becher Schor, *Ein Nordfranzösischer Bibelerklärer des XII Jahrhunderts* (Leipzig: 1908), pp. 41–61; Joshua Halberstam, "From Kant to Auschwitz," *Social Theory and Practice* 14/1 (1988): 41–54. For further discussion of the Jews within the European Enlightenment, see chapter 2 of this volume.

22   John Rawls, *The Law of Peoples: The Law of Peoples, with "The Idea of Public Reason" Revisited* (Cambridge, MA: Harvard University Press, 1999).

23   Charles Beitz, *Political Theory and International Relations*, revised edition (Princeton, NJ: Princeton University Press, [1979]

1999); Charles Beitz, "Rawls's Law of Peoples," *Ethics* 110/4 (July 2000): 669–96; Allan Buchanan, "Rawls's Law of Peoples: Rules for a Vanished Westphalian World," *Ethics* 110/4 (July 2000): 697–721; Andrew Kuper, "Rawlsian Global Justice: Beyond *The Law of Peoples* to a Cosmopolitan Law of Persons," *Political Theory* 28 (2000): 640–74.

24 John Rawls, "The Law of Peoples" [1993], in J. Rawls, *Collected Papers*, ed. Samuel Freeman (Cambridge, MA: Harvard University Press, 1999), pp. 529–64; here p. 552. There are interesting differences in formulation between this early article and Rawls's later book *The Law of Peoples*, which I leave uncommented in this Introduction, but see chapter 5 of this volume.

25 For a defense of Rawls, see Joshua Cohen, "Minimalism About Human Rights: The Most We Can Hope For?," in *The Journal of Political Philosophy* 12/2 (2004): 190–213; here 192.

26 Cohen, "Minimalism About Human Rights," p. 192.

27 Seyla Benhabib, *Situating the Self: Gender, Community and Postmodernism in Contemporary Ethics* (New York and London: Routledge and Polity, 1992), pp. 148–78.

28 The Lisbon Treaty was signed by the EU member states on December 13, 2007, and entered into force on December 1, 2009. It amends the Treaty on European Union (TEU; also known as the Treaty of Maastricht) and the Treaty establishing the European Community (TEC; also known as the Treaty of Rome). It has been renamed "Treaty of Lisbon Amending the Treaty on European Union and the Treaty establishing the European Community." See: <http://eur-lex.europa.eu/LexUriServ/LexUriServ.do?uri=OJ:C:2007:306:0001:0010:EN:PDF>.Accessed on August 31, 2010, and December 1, 2010.

29 UDHR, Preamble, para 5. Available at: <http://www.un.org/en/documents/udhr/index.shtml>. Accessed September 10, 2010.

30 Ibid., Article 2.

31 Cheah, *Inhuman Conditions*, p. 10.

32 Samuel Moyn's, *The Last Utopia: Human Rights in History* (Cambridge, MA: Harvard University Press, 2010), is an attempt to "deflate" the significance of human rights discourse and politics by tracing the ironical shifts that have influenced both. Moyn sees the evolution of human rights discourse in modernity as having moved from an alliance between national sovereignty and the nation-state (12–14) to a "morality, global in its scope," that became the aspiration of mankind (213). The current

confusion seems to be that "Born of the yearning to transcend politics, human rights have become the core language of a new politics of humanity that has sapped the energy from old ideological contests of left and right" (227). Moyn's account damns with "faint praise." It is also based upon a series of unexamined juxtapositions between morals and politics, human rights and democracy, human rights and sovereignty that avoid an analysis of their interconnections. Human rights are both moral and political concepts; human rights both enable democracy and establish limits on democratic sovereignty; rights can only be actualized in some form of self-determining entity that must institutionalize some decisional closure, but this is not equivalent to the *suprema potestas* view of traditional concepts of sovereignty.

33 "Committee for Human Rights Guidelines," *American Anthropological Association*, written by Leslie Sponsel (Chair), available at: <http://www.aaanet.org/cmtes/cfhr/Committee-for-Human-Rights-Guidelines.cfm>; accessed on May 31, 2010.

34 See Robert Cover, "Foreword: Nomos and Narrative," The Supreme Court 1982 Term, *Harvard Law Review* 97/4 (1983/84): 4–68.

35 Cover, ibid., p. 18.

36 See Seyla Benhabib, *Another Cosmopolitanism: The Berkeley Tanner Lectures*, with Jeremy Waldron, Bonnie Honig, and Will Kymlicka, ed. Robert Post (Oxford: Oxford University Press, 2006), pp. 45ff. For a clarification of the status of democratic iterations as processes of generating democratic legitimacy, see chapter 8 of this volume.

37 See Ernst Bloch, *The Principle of Hope* [1959], vol. 1, trans. Neville Plaice, Stephen Plaice, and Paul Knight (Cambridge, MA: MIT Press, 1986).

38 "Dergestalt also, dass menschliche Würde (die im Naturrecht wesentlich intendiert ist . . .) ohne ökonomische Befreiung überhaupt nicht möglich ist, dass auch nicht ökonomische Befreiung geschehen kann, ohne die Sache Menschenrechte in ihr . . . Keine wirkliche Installierung der Menschenrechte also ohne Ende der Ausbeutung, aber auch kein wirkliches Ende der Ausbeutung ohne Installierung der Menschenrechte." E. Bloch, "Naturrecht und menschliche Würde. Rundfunkvortrag 1961," in *Bloch-Almanach. 5te Folge* (Baden-Baden: 1985), pp. 165–79; here p. 173.

CHAPTER 2 FROM *THE DIALECTIC OF ENLIGHTENMENT* TO *THE ORIGINS OF TOTALITARIANISM*: THEODOR ADORNO AND MAX HORKHEIMER IN THE COMPANY OF HANNAH ARENDT

1   Martin Jay, *The Dialectical Imagination: A History of the Frankfurt School and the Institute of Social Research, 1923–50* (Boston, MA: Beacon Press, 1973); reissued Berkeley and Los Angeles, CA, 1996. All references in the text are to the first edition. Jay's pioneering work was followed by several other monographs in the 1970s and 1980s. See Susan Buck-Morss, *The Origin of Negative Dialectics* (New York: Free Press, 1977); Andrew Arato and Eike Gebhardt, eds, *The Essential Frankfurt School Reader* (New York: Urizen Books, 1978); Thomas McCarthy, *The Critical Theory of Jürgen Habermas* (Cambridge, MA: MIT Press, 1978); David Held, *Introduction to Critical Theory* (Berkeley and Los Angeles, CA: University of California Press, 1980); Helmut Dubiel, *Wissenschaftsorganization und politische Erfahrung: Studien zur frühen kritischen Theorie* (Frankfurt: Suhrkamp, 1978); trans. Benjamin Gregg (Cambridge, MA.: MIT Press, 1985); Wolfgang Bonss and Axel Honneth, eds, *Sozialforschung als Kritik* (Frankfurt: Suhrkamp, 1982); Axel Honneth, *Kritik der Macht: Reflexionsstufen einer kritischen Gesellschaftstheorie* (Frankfurt: Suhrkamp, 1985); Seyla Benhabib, *Critique, Norm and Utopia: A Study of the Foundations of Critical Theory* (New York: Columbia University Press, 1986). More than a decade later, and relying upon recently available archival material, Rolf Wiggershaus published *Die Frankfurter Schule: Geschichte, Theoretische Entwicklung, Politische Bedeutung* (Munich, Vienna: Hanser Verlag, 1986). Wiggershaus was less ceremonial and less protective of Max Horkheimer's intellectual and personal failings as the Institut's Director than Jay.

2   As Jay explains in *The Dialectical Imagination*, with Erich Fromm as the project's director, and the cooperation of Paul Lazarsfeld, Ernst Schachtel, and others, three thousand questionnaires were distributed to workers, "asking their views on such issues as the education of children, the rationalization of industry, the possibility of avoiding a new war, and the locus of real power in the state" (p. 116). Cf. *Studien über Autorität und Familie* (Paris: Librairie Alcan, 1936). The individually conducted interviews, which were taken down verbatim, were then

analyzed for the latent personality traits they disclosed. Of the 586 respondents, 10 percent exhibited an "authoritarian" character; 15 percent were deemed anti-authoritarian, even revolutionary; "The vast majority, however, were highly ambivalent. As a result, the Institut concluded that the German working class would be far less resistant to a right-wing seizure of power than its militant ideology would suggest" (Jay, *The Dialectical Imagination*, p. 117). The empirical sections, penned by Erich Fromm, were not included in the original study and were published much later as *Arbeiter und Angestellte im Vorabend des dritten Reichs: Eine sozialpsychologische Untersuchung (Workers and Civil Servants on the Eve of the Third Reich: A sociopsychological Study)*, ed. Wolfgang Bonss (Stuttgart: Deutsche Verlaganstalt, 1980).

3 See *The Authoritarian Personality*, by T. W. Adorno, Else Frenkel-Brunswik, Daniel J. Levinson, and R. Nevitt Sanford, abridged edition, in *Studies in Prejudice*, ed. Max Horkheimer and Samuel H. Flowerman (New York and London: W.W. Norton and Company, 1950); reissued as Norton paperback in 1969 and 1982. There were actually two studies conducted by members of the Institute: one, the study of anti-Semitism within American labor, sponsored by the Jewish Labor Committee, and the other, on the authoritarian personality, sponsored by the American Jewish Committee.

4 Jay, *The Dialectical Imagination*, p. 133. Right after the publication of Jay's book, there were some caustic criticisms of the Frankfurt School's neglect of anti-Semitism, drawing attention precisely to these passages. See Erhard Bahr, "The Anti-Semitism Studies of the Frankfurt School: The Failure of Critical Theory," *German Studies Review* 1/2 (May 1978): 125–38.

5 Cf. Gershom Scholem on the failure of the "German-Jewish" symbiosis, "Jews and Germans," in Gershom Scholem, *On Jews and Judaism in Crisis: Selected Essays*, ed. Werner J. Dannhauser (New York: Schocken Books, 1976), pp. 82 ff.; Leo Strauss, *Jewish Philosophy and the Crisis of Modernity: Essays and Lectures in Modern Jewish Thought*, ed. and with an Introduction by Kenneth Hart Green (Albany, NY: SUNY Press, 1997); Leo Strauss, "German Nihilism," Lecture Delivered on February 26, 1941, in *Interpretation* 26 (1999): 353–78 (I thank my colleague Steven Smith for helpful references to Strauss's work); Jacob Taubes, *The Political Theology of Paul*, trans. Dana Hollander (Stanford, CA: Stanford University Press, 2004 [1987]);

Martin Buber, *Zwei Glaubensweisen* [1950], in *Werke.* (Munich: Koesel, 1962), vol. 1, pp. 651–782; Leo Baeck, *Das Wesen des Judentums*, 3rd edn (Darmstadt: Melzer, 1985 [1923]); Kurt Blumenfeld, *Erlebte Judenfrage: Ein Vierteljahrhundert Deutscher Zionismus.* Publication of the Leo Baeck Institut (Stuttgart: Deutsche Verlagsanstalt, 1962).

6 On the defiance of instrumental logic by the Nazis and hence the uselessness of the category of "instrumental reason" generally to understand Nazi anti-Semitism, see Dan Diner, "Historical Understanding and Counterrationality: The Judenrat as Epistemological Vantage," in Saul Friedlander, ed., *Probing the Limits of Representation: Nazism and the "Final Solution"* (Cambridge, MA: Harvard University Press, 1992), and, most recently, Dan Diner, *Gegenläufige Gedächtnisse: Über Geltung und Wirkung des Holocaust*, in *Toldot: Essays zur jüdischen Geschichte und Kultur*, vol. 7 (Göttingen: Vandenhoeck and Ruprecht, 2007).

7 I am thinking, of course, of Daniel Goldhagen's *Hitler's Willing Executioners: Ordinary Germans and the Holocaust* (New York: Alfred Knopf, 1996), versus Christopher Browning, *Ordinary Men: Reserve Police Batallion 101 and the Final Solution in Poland* (New York: HarperCollins, 1992); Christopher Browning, *The Origins of the Final Solution: The Evolution of Nazi Jewish Policy, September 1939–March 1942* (Jerusalem: Yad Vashem and University of Nebraska Press, 1992); and Dan Stone, ed., *The Historiography of the Holocaust* (Basingstoke: Palgrave Macmillan, 2004). George Steiner has continued to emphasize the unique position of the Jews within Western and Christian culture as outsiders, as "guests," who through their irredeemable otherness also remind Western culture of its failed aspirations and cosmopolitan ideals. See George Steiner, "The Wandering Jew," *Petahim* 1/ 6 (1988); George Steiner, *Errata: An Examined Life* (London: Weidenfeld and Nicholson, 1997). I am relying here on the critical but very insightful essay by Assaf Sagiv, "George Steiner's Jewish Problem," in *Azure* 5763 (summer 2003): 130–54. Sagiv approaches Steiner's work from a Zionist perspective that is skeptical of cosmopolitan aspirations.

8 There are many other themes and concepts which may serve as entry points for a useful, and long-overdue, conversation between Arendt and the Frankfurt School, such as the critique of liberalism, mass society, and bureaucracy; the skepticism toward

orthodox Marxism and its philosophy of history; the critique of Hegel and the move back to Kant; and, of course, the shared admiration, on the part of Adorno and Arendt in particular, toward Walter Benjamin. I choose the topic of "anti-Semitism," because I have always believed that the origins of Hannah Arendt's political philosophy owe more to her reflections on the Jewish question, and the rise of European anti-Semitism, than to Heidegger's influence upon her. It is around this point as well that some of the most striking differences between Arendt and Horkheimer and Adorno come to the fore.

9 I use this term with reference to Weber's distinction between "generalizing" and "ideographic" social science. On the difficulties of characterizing Arendt's methodology, see the early review essay by Eric Vogelin of *The Origins of Totalitarianism* (*Review of Politics* 15 (January 1953)) and my discussion, in Seyla Benhabib, "Hannah Arendt and the Redemptive Power of Narrative," in *Social Research* 57/1 (1990): 167–96.

10 See Martin Jay and Leon Botstein, "Hannah Arendt: Opposing Views," *Partisan Review* xlv/3 (1978): 348–81. (This text has been reprinted with no revisions in Martin Jay, *Permanent Exiles: Essays on the Intellectual Migration From Germany to America* (New York: Columbia University Press, 1986), as "Hannah Arendt's Political Existentialism," pp. 237–57. I am using the original *Partisan Review* essay here.) In the "Introduction" to *Permanent Exiles*, Jay discusses the controversy his essay has generated, but sees no need to revise its claims: see pp. xix–xx.

On the supposed influence of Carl Schmitt and Alfred Baeumler on Arendt, see Jay, p. 353, who writes: "As its own end, politics should not be conceived as a means to anything else whether it be domination, wealth, public welfare, or social justice; in short, *politique pour la politique*" (p. 363). There is very little textual evidence in any of Arendt's oeuvre that she was influenced either by Schmitt (to whom there are barely more than two references in *The Origins of Totalitarianism*) or by Alfred Baeumler. These assertions, as Jay himself acknowledges, are a matter of conjectural contextualization (ibid., p. 351). What is certainly not open to dispute is the influence of Heidegger's thought on Arendt, however one is to interpret it. Jay also focuses on Arendt's early essay in *Partisan Review* to support his claims about her "political existentialism," but he does not clearly distinguish this from "political decisionism."

(See Hannah Arendt, "What is Existenz Philosophy?," *Partisan Review* 18/1 (1946): 35–46; republished as "What is Existential Philosophy?," in Jerome Kohn, ed., *Arendt: Essays in Understanding: 1930–1954* (New York: Harcourt, Brace and Jovanovich, 1994), pp. 163–87. I note the differences between the original title and this later version and comment on it, in Seyla Benhabib, *The Reluctant Modernism of Hannah Arendt*, new edition (New York: Rowman and Littlefield Publishers, 2003, fn. 35, pp. 59–60).) Political existentialism and political decisionism are not the same: one can be a political existentialist, believing that there are no ultimate guarantees and foundations in the political sphere which can be provided either by reason or history, without at the same time accepting the characteristic theses of political decisionism about the significance of the single, individual act upon which sovereignty is grounded, such as in Schmitt's claim that "Sovereign is he who decides on the exception" (*Carl Schmitt, Political Theology: Four Chapters on the Concept of Sovereignty* [1922], trans. and with an Introduction by George Schwab (Chicago, IL: University of Chicago Press, 1985), p. 5.) Jay does not cite the all too crucial passage in Arendt's critique of Heidegger in this essay, which applies equally to all politically decisionist illusions. Arendt writes about Heideggerian *Dasein*: "The essential character of the Self is its absolute Self-ness, its radical separation from all its fellows . . . Later, and after the fact, Heidegger has drawn on mythologizing and muddled concepts like 'folk' and 'earth' in an effort to supply his isolated Selves with a shared, common ground to stand on . . . All that can result from that is the organization of these Selves intent only on themselves into an Over-self in order somehow to affect a transition from resolutely accepted guilt to action" (Arendt, "What is Existenz Philosophy?," in *Arendt: Essays in Understanding*, pp. 181–2). This passage hardly displays political decisionism; in fact, it is ironical and almost contemptuous of the amateurish way in which Heidegger seeks to proceed from the isolated self – *Dasein* – to politics, which always means engagement with others. Whatever Arendt's later predilections in minimizing Heidegger's involvement with National Socialism, she never abandoned her thesis that to think politically one needs to proceed from the premise of irreducible human plurality and not from an isolated *Dasein*. On Arendt and Heidegger, see chapter 4 in my *The Reluctant Modernism of Hannah Arendt*, "The Dialogue with Martin Heidegger: Arendt's Ontology of

The Human Condition," pp. 102–23. On their relationship and
its misinterpretation, see Elzbietta Ettinger, *Hannah Arendt–
Martin Heidegger* (New Haven, CT: Yale University Press,
1995)) and Richard Wolin, *Heidegger's Children: Hannah
Arendt, Karl Löwith, Hans Jonas and Herbert Marcuse* (Princ-
eton, NJ: Princeton University Press, 2003), and Seyla Benhabib,
"The Personal is not the Political," *Boston Review* (October–
November 1999): 45–48; reprinted in revised and enlarged form
as "Appendix" to *The Reluctant Modernism of Hannah Arendt*,
2nd edition, pp. 221–33. See also my review of Richard Wolin's
Heidegger's Children, "Taking Ideas Seriously," in *Boston
Review: A Political and Literary Forum* 11 (December 2002/
January 2003): 40–4.

11 Max Horkheimer, "Die Juden und Europa," in *Zeitschrift für
Sozialforschung*, ed. Max Horkheimer, dtv Reprint of vol. viii
(1939); edition used (Deutscher Taschenbuch Verlag: Munich,
1980), pp. 115–37; here p. 115; my translation.

12 The whole quote, with its obscure syntax, reads, "Der Faschis-
mus ist die Wahrheit der modernen Gesellschaft, die von der
Theorie von Anfang an getroffen war. Er fixiert die extremen
Unterschiede, die das Wertgesetz am Ende produzierte." (Fascism
is the truth of modern society, which was identified by Theory
since its inception. Fascism fixates the extreme differences which
are ultimately produced by the law of value.) Ibid., p. 116.

13 See Friedrich Pollock's subsequent article, "State Capitalism: Its
Possibilities and Limitations," *Studies in Philosophy and Social
Sciences* IX/2 (1941): 200–25. On Pollock's diagnosis on how
to achieve a stabilized capitalist economy despite the Depression,
and his rejection of orthodox Marxist crisis theory, see also Jay,
The Dialectical Imagination, pp. 153 ff.

14 Ibid., p. 115.

15 Ibid., p. 129. Allegedly concluded in September 1939, this article
expresses extreme skepticism toward British and French intentions and capacities to fight National Socialism. Horkheimer
sees the coming war as an imperial, and indeed a global one, for
world domination among "the superpowers" (see pp. 128 and
135). Much of the poisonous quality of his comments about
liberalism can be accounted for in the light of his deep skepticism
that Great Britain and France would or could really resist
National Socialism alone, without the aid of the United States.

16 Martin Jay, "The Jews and the Frankfurt School: Critical Theory's Analysis of Anti-Semitism," *Permanent Exiles: Essays*

on the Intellectual Migration from Germany to America, pp. 90–100.

17   Max Horkheimer to Herbert Marcuse, 17 July 1943, in Alfred Schmidt and Gunzlein Schmid Norr, eds, *Gesammelte Schriften* 17 (Frankfurt am Main: Fischer, 1985), p. 463. Cited in Anson Rabinbach, "Why Were the Jews Sacrificed?: The Place of Anti-Semitism in *Dialectic of Enlightenment,*" *New German Critique* 81, special issue on *Dialectic of Enlightenment* (autumn 2000): 49–64; here 51–2.

18   Rabinbach, "Why Were the Jews Sacrificed?: The Place of Anti-Semitism in *Dialectic of Enlightenment,*" p. 52.

19   Theodor Adorno and Max Horkheimer, *Dialektik der Aufklärung* (1944). 7th edn (Frankfurt: Fischer Verlag, 1980), here p. 27; English trans. John Cumming, *Dialectic of Enlightenment* (New York: Herder and Herder, 1972); referred to in the text with the abbreviation DA; I have mostly used my own translations. I have discussed this text as well as Horkheimer's concept of "self-preservation" more extensively in Seyla Benhabib, *Critique, Norm and Utopia: A Study of the Foundations of Critical Theory,* pp. 163–71 and 190–205.

20   Adorno and Horkheimer, *Dialectic of Enlightenment,* p. 207; see also Benhabib, *Critique, Norm and Utopia,* pp. 166–7.

21   On the origins and significance of this concept, see Jay, *The Dialectical Imagination,* pp. 269–73; Rabinbach, "Why Were the Jews Sacrificed?," pp. 56–9.

22   See Yirmiyahu Yovel, *Dark Riddle. Hegel, Nietzsche and the Jews* (Pennsylvania, PA: Pennsylvania State University Pres, 1998).

23   A. Rabinbach, "Why Were the Jews Sacrificed?," p. 61.

24   Thomas Baumeister and Jens Kulenkampff, "Geschichtsphiloso-phie und philosophische Ästhetik," *Neue Hefte für Philosophie* 6 (1974): 74 ff.

25   Jay, "The Jews and the Frankfurt School: Critical Theory's Analysis of Anti-Semitism," p. 99.

26   See Erhard Bahr, "The Anti-Semitism Studies of the Frankfurt School," pp. 133 ff; on Arendt, see Leon Weiseltier, "Under-standing Anti-Semitism: Hannah Arendt on the Origins of Preju-dice," *The New Republic* 7/32 (1981): 20 ff.

27   Hannah Arendt, *Eichmann in Jerusalem: A Report on the Banal-ity of Evil,* revised and enlarged edn (New York: Penguin Books, 1965); originally published in 1963; this reprint 1992. This edition is abbreviated throughout as EJ. On Arendt's meeting Blumenfeld, see Elisabeth Young-Brühl, *For Love of the* World

(New Haven, CT: Yale University Press, 1982), pp. 70ff. On the correspondence of Hannah Arendt and Kurt Blumenfeld, see -*in keinem Besitz verwurzelt. Die Korrespondenz,* ed. Ingeborg Nordmann and Iris Philling (Nördlingen: Rotbuch, 1995), pp. 257–65, and Ingeborg Nordmann, "Nachwort. Eine Freundschaft auf des Messers Schneide," in -*in keinem Besitz verwurzelt. Die Korrespondenz,* pp. 349 ff.

28 For more details on the family background, see Young-Brühl, *For Love of the World,* pp. 8 ff.

29 In a letter to Heinrich Blücher, her husband, who is here playfully referred to as "the Golem," Arendt writes: "The Golem is wrong when he argues that the Jews are a people, or a people which, like others, is in the process of realizing itself. In the East they are already a people without a territory. And in the West, God knows what they are (including myself)" (*Hannah Arendt–Heinrich Blücher, Briefe. 1936–1968,* ed. Lotte Köhler (Munich: R. Piper Verlag, 1996), p. 58 (my translation)). For further discussions, see also Seyla Benhabib, "Arendt's *Eichmann in Jerusalem,*" in *The Cambridge Companion to Hannah Arendt,* ed. Dana Villa (Cambridge: Cambridge University Press, 2000), pp. 65–86.

30 Hannah Arendt, *Rahel Varnhagen: The Life of a Jewish Woman,* rev. edn, trans. Richard and Clara Winston (New York: Harcourt, Brace, Jovanovich, 1974).

31 The phrase is from Arendt's "Preface" to *Rahel Varnhagen,* pp. xv–xvi. I have discussed this work at great length in Benhabib, *The Reluctant Modernism of Hannah Arendt,* chapter 1, "The Pariah and Her Shadow: Hannah Arendt's Biography of Rahel Varnhagen," pp. 1–34.

32 Dana Villa is certainly correct in noting that Arendt's characterization of "the social" owes a great deal to Heidegger's characterization of "das Man" in *Being and Time* (Dana Villa, *Arendt and Heidegger: The Fate of the Political* (Princeton, NJ: Princeton University Press, 1995)). But equally interesting is the way in which Arendt commingles the three dimensions of the social: mass society, society based on commodity exchange, and the new sphere of social relations in modern society or "civil society." This categorical conflation of the various dimensions of the social is the major weakness of Arendt's social theory and at the root of her neglect of economics in political life. See Benhabib, "The Social and the Political: An Untenable Divide," in *The Reluctant Modernism of Hannah Arendt,* pp. 138–72.

33 Hannah Arendt, *The Origins of Totalitarianism* [1951] (New York: Harcourt, Brace and Jovanovich, 1979 edn); abbreviated in the text as *OT* and all references in parantheses are to this edition. Originally published in Britain as *The Burden of Our Time* (London: Secker and Warburg, 1951), p. 54.

34 Parts of this section have previously appeared in Seyla Benhabib and Raluca Eddon, "From Anti-Semitism to the 'Right to Have Rights.' The Jewish Roots of Hannah Arendt's Cosmopolitanism," in *Babylon: Beiträge zur jüdischen Gegenwart* 22 (Frankfurt: Verlag Neue Kritik, 2007): 44–62. For general discussions on the significance of Jewish politics for Arendt's conception of politics and philosophy, see Richard Bernstein, *Hannah Arendt and the Jewish Question* (Cambridge, MA: MIT Press, 1996). Cf. also Jerome Kohn, "Preface: A Jewish Life: 1906–1975," in Jerome Kohn and Ron H. Feldman, eds, *Hannah Arendt: The Jewish Writings* (New York: Schocken Books, 2007), pp. ix–xxxiii.

35 Arendt's insistence on the centrality of Jews to the larger story of the moral and political collapse of Europe reveals a complex and ambivalent philosemitism that underpins her theory of anti-Semitism. While she famously declared that "I have never in my life 'loved' any people or collective," and, indeed, that the " 'love of the Jews' would appear to me, since I am myself Jewish, as something rather suspect," she nevertheless attributed to Jews a privileged cultural as well as political role in European history (see Hannah Arendt, *The Jew as Pariah*, ed. and with an introduction by Ron H. Feldman (New York: Grove Press, 1978), p. 247; see also the expanded and revised edition of the essays from *The Jew as Pariah*, supplemented by other materials, in Jerome Kohn and Ron H. Feldman, eds, *Hannah Arendt. The Jewish Writings*). In one sense, for example, in the figure of the *schlemiel* as embodied by Heinrich Heine and in Bernard Lazare's *pariah*, Arendt discerned a unique model of humanity, which, "excluded from the world of political realities," could at one time "preserve the illusion of liberty." Even if Nazi totalitarianism erased this illusion, Arendt regarded the pariah's humanity and independence of mind as eminently political qualities in her own time – indeed, as the conditions *sine qua non* of human freedom.

36 What, exactly, the "mob" is and who falls into that category is an issue of some difficulty in Arendt. As Margaret Canovan explains, Arendt "speaks of the Mob as the 'residue' or even 'the

refuse of all classes' accumulated from those left behind after each of capitalism's economic cycles. These individuals have lost their place in the class structure. They are burning with resentment against ordered society, and easily mobilized for violence by demagogues" (Margaret Canovan, "The People, the Masses and the Mobilization of Power: The Paradox of Arendt's Populism," in *Social Research* 69/2 (summer 2002): 403–22; here 405). Nevertheless, one thing is clear: the mob has no interest in, or regard for, any of the institutions that had sustained the nation-state and it disdains especially the institution at its very heart, the rule of law.

37 In the opening sections of Part II of *OT*, entitled "Imperialism," Arendt's thesis is that the encounter with Africa allowed the colonizing white nations such as the Belgians, the Dutch, the British, the Germans, and the French, to transgress those moral and civil limits abroad which would normally control the exercise of power at home. In the encounter with Africa, civilized white men regressed to levels of inhumanity by plundering, looting, burning, and raping the "savages" whom they encountered. Arendt uses Joseph Conrad's famous story, "The Heart of Darkness," as a parable of this encounter. The "heart of darkness" is not in Africa alone; twentieth-century totalitarianism brings this center of darkness to the European continent itself. The lessons learned in Africa seem to be practiced in the heart of Europe. Her discussion of imperialism, which begins with the European "scramble for Africa," concludes with "The Decline of the Nation-State and the End of the Rights of Man." Arendt was ahead of her times here. On recent explorations of the relationship between the Holocaust and Imperialism, see Richard King and Dan Stone, eds, *Hannah Arendt and the Uses of History: Imperialism, Nation, Race and Genocide* (London and New York: Berghan Books, 2007).

38 As Arendt explains: "Only when the nation state proved unfit to be the framework for the further growth of the capitalist economy did the latent fight between state and society become openly a struggle for power. During the imperialist period neither the state nor the bourgeoisie won a decisive victory. [. . .] This changed when the German bourgeoisie staked everything on the Hitler movement and aspired to rule with the help of the mob, but it then turned out to be too late" (*OT*: 124).

39 These philosophical theses about the contradictions between human rights and national sovereignty are more clearly analyzed

in Hannah Arendt's *On Revolution* (New York: Penguin Books, 1963). Arendt's antagonism toward the concept of sovereignty in political thought shows again that she does not share "decisionist" premises. For a more detailed discussion of these themes, see Seyla Benhabib, *The Rights of Others: Aliens, Citizens and Residents*, chapter 2.

40 Cf. Herbert Marcuse, "Der Kampf gegen den Liberalismus in der totalitären Staatsauffassung," in *Zeitschrift für Sozialforschung* 3/1 (1934): 161–95.

41 Carole Fink, "Defender of Minorities: Germany in the League of Nations, 1926–1933," *Central European History* 4: 330 ff; here p. 331. Also, Carole Fink, *Defending the Rights of Others: The Great Powers, the Jews and International Minority Protection* (Cambridge: Cambridge University Press, 2004).

42 We should not forget that this phrase also has a history within Critical Theory and was used to describe the transformation of critical theory in the wake of Friedrich Pollock's very important essays on "State Capitalism," in *Studies in Philosophy and Social Science* IX/2 (1941): 200–25, and "Is National Socialism a New Order?," *Studies in Philosophy and Social Science* 9 (1941): 440–55. For a critical discussion of Pollock's position, see Moishe Postone, *Time, Labor and Social Domination: A Reinterpretation of Marx's Critical Theory* (Cambridge: Cambridge University Press, 1993), section on "Friedrich Pollock and the Primacy of the Political," pp. 90–6.

43 There is yet another source of "the primacy of the political" in Arendt's work. This is the critique of orthodox Marxism-Leninism, which her husband Heinrich Blücher shared with other members of the *Spartacist* party. Arendt was much more aware of these discussions among various communist and ex-communist militants, many of whom, like her, were in exile in Paris in the mid- to late 1930s, than we are wont to believe. On the significance of the Paris exile for Arendt, see my "Hannah Arendt's Political Engagements," in Roger Berkowitz, Jeffrey Katz, and Thomas Keenan, eds, *Thinking in Dark Times: Hannah Arendt on Ethics and Politics* (New York: Fordham University Press, 2009), pp. 55–62.

As Jay perceptively notes, Rosa Luxemburg's polemic against Lenin was quite significant for Arendt's own understanding of the significance of democratic participation of the masses in self-governance (Jay, "Hannah Arendt: Opposing Views," p. 358). "The primacy of the political" has returned in the writings of

East European dissidents like Vaclav Havel, Adam Michnik, Jacek Kuron, Janos Kis, and others since 1989, precisely because this faith in "the unforced combination of objective and subjective factors" has revealed itself to be exactly what Arendt said the Marxian conception of history had been all along, namely, the unproven faith that one possessed the key whereby to unlock the meaning of history. For Arendt's oft-misunderstood critique of Marx, see the important and neglected section on "The Labor Movement," in H. Arendt, *The Human Condition* (Chicago, IL, and London: University of Chicago Press, 1958), pp. 212–20.

44 Jay, *Dialectical Imagination*, chapter 1.

45 John Rawls, *Political Liberalism* (New York: Columbia University Press, 1993; paperback edition, 1996). The core of political liberalism is the free-standing justification of the principles which legitimize political rule in terms of non-sectarian and non-divisive understandings of what constitutes "the right" for us all, as opposed to what we may conceive of individually as "the good." There would be many other respects in which a Frankfurt School perspective would be critical of political liberalism, but the conflation of political liberalism as a theory of government with the free market is a non-starter. Political liberalism is not dependent upon economic liberalism; and in fact requires a social democratic restructuring of the economy.

46 There is an important distinction in Arendt's work between "emancipation" and "freedom." See *On Revolution* (New York: Viking, 1963), pp. 54 ff, and also Benhabib, *The Reluctant Modernism of Hannah Arendt*, pp. 157 ff.

47 Raphael Lemkin, *Axis Rule in Occupied Europe: Laws of Occupation, Analysis of Government, Proposals for Redress* (Washington, DC: Carnegie Endowment for International Peace, 1944), p. xi.

48 Dan Stone, "Raphael Lemkin on the Holocaust," in *Journal of Genocide Research* 7/4 (December 2005): 539–50; here 546.

49 Lemkin, *Axis Rule*, p. 79.

CHAPTER 3 INTERNATIONAL LAW AND HUMAN PLURALITY IN THE SHADOW
OF TOTALITARIANISM: HANNAH ARENDT AND RAPHAEL LEMKIN

1 This, and other biographical information on Ralph Lemkin, is drawn from Samantha Power, *"A Problem from Hell": America and the Age of Genocide* (New York: Basic Books, 2002),

pp. 17–87; Ann Curthoys and John Docker, "Defining Genocide," in Dan Stone, ed., *The Historiography of Genocide* (Palgrave Macmillan, 2008), pp. 9 ff. See also Dominik J. Schaller
and Jurgen Zimmerer, "From the Guest Editors: Raphael Lemkin:
the 'founder of the United Nation's Genocide Convention' as a
historian of mass violence," in *Journal of Genocide Research*
7/4 (December 2005): 447–52.

2　Cf. Raphael Lemkin, *Axis Rule in Occupied Europe: Laws of
Occupation, Analysis of Government, Proposals for Redress*
(Washington, DC: Carnegie Endowment for International Peace,
1944). Abbreviated in the text as *ARiE*. Upon the publication
of *Axis Rule in Occupied Europe*, the *New York Times Book
Review* devoted its January 1945 cover to this work. It is hard
to believe that Arendt, who resided in New York City at that
time, and in view of her general interest in and knowledge of
these questions, would not have been familiar with Lemkin's
book. See Otto D. Tolischus, "Twentieth Century Moloch: The
Nazi-Inspired Totalitarian State, Devourer of Progress – and of
Itself," *New York Times Book Review* (January 21, 1945): 1,
24, as cited by Samantha Power, *"A Problem from Hell":
America and the Age of Genocide*, p. 525, n.35.

3　A subtle analysis of the sensibilities of Arendt, Lemkin, and
others in terms of the category of "citizen of the world" is given
by Ned Curthoys, who writes: "As émigré scholars and public
intellectuals, Arendt, Jaspers, Spitzer, Auerbach and Lemkin
were dedicated to illuminating generous and unorthodox methodological approaches imbued with the restless exigencies of
personal experience and hermeneutic intuition" (Ned Curthoys,
"The Émigré Sensibility of 'World Literature': Historicizing
Hannah Arendt and Karl Jaspers' Cosmopolitan Intent," *Theory
and Event* 8/3, accessed online at: <http://muse.jhu.edu/journals/
theory_and_event/v008/8.3curthoys.html>).

4　I am being tentative here because there is still no exhaustive
cataloguing of the contents of some 80 odd boxes deposited in
the Library of Congress in Washington, DC, although microfilm
collections exist in several universities. The same is true of the
extensive Hannah Arendt and Heinrich Blücher Library, which
is located in Bard College. Attempts are under way to catalogue
its holdings. The electronic catalogue contains no references to
Lemkin.

5　Contentious exchanges surround Hannah Arendt's concept and
justification of human rights. See Jeffrey Isaac, "Hannah Arendt

on Human Rights and the Limits of Exposure, or Why Noam Chomsky is Wrong About the Meaning of Kosovo," *Social Research* 69/2 (2002): 263–95; S. Benhabib, *The Rights of Others: Aliens, Citizens and Residents*, pp. 49–61; Christoph Menke, "The 'Aporias of Human Rights' and the 'One Human Right': Regarding the Coherence of Hannah Arendt's Argument," in *Social Research: Hannah Arendt's Centennary* 74/3 (fall 2007): 739–62; Peg Birmingham, *Hannah Arendt and Human Rights: The Predicament of Common Responsibility* (Bloomington, IN: Indiana University Press, 2006), and chapter 4 of this volume, "Another Universalism: On the Unity and Diversity of Human Rights."

6   See Leora Bilsky, "The Eichmann Trial and the Legacy of Jurisdiction," in Seyla Benhabib, *Politics in Dark Times: Encounters with Hannah Arendt*, pp. 198–219. See also, for an in-depth discussion of the jurisprudential issues behind the Eichmann trial, Benhabib, *Another Cosmopolitanism: The Berkeley Tanner Lectures*, pp. 13–44.

7   United Nations Convention on the Prevention and Punishment of the Crime of Genocide. Adopted by Resolution 260 (III) A of the UN General Assembly on December 9 1948 (chapter II). See the rather dramatic description of the events surrounding and leading up to the adoption of this Convention, in Samantha Power, *"A Problem from Hell": America and the Age of Genocide*, pp. 54–60.

8   See Christian Volk, "The Decline of Order: Hannah Arendt and the Paradoxes of the Nation-State," in Benhabib, ed., *Politics in Dark Times*, pp. 172–98.

9   "In my early boyhood, I read *Quo Vadis* by Henry Sienkiewicz – this story full of fascination about the sufferings of the early Christians and the Romans' attempt to destroy them solely because they believed in Christ . . . It was more than curiosity that led me to search in history for similar examples, such as the case of the Huguenots, the Moors of Spain, the Aztecs of Mexico, the Catholics in Japan, and so many races and nations under Genghis Khan . . . I was appalled by the frequency of evil, by great losses in life and culture, by the despairing impossibility of reviving the dead or consoling the orphans, and above all, by the impunity coldly relied upon by the guilty" (Raphael Lemkin, "Totally unofficial," manuscript, undated, New York Public Library, Manuscripts and Archives Division, The Raphael Lemkin Papers, Box 2); Bio- and autobiographical sketches of

Lemkin, as cited in Dominik J. Schaller and Jürgen Zimmerer, "From the Guest Editors: Raphael Lemkin: the 'founder of the United Nation's Genocide Convention' as a historian of mass violence," *Journal of Genocide Research* 7/4 (December 2005): 447–52; here 450–51.

10 The full quote is: "Only man has law . . . You must build the law!" Quoted in Samantha Power, *"A Problem from Hell": America and the Age of Genocide*, pp. 47 and 55.

11 Ann Curthoys and John Docker report that only 11 months after the Genocide Convention went into effect, in December 1951, "a petition entitled *We Charge Genocide* was presented by Paul Robeson and others to the UN Secretariat in New York" on behalf of African-Americans, charging that slavery was a form of genocide. See "Defining Genocide," pp. 15 ff. The General Assembly did not adopt the petition and furthermore "Without exception, law academics were adamantly opposed because any attempt to apply the Genocide Convention to the US situation would affect the integrity of 'our nation'" (ibid., p. 19). Lemkin was among these academics and, within the context of the Cold War, he saw these accusations as Soviet attempts to "divert attention from the crimes of genocide committed against Estonians, Latvians, Lithuanians, Poles and other Soviet-subjugated peoples" (from a *New York Times* interview of December 18, 1951, as quoted in Curthoys and Docker, ibid., p. 19). See also for further discussion, Anson Rabinbach, "The Challenge of the Unprecedented – Raphael Lemkin and the Concept of Genocide," in *Simon Dubnow Institute Yearbook*, vol. 4 (2005), pp. 397–420.

In Lemkin's case too, we encounter a certain "color blindness," an insensitivity to the problem of race as color, as opposed to race defined through ethnicity, language, and religion. Hannah Arendt has often been criticized on this account and in particular for her controversial essay on school desegregation in Southern Schools, published as "Reflections on Little Rock," in *Dissent* 6/1 (1959): 45–56. See my analysis of Arendt on black–white relations in the US and on race in Africa in *The Reluctant Modernism of Hannah Arendt,* pp. 146–55, and Richard King's essay on the invisibility of race among émigré intellectuals, "On Race and Culture: Hannah Arendt and Her Contemporaries," in *Politics in Dark Times*, pp. 113–37 .

12 For further considerations on the concept of groups, see A. Dirk Moses, "Moving the Genocide Debate Beyond the History

Wars," *Australian Journal of Politics and History* 54/2 (2008): 248–70; here 267. See also Daniel Marc Segesser and Myriam Gessler, "Raphael Lemkin and the International Debate on the Punishment of War Crimes (1919–1948)," *Journal of Genocide Research* 7/4 (2005): 453–68.

13 On the place of *existential* as distinct from *moral* values in Arendt's work, see the illuminating essay by George Kateb, "Existential Values in Arendt's Treatment of Evil and Morality," in Seyla Benhabib, ed., *Politics in Dark Times*, pp.342–75; an earlier version of Kateb's essay has appeared in *Hannah Arendt's Centennary: Political and Philosophic Perspectives*, Guest Editor Jerome Kohn, Part I, 74/3 (fall 2007): 811–55.

14 United Nations Convention on the Prevention and Punishment of the Crime of Genocide. Adopted by Resolution 260 (III) A of the UN General Assembly on December 9 1948 (Chapter II).

15 Anson Rabinbach, "The Challenge of the Unprecedented – Raphael Lemkin and the Concept of Genocide," in *Simon Dubnow Institute Yearbook*, vol. 4 (2005), pp. 397–420; here p. 401.

16 This broad conception of genocide in the meantime has spawned a new field of "comparative genocide studies." See the special issue of the *Journal of Genocide Research* 7/4 (December 2005), devoted to the work of Raphael Lemkin; Michael A. McDonnell, and A. Dirk Moses, "Raphael Lemkin as Historian of Genocide in the Americas," in the same issue, pp. 501–29, and A. Dirk Moses, "The Holocaust and Genocide," in Dan Stone, ed., *The Historiography of the Holocaust* (Basingstoke: Palgrave Macmillan, 2004), pp. 533–55.

17 Cf. the illuminating article by Dan Stone, "Raphael Lemkin on the Holocaust," *Journal of Genocide Research* 7/4 (December 2005): 539–50.

18 The Rousseau-Portalis doctrine provided the basis for the combatant–non-combatant distinction. In the 1801 opening of the French Prize Court, borrowing heavily from Jean-Jacques Rousseau (*The Social Contract*, Book 1, ch. 4), Portalis said: "war is a relation of state to state and not of individual to individual. Between two or more belligerent nations, the private persons of whom these nations are composed are only enemies by accident; they are not so as men, they are not so even as citizens, they are so only as soldiers" (quoted A. Pearce Higgins and William Edward Hall, *International Law* 611, 8th edn (Oxford: Clarendon Press, 1924)); in turn cited by Myres Smith McDougal and Florentino P. Feliciano, *Law and*

Minimum World Public Order (New Haven, CT: Yale University Press, 1994), p. 543, Notes.
19 Ralph Lemkin, "Genocide as a Crime Under International Law," *American Journal of International Law* 41/1 (1947): 147.
20 It is all the more puzzling therefore that Lemkin would be so resistant to extend the Genocide Convention to cover conditions of slavery in the Americas. See n.9 of this chapter, above.
21 Mark Mazower points out that "the Genocide Convention only passed once a clause that made 'cultural genocide' a crime – the clause that Lemkin himself described as 'the soul of the Convention' – was dropped. Resolute opposition from colonial powers and South African states in particular thus prevented minority rights being smuggled into the UN by the back door" (in *No Enchanted Palace. The End of Empire and the Ideological Origins of the United Nations* (Princeton, NJ: Princeton University Press, 2009), p. 130).
22 Lemkin, "Genocide," *American Scholar* 15/2 (1946): 228; quoted in Samantha Power, *"A Problem from Hell": America and the Age of Genocide*, p. 53.
23 See Will Kymlicka, *Multicultural Citizenship: A Liberal Theory of Minority Rights* (Oxford: Oxford University Press, 1995); Will Kymlicka, *Citizenship in Diverse Societies* (Oxford: Oxford University Press, 2000); for a general discussion of these issues in contemporary debates, cf. Seyla Benhabib, *The Claims of Culture: Equality and Diversity in the Global Era* (Princeton, NJ: Princeton University Press, 2002); within the American context of dilemmas raised by group-based classifications, see Robert Post and Michael Rogin, eds, *Race and Representation: Affirmative Action* (New York: Zone Books, 1998); James Sleeper, *Liberal Racism* (New York: Viking, 1997).
24 There has been ongoing debate about Johann Gottfried Herder's legacy. Some classify him as a "German nationalist." Karl Popper, for example, in *The Open Society and its Enemies* (London: 1945), "includes Herder in a sort of Hall of Shame recapitulating the rise of German nationalism," as noted by Michael N. Forster, ed. and trans., "Introduction," in Johann Gottfried Herder, *Philosophical Writings: Cambridge Texts in the History of Philosophy* (Cambridge: Cambridge University Press, 2002), p. xxxi, n.33. Others such as Isaiah Berlin and Charles Taylor view Herder as a precursor of a kind of cultural and value pluralism which is distinct from relativism. See, for example, Charles Taylor, "The Importance of Herder," in

E. Avishai Margalit, ed., *Isaiah Berlin: A Celebration* (Chicago, IL: University of Chicago Press, 1992).

By pointing to this Herderian connection, my aim is not to charge Lemkin with a kind of "relativist nationalism of vulnerable peoples"! Rather, I wish to draw attention to the concept of the group in his writings, which is philosophically underexplored, inasmuch as language, race, ethnicity, and religion are often used, either together or individually, as markers of group identities. Lemkin does not explore either the conflicts or ambiguities that the use of these markers can give rise to in the law or society. We know, by contrast, that for Herder the nation is a linguistic and cultural and not a racial group. See, for example, J. G. Herder, "Treatise on the Origin of Language" [1772], in *Philosophical Writings: Cambridge Texts in the History of Philosophy*, ed. and trans. Michael N. Forster, pp. 65–167. See also Letter 114 in "Letters for the Advancement of Humanity. Tenth Collection," and the Fragment on "Purified Patriotism" for Herder's condemnation of wars among nations and of imperialism (in *Philosophical Writings: Cambridge Texts in the History of Philosophy*, ed. and trans. Michael N. Forster, pp. 380 ff. and p. 406). Lemkin undoubtedly would have fully shared Herder's sentiments as expressed by the following: "What, generally, is a foisted, foreign culture, a formation [*Bildung*] that does not develop out of [a people's] own dispositions and needs? It oppresses and deforms, or else it plunges straight into the abyss. You poor sacrificial victims who were brought from the south sea islands to England in order to receive culture . . . It was therefore no otherwise than justly and wisely that the good *Ch'ien-lung* acted when he had the foreign viceking rapidly and politely shown the way out of his realm with a thousand fires of celebration. If only every nation had been clever and strong enough to show the Europeans this way" (ibid., p. 382).

In "Perpetual Peace," Kant responded to Herder that one needs to distinguish between desired contact among nations, which is grounded in the "right of hospitality," and imperialist, exploitative, and belligerent intentions harbored by some nations against others in seeking contact. Cultural isolationism is not defensible. See Immanuel Kant [1795], "Perpetual Peace: A Philosophical Sketch," in *Kant: Political Writings*, pp. 93–131.

Cf. also Arendt's very interesting reflections on Herder's significance for the Jews after the Enlightenment. She credits Herder with rendering Jewish history visible in Germany "as history defined essentially by their possession of the Old Testament" (Hannah Arendt, "The Enlightenment and the Jewish Question," in Jerome Kohn and Ron H. Feldman, eds, *Hannah Arendt: The Jewish Writings* p. 12). At the same time, insofar as this history is theological history and not history connected to that of the world at large, for Herder, "the Jews have become a people without history within history. Herder's understanding of history deprives them of their past" (ibid., p. 16). Philosophically, as well as historiographically, the question is one of balancing the universal and the particular, the general history of humanity and the specific memories, trajectories, and suffering of specific peoples.

25 Doesn't this voluntarist concept of the group contradict Hannah Arendt's own assertive defense of her own Jewish identity? I would argue that it does not in that Arendt insists on defining the conditions and the meaning of her own belonging to the Jewish people. For her, it is not the Halachachic definition of the Jew, as one born to a Jewish mother that is paramount, but rather one's conscious and self-chosen identification with the fate of a collectivity and a people. This individualist, perhaps existentialist, dimension of Arendt's Judaism is at the root of her conflict with Gershom Scholem and distinguishes her from other thinkers such as Leo Strauss who argued that one could not separate out the cultural and theological meanings of Judaism as sharply as Arendt herself wished to.

26 Hannah Arendt, "The Promise of Politics," in *The Promise of Politics*, ed. and with an Introduction by Jerome Kohn (New York: Schocken Books, 2005), p. 175.

27 Patricia Owens, *Between War and Politics: International Relations and the Thought of Hannah Arendt* (Oxford: Oxford University Press, 2007), p. 110.

28 Hannah Arendt, *The Human Condition*, p. 7.

29 For further discussion of these dimensions of Arendt's thought, see Patchen Markell, "The Rule of the People: Arendt, Arche and Democracy," in Seyla Benhabib, ed., *Politics in Dark Times*, pp. 58–83 (an early version of this essay appeared in *The American Political Science Review* 100/1 (February 2006): 1–14), and Roy Tsao, "Arendt's Augustine," in *Politics in Dark Times*, pp. 39–58. For the roots of these Arendtian themes in Martin Heidegger's philosophy, see Dana Villa, *Arendt and Heidegger: The Fate of the Political*, and Seyla Benhabib, ch. 4, "The

Dialogue with Martin Heidegger," *The Reluctant Modernism of Hannah Arendt.*

30 Arendt's almost militant defense of capital punishment will shock and disturb many readers. Was she perhaps indulging in some form of vengeance herself rather than just defending justice? These are questions that go beyond the scope of the present discussion. I am grateful to Professor Hans Joas of the Max-Weber Kollegium in Erfurt for having pointed out this problem to me in the course of a discussion.

31 For an illuminating discussion of the legal details of some of the issues involved, see Bilsky, "The Eichmann Trial and the Legacy of Jurisdiction," in Seyla Benhabib, ed., *Politics in Dark Times*, pp. 198–219.

32 For a more skeptical consideration of Arendt's claims with regards to sovereign power and executive privilege in the US experience, see Andrew Arato and Jean L. Cohen, "Banishing the Sovereign: Internal and External Sovereignty in Arendt," in Seyla Benhabib, ed., *Politics in Dark Times*, pp. 137–72; originally published in *Constellations* 16/2 (June 2009): 307–31. See also on the Eichmann trial, Benhabib, *Another Cosmopolitanism: The Berkeley Tanner Lectures*, ch. 1, pp. 13–44.

33 Power, *"A Problem from Hell": America and the Age of Genocide*, p. 56.

34 Mazower, *No Enchanted Palace*, p. 131.

CHAPTER 4   ANOTHER UNIVERSALISM: ON THE UNITY
AND DIVERSITY OF HUMAN RIGHTS

1 Edmund Husserl, *The Crisis of European Sciences and Transcendental Phenomenology: An Introduction to Phenomenological Philosophy*, trans. with an introduction by David Carr, Northwestern University Studies in Phenomenology and Existential Philosophy (Evanston, IL: Northwestern University Press, 1970). All references in the text are abbreviated as *Crisis* and are to this edition. See also *Die Krisis der europäischen Wissenschaften und die transzendentale Phänomenologie*, ed. and introduced by Elisabeth Stroker (Hamburg: Felix Meiner Verlag, 1977).

2 Caught between the positivism of the Vienna School and the existential-ontology of his former student Martin Heidegger, Husserl saw the mission of philosophy as a dual-pitched battle: to show that the modern mathematical sciences of nature, despite

their considerable achievements, could not define what counts as "reason" alone. Philosophical questions concern "man as free, self-determining being in his behavior toward the human and extrahuman surrounding world" and the sciences have nothing to say "about us men as subjects of this freedom," he wrote (*Crisis*, p. 6). Husserl was equally concerned with another approach prevalent in the "human-historical sciences" or the *Geisteswissenschaften*. According to this relativist historicism, "all the shapes of the spiritual world, all the conditions of life, ideals, norms upon which man relies, form and dissolve themselves like fleeting waves, that it always was and ever will be so, that again and again reason must turn into nonsense, and well-being into misery" (*Crisis*, p. 7). "Can we console ourselves with that?" he asks.

3 Husserl, "The Vienna Lecture," Appendix I: "Philosophy and the Crisis of European Humanity," in *The Crisis of the European Sciences*, p. 273.

4 I introduce this qualification because Husserl also states that in India as well as China, "similar philosophies" developed, which aimed at universal knowledge of the world (Husserl, "The Vienna Lecture," p. 280). These pursuits gave rise to vocational communities who then transmitted their knowledge from generation to generation. What distinguishes the Greek pursuit of *theoria* from these other efforts is its detachment from cosmological and religious-communal interests, precipitated by the emergence of a community of men, who "strive for and bring about *theoria* and nothing but *theoria*" (ibid.).

Here Husserl is repeating some well-established sociological assumptions of his time that in other high cultures, and in contrast with the Greek experience, the pursuit of "universal knowledge of the world" never freed itself from the interests and vocations of a cultured literati (the Brahmins in India), a priestly caste (Buddhist monks throughout Asia), or of a state bureaucracy (the Chinese mandarins). See Reinhard Bendix, *Max Weber: An Intellectual Portrait*, with a new Introduction by Guenther Roth (Berkeley, CA: University of California Press, 1977), pp. 90 ff. Cf. Max Weber's statement: "which chain of circumstances has led to the fact that in the West, and in the West alone, cultural phenomena have appeared, which nonetheless – or at least we like to think – lie in a line of development having universal significance [*Bedeutung*] and validity [*Gültigkeit*]?" (Max Weber, "*Die Protestantische Ethik und der Geist des Kapitalismus,"* in *Gesammelte Aufsätze zur Religionssozio-logie* (Mohr Verlag: Tübingen, 1920), p. 1). English translation: *The Protestant Ethic and the Spirit of Capitalism,* trans. Talcott Parsons (New York: Scribner's, 1958). For reasons that I explain elsewhere, I have used my own translation of this passage rather than Talcott Parsons'. See Seyla Benhabib, *Critique, Norm and Utopia: A Study of the Foundations of Critical Theory* (New York: Columbia University Press, 1986), p. 395, fn. 64.

In a series of influential articles, Amartya Sen has contended that some of the most prized aspects of Western rationalism, such as public discussion, toleration, and consultation with the governed, have been developed and prized by other traditions as well. See Amartya Sen, "Elements of a Theory of Human Rights," in *Philosophy and Public Affairs* 32/4 (2004): 315–56; here 352; A. Sen, "Human Rights and Asian Values," *The New Republic* 217/2–3 (July 14–July 21, 1997): 33–40; A. Sen, "The Reach of Reason: East and West," *The New York Review of Books* 47/12 (July 20, 2000): 33–8; A. Sen, "Democracy and its Global Roots," *The New Republic* 229/14 (October 2003): 28–35. Clearly, Husserl and Weber relied upon a comparative theory of cultures and civilizations that needs serious updating for our times.

5   See Michael Ignatieff, in Amy Gutmann, ed., *Human Rights as Politics and Idolatry* (Princeton, NJ: Princeton University Press, 2001). I use the concept of "a public vocabulary" to distinguish it from the Rawlsian concept of "public reason." Public reason for Rawls is primarily the deployment of reason as a justificatory enterprise in a pluralistic, liberal society, in which many world-views compete for the allegiance of citizens. See John Rawls, *Political Liberalism* (New York: Columbia University Press, 1996). For an exploration of the epistemological and method-ological differences between the Rawlsian concept of public reason and the discourse-theoretic model, see chapter 5 of this volume. For my early critique of Rawls, see Seyla Benhabib, "Toward a Deliberative Model of Democratic Legitimacy," in Seyla Benhabib, ed., *Democracy and Difference* (Princeton, NJ: Princeton University Press, 1996), pp. 67–95.

6   The phrase "the right to have rights," as we saw in the previous chapters, was introduced by Hannah Arendt, in *The Origins of Totalitarianism* [1951] (1979 edn), p. 296. Hegel, too, starts his *Philosophy of Right* with the right of "personality," which is the right of the individual to be considered as a being entitled to

rights. Like Arendt, Hegel considers this status to emerge as a consequence of political, cultural, and social struggles in world history, but also as being the only standpoint compatible with the modern concept of freedom. See. G. W. F. Hegel, *Grundlinien der Philosophie des Rechts,* in *Werke in zwanzig Bänden,* vol. 7, ed. Eva Moldenhauer and K. Markus Michel (Frankfurt: Suhrkamp, 1970); *Hegel's Philosophy of Right,* trans. T. M. Knox (Oxford: Oxford University Press, 1973). See section on "Abstraktes Recht."

7 Susan Mendus, "Human Rights in Political Theory," *Political Studies* xliii (1995): 10. Since the original publication of this chapter in 2007, the topic of human rights, their justification, scope, and relationship to international law have garnered increasing attention in philosophical circles. A very good analysis of developments in Anglo-American moral and political philosophy on these topics is given by Allen Buchanan, "The Egalitarianism of Human Rights," *Ethics* 120 (July 2010): 679–710; here 679–83. So Mendus's observation needs to be qualified somewhat.

8 John Rawls, "The Law of Peoples" [1993], in J. Rawls, *Collected Papers,* ed. Samuel Freeman (Cambridge, MA: Harvard University Press, 1999), pp. 529–64; here p. 552. There are interesting differences in formulation between this early 1993 article and Rawls's later book, *The Law of Peoples,* which I comment upon below. See J. Rawls, *The Law of Peoples with "The Idea of Public Reason Revisited."*

9 Michael Walzer, *"Thick and Thin: Moral Argument at Home and Abroad."*

10 Charles Beitz, "Human Rights as a Common Concern," in *American Political Science Review* 95/2 (June 2001): 272.

11 Martha C. Nussbaum, "Capabilities and Human Rights," in *Fordham Law Review* 66/273 (1997–8): 273–300. See also Martha Nussbaum, *Frontiers of Justice: Disability, Nationality, Species Membership* (Cambridge, MA: Harvard University Press, 2006), pp. 281–91.

12 The UN Commission on Human Rights, created in 1946, drafted "major international human rights standards, including the two international human rights covenants, which, together, with the earlier adopted Universal Declaration of Human Rights (1948), form what is known as the International Bill of Human Rights" (Yvonne Terlingen, "The Human Rights Council: A New Era in UN Human Rights Work?," in *Ethics and International Affairs*

21/2 (summer 2007): 167–79; here 168.) For the documentation of the Declaration and Covenants, see Henry J. Steiner and Philip Alston, *International Human Rights in Context: Law, Politics, Morals,* 2nd edn (Oxford: Oxford University Press, 2000); Louis Henkin, "Ideology and Aspiration, Reality and Prospect," in Samantha Power and Graham Allison, eds, *Realizing Human Rights: Moving From Inspiration to Impact* (St Martin's Press: New York, 2000), pp. 3–39.

13 Rawls, *The Law of Peoples* (1999), p. 65. The earlier list in the 1993 article of the same title presented a slightly different formulation: included here as human rights were "the elements of the rule of law, as well as the right to a certain liberty of conscience and freedom of association, and the right to emigration" (Rawls (1993), p. 554).

14 See "The Law of Peoples" (1993), pp. 553–4; *The Law of Peoples* (1999), pp. 79–80. This thesis and Joshua Cohen's spirited defense will be taken up in chapter 5. See Joshua Cohen, "Minimalism About Human Rights: The Most We Can Hope For?," pp. 190–213; here p. 192. For a critique of the methodological holism and Rawls's faulty sociology in *The Law of Peoples,* see Seyla Benhabib, "*The Law of Peoples,* Distributive Justice, and Migrations," in *Fordham Law Review* LXXII/5 (April 2004): 1761–87.

15 For a lucid account of this Rawlsian position, cf. Joshua Cohen, "Is There a Human Right to Democracy?," in *The Egalitarian Conscience: Essays in Honor of G. A. Cohen,* ed. Christine Sypnowich (Oxford: Oxford University Press, 2006), pp. 226–48. In contrast to Cohen, I will argue that the human right to democracy is crucial for being able to articulate what Cohen himself names an account of human rights as "entitlements that serve to ensure the bases of membership." See pp. 78ff. of this volume.

16 Cf. Johannes Morsink, *The Universal Declaration of Human Rights: Origins, Drafting and Intent* (Philadelphia, PA: University of Pennsylvania Press, 1999).

17 James Griffin, "Discrepancies Between the Best Philosophical Account of Human Rights and the International Law of Human Rights," The Presidential Address, *Proceedings of the Aristotelian Society* 101 (2001): 1–28. The result of such an examination may be that "Some of the items on the lists are so flawed that they should be given, as far as possible, the legal cold shoulder" (ibid., p. 26). I agree, but Griffin proceeds from a rather conventional

account of human rights as "centered on the notion of agency . . . We value our status as agents especially highly, often more highly than our happiness. Human rights can then be seen as protections for our agency – what one might call our personhood" (p. 4). This defense of human rights is subject to the same criticisms as all other agent-centric views: that some condition is necessary for the exercise of *my* agency does not impose an obligation upon *you* to respect this condition, unless you and I also recognize each other's equality and reciprocity as moral beings. This is the first justificatory step in the argument.

18 For an interesting critique of Rawls on the right to democracy, see Alessandro Ferrara, "Two Notions of Humanity and the Judgment Argument for Human Rights," in *Political Theory* 31/X (2003): 1–30; here 3 ff.

19 Rainer Forst, "The Justification of Human Rights and the Basic Right to Justification: A Reflexive Approach," *Ethics* 120 (July 2010): 711–40; here 718. The "basic right to justification," as I will argue, is dependent upon our conception of the person as a being capable of communicative reason – every person capable of the use of a natural and a symbolic language can fulfill this minimum criterion.

20 I have developed an early version of this analysis in *The Claims of Culture: Equality and Diversity in the Global Era* , pp. 26–8.

21 Richard Rorty's defense of "postmodernist bourgeois liberalism" fits this paradigm, as does Jacques Derrida's many interventions against apartheid and on behalf of minorities and civil rights in the decade before his death. They all attempt to disassociate the "right" from the "good," and distinguish what I am calling "juridical universalism" from essentialism, whether cognitive or moral. Universalism, such is their claim, can be political without being metaphysical. Cf. Richard Rorty, "Postmodernist Bourgeois Liberalism," *Journal of Philosophy* 80 (1983): 583–9; R. Rorty, "Human Rights, Rationality and Sentimentality," in Stephen Shute and Susan Hurley, eds, *On Human Rights: The Oxford Amnesty Lectures 1993* (New York: Basic Books, 1993), pp. 11–34. See also Jacques Derrida, "Declarations of Independence," in *New Political Science* (summer 1986): 6–15.

22 For a most illuminating account of this development, see Richard J. Bernstein, *The Pragmatic Turn* (Cambridge and Malden, MA: Polity, 2010), and in particular pp. 32–53, 89–106.

23 Alan Gewirth, *The Community of Rights* (Chicago, IL: University of Chicago Press, 1996); cf. also *Human Rights: Essays on*

Justification and Applications (Chicago, IL: University of Chicago Press, 1982), and James Griffin, *On Human Rights* (Oxford: Oxford University Press, 2009).

24 A. MacIntyre, *After Virtue* (London: Duckworth, 1981), p. 67. Cf. Jeremy Bentham: "*Right*, the substantive *right*, is the child of law; from *real* laws come *real* rights; but from *imaginary* laws, from "law of nature" [can come only] "*imaginary* rights" (Jeremy Bentham, "Anarchical Fallacies," in *The Works of Jeremy Bentham*, ed. John Bowring, vol. 2 (Edinburgh and London: W. Tait, 1843), p. 523).

25 Jeremy Bentham, "Anarchical Fallacies," ibid., p. 501.

26 For a careful analysis of the self-contradictions of MacIntyre's own appeal to reason, see Rainer Forst, *Contexts of Justice: Political Philosophy beyond Liberalism and Communitarianism*, trans. John M. Farrell (Berkeley and Los Angeles, CA: University of California Press, 2002), pp. 200–15.

27 Richard Tuck, *Natural Rights Theories* (Cambridge: Cambridge University Press, 1979); see also Anthony Pagden, "Human Rights, Natural Rights, and Europe's Imperial Legacy," for a good historical account of the evolution of the discourse of rights, which nonetheless avoids endorsing or denouncing Eurocentrism, in *Political Theory* 31/2 (April 2003): 171–99.

28 Jeremy Waldron, "Introduction," *Theories of Rights* (Oxford: Oxford University Press, 1984), p. xxx. I have also found very helpful, Matthew Noah Smith, "The Normativity of Human Rights" (manuscript on file with the author).

29 Immanuel Kant [1797], *The Metaphysics of Morals*, ed. and trans. Mary Gregor, Cambridge Texts in the History of Political Thought (Cambridge: Cambridge University Press, 1996), p. 133.

30 Rainer Forst, "The Justification of Human Rights and the Basic Right to Justification," p. 719.

31 This raises an important question concerning the rights of those whose capacity to engage in communicative freedom is either limited – children, the handicapped – or impaired, for example, the mentally ill. My claim is that our obligation to treat others as beings entitled to rights, who are equally entitled to our moral concern, presupposes some understanding of their human agency as generalized and as concrete others. When I conceive of the other as a concrete other, then I can see that my obligations toward them entail concern for their special needs, which they would have been able to express were they fully capable of com-

municative freedom. And we can have very deep and at times pre-verbal forms of communication with infants, the handicapped, and the mentally ill, all beings who share in our common humanity.

32   My position on these matters is closet to Rainer Forst's among other discourse theorists – including Jürgen Habermas himself, whose justification of human rights seems to me to be evolving in different directions when compared to his earlier views. Cf. Rainer Forst, "The Justification of Human Rights and the Basic Right to Justification," and R. Forst, *Das Recht auf Rechtfertigung: Elemente einer konstruktivistischen Theorie der Gerechtigkeit* (Frankfurt: Suhrkamp, 2007); on Habermas's view of human rights, see chapter 7 of this volume.

33   This is the major flaw in James Griffin's otherwise instructive account, "Discrepancies Between the Best Philosophical Account of Human Rights and the International Law of Human Rights," here pp. 4 ff. See also Griffin, *On Human Rights*, pp. 3–39, 44–8. Buchanan puts the point more sharply: "Griffin's view of normative agency and dignity is essentially nonsocial. On his view, it is possible to give a full characterization of the kind of life human rights are supposed to protect without any consideration of the social standing of the normative agent. For Griffin, social standing is relative to normative agency, and hence to human rights, only if it happens to be true that having an inferior social standing undermines one's own normative agency" (in "The Egalitarianism of Human Rights," p. 703).

34   For an analysis of the two meanings of "the right to have rights," in terms of its moral and juridico-civil components, see Seyla Benhabib, *The Rights of Others: Aliens, Residents and Citizens*, pp. 56–61.

35   See Seyla Benhabib, *Situating the Self: Gender, Community and Postmodernism in Contemporary Ethics*, pp. 35–7.

36   For a thoughtful statement which I endorse, cf. Heiner Bielefeldt, "The history of human rights in the West is not a binding 'model' that allows us to make forecasts about the prospects of human rights in other parts of the world . . . Rather, the history of human rights in the West gives us an *example* – not the paradigm per se but merely an example – of the various obstacles, misunderstandings, learning processes, achievements, and failures in the long-lasting struggle for human rights" (in " 'Western' versus 'Islamic' Human Rights Conceptions?: A Critique of Cultural

Essentialism in the Discussion of Human Rights," *Political Theory* 28/1 (February 2000): 90–121; here 101–2.

37 I wish to thank Richard J. Bernstein for pressing me on this point. In *The Claims of Culture*, I addressed this question from within a mode of deliberative democracy and distinguished between "the syntax" and "semantics" of public-reason giving. Reasons, I suggested, would be counted as good reasons because they could be considered as being in the "best interest of all considered as moral and political beings." And to parse X or Y – a policy, a law, a principle of action, to be "in the best interests of all," would mean "that we have established X or Y through processes of public deliberation in which all affected by these norms and policies take part as participants in a discourse" (Benhabib, *The Claims of Culture*, pp. 140 ff.). I said that there is no way to know in advance which semantically specific claims or perspectives may count as "good reasons." What discourse ethics, as well as deliberative democracy modeled on discourse ethics, rules out are *some kinds of reasons* – these are ones that cannot be syntactically generalizable.

38 See the very instructive reflections by Norberto Bobbio, "Human Rights Now and in the Future," in *The Age of Rights*, trans. Allan Cameron (Cambridge: Polity, 1996), pp. 12–32.

39 For a position which strongly differentiates between the moral and ethical dimension of human rights and their legal articulation, see Amartya Sen, "Elements of a Theory of Human Rights," p. 319. Sen's theses are discussed in detail in this volume, pp. 80–2.

40 See Seyla Benhabib, *Another Cosmopolitanism: Sovereignty, Hospitality, and Democratic Iterations,* pp. 67 ff., and see chapters 7 and 8 in this volume.

41. I have omitted section V of the original article here since the argument presented therein has now been expanded into the next three chapters. See Benhabib, "Another Universalism," *Proceedings and Addresses of the American Philosophical Association*, pp. 19–22.

42 See Jürgen Habermas, *Faktizität und Geltung* (Frankfurt: Suhrkamp, 1992); *Between Facts and Norms: Contributions to a Discourse Theory of Law and Democracy*, trans. William Regh (Cambridge, MA: MIT Press, 1996), pp. 121–3.

43 See the classical essay by Ronald Dworkin, "Taking Rights Seriously" (1970), in *Taking Rights Seriously* (Cambridge, MA: Harvard University Press, 1978), pp. 184 ff.

44 I will distinguish more precisely between self-government and democracy in chapter 5, below.

45 For the concept of "complex cultural dialogues," see Benhabib, *The Claims of Culture: Equality and Diversity in the Global Era*, chs 1 and 2, and Boaventura de Sousa Santos who observes: "all cultures are incomplete and problematic in their conceptions of human dignity. The incompleteness derives from the very fact that there is a plurality of cultures and this is best visible from the outside, from the perspective of another culture. If each culture were as complete as it claims to be, there would be just one single culture. To raise the consciousness of cultural incompleteness to its possible maximum is one of the most crucial tasks in the construction of a multicultural conception of human rights," in "Toward a Multicultural Conception of Human rights," in Berta Hernandez-Truyol, ed., *Moral Imperialism: A Critical Anthology* (New York: New York University Press, 2002), pp. 46–47.

CHAPTER 5 IS THERE A HUMAN RIGHT TO DEMOCRACY? BEYOND INTERVENTIONISM AND INDIFFERENCE

1 See Joshua Cohen, "Minimalism About Human Rights: The Most We Can Hope For?," pp. 190–213; here p. 192.

2 Michael Ignatieff, *Human Rights as Politics and Idolatry*, p. 173.

3 Thomas Nagel, "The Problem of Global Justice," *Philosophy and Public Affairs* 33/2 (2005): 1508–42; see here 1522. For Nagel, "negative rights like bodily inviolability, freedom of expression, and freedom of religion" are "morally unmysterious" in their defense. (1522). To call "freedom of expression" and "freedom of religion" negative rights displays a very limited view of the meaning of human rights of association, worship, and citizenship. In strict terms, Nagel is both a "substantive" and a "justificatory" minimalist, but I will not pursue this issue further here.

4 Cohen, "Minimalism About Human Rights," p. 192.

5 Cohen, "Minimalism About Human Rights," p. 213.

6 It is interesting that Risse and Baynes, who enthusiastically endorse a "political conception of human rights," are silent about this particular aspect of Cohen's discussion. See Mathias Risse, "What are Human Rights? Human Rights as Membership

Rights in the Global Order," presented to the Workshop on Law and Globalization, Yale Law School, February 11, 2008, and Kenneth Baynes, "Toward a Political Conception of Human Rights?," *Philosophy and Social Criticism* 35/4 (2009): 371–90.

7   Again, there is a fascinating overlap here between Joshua Cohen's claim "that human rights norms are best thought of as norms associated with an idea of *membership* or *inclusion* in an organized political society," and the "right to have rights." See Cohen, "Minimalism About Human Rights," p. 197.

8   The juxtaposition of a "political" versus "metaphysical" conception of human rights, from which Baynes proceeds (see above, "Toward a Political Conception of Human Rights"), strikes me as being narrow. This contrast is by no means exhaustive of the range of justification of human rights. I do not believe that one can develop a conception of rights without basing it on some view of human agency. Such a conception of the rights-bearing person as an agent can certainly entail strong metaphysical and other kinds of assumptions deriving from comprehensive worldviews, but they need not be. Discourse ethics and the view of human agency, I articulate here, correspond best to what Risse has called "a principle-driven" account of human rights. See Risse, "What are Human Rights?," p. 5.

9   Martha C. Nussbaum, "Capabilities and Human Rights," in *Fordham Law Review* 66/273 (1997–98): 273–300.

10 Membership is not identical with citizenship, which is the highest form of political membership in a nation-state-centric system. There are forms of non-political as well as political membership, which all need to be protected by the law. See pp. 111–16 of this volume.

11 I am grateful to my colleague Alex Stone Sweet for bringing the relevance of Article 29 of the UDHR to my attention in this respect: "(1) Everyone has duties to the community in which alone the free and full development of his personality is possible. (2) In the exercise of his rights and freedoms, everyone shall be subject only to such limitations as are determined by law solely for the purpose of securing due recognition and respect for the rights and freedoms of others and of meeting the just requirements of morality, public order and the general welfare in a democratic society." Available at: <http://www.un.org/en/documents/udhr/index.shtml>. All human rights principles need articulation and contextualization.

12 This critique of Martha Nussbaum's position was first developed without reference to her book, *Frontiers of Justice: Disability, Nationality, Species Membership* (Cambridge, MA: The Belknap Press of Harvard University Press, 2006). This later publication does not affect the criticisms I raise in this chapter. Nussbaum defines her capabilities approach as "a species of the human rights approach" (*Frontiers of Justice*, p. 285), and holds that "the relevant entitlements are prepolitical, nor merely artifacts of laws and institutions" (ibid., p. 265). Yet Nussbaum also stresses that the capabilities approach, "Like the human rights approach, . . . is in one way nation-centered, *recommending that the capabilities list be used as a criterion for social justice internally to each society, as in an account of basic constitutional entitlements*" (ibid., p. 291, emphasis added). But this is not consistent: if the relevant entitlements are "prepolitical," they cannot be simply used as a "criterion" for each nation to develop its own account of basic constitutional entitlements. Some rules and procedures of translation are needed here between the account of human capabilities on the one hand and the juridical or justiciable form of human rights on the other. There is not much detail in Nussbaum's later argument as to how this is to be accomplished. My approach, which explores the relationship between the juridification of human rights and the right to democratic self-governance, is an attempt to provide such criteria of translation.

13 See Amartya Sen, "Elements of a Theory of Human Rights," pp. 315–56; here p. 333, fn. 31.

14 Amartya Sen, *The Idea of Justice* (Cambridge, MA: The Belknap Press of Harvard University Press, 2009), pp. 357–60.

15 Sen, *The Idea of Justice*, p. 363.

16 Ibid., pp. 364–5.

17 Sen, *The Idea of Justice*, pp. 365–6. I cannot do justice to the complexities of Sen's argument in this article. There is much else that I deeply admire and endorse in this book such as the excavation of Enlightenment-friendly ideals formulated by non-Western societies as well as the assessment of democracy in terms of "the capacity to enrich reasoned engagement" (p. xiii).

18 Joshua Cohen, "Minimalism About Human Rights: The Most We Can Hope For?," p. 192.

19 Terence Turner, "Anthropology and Multiculturalism: What is Anthropology that Multiculturalists Should be Mindful of it?," *Cultural Anthropology* 8/4 (1993): 411–29. See Benhabib, *The Claims of Culture: Equality and Diversity in the Global Era*,

pp. 5 ff., for further discussion. Thomas Pogge, Charles Beitz, and Martha Nussbaum all criticize Rawls's "nation-centered" approach, but my point here is somewhat different. I am criticizing the *social theory* behind Rawls's privileging of the standpoint of the nation and not his normative premises alone. Cf. Thomas Pogge, *Realizing Rawls* (Ithaca, NY: Cornell University Press, 1989); Charles Beitz, *Political Theory and International Relations* (Princeton, NJ: Princeton University Press, 1979); Martha Nussbaum, *Frontiers of Justice*, pp. 272–324.

20 For an extended discussion of the problem of "methodological holism" in Rawls's work, see Seyla Benhabib, "*The Law of Peoples,* Distributive Justice, and Migrations," *Fordham Law Review* LXXII/5 (April 2004): 1761–87.

21 Cf. Joshua Cohen, "Is There a Human Right to Democracy?," pp. 226–48.

22 See Cohen, "Is There a Human Right to Democracy?," where he writes: "The distinction between the rights that must be assured in a just political society and human rights is associated with Rawls's distinction between liberal and decent but non-liberal peoples," p. 228.

23 Ibid., pp. 237–8.

24 Cohen, "Is there a Human Right to Democracy?," p. 233.

25 Cohen, "Is There a Human Right to Democracy?," pp. 242–3. I am assuming that the equal right of persons to take part in the affairs governing their collective existence through the medium of law and the articulation of their opinions and preferences in a political community through the rights of freedom of speech and association is the essence of the democratic form of government. Whether this is institutionalized through periodic elections, a multi-party system, proportional representation, mandates and recalls, and the like are questions which do not belong to the *idea of democracy* itself but to its concretization in specific socio-historical circumstances, and there can be quite an acceptable range of variation here. A much more robust conception of democracy can be found principally in the writings of John Dewey. Cf. Dewey's statement: "To say that democracy is *only* a form of government is like saying that a home is a more or less geometrical arrangements of bricks and mortar; that the church is a building with pews, pulpit and spire. It is true; they certainly are so much. But it is false; they are infinitely more. Democracy, like any other polity, has been finely termed the memory of an historic past, the consciousness of a living

present, the ideal of a coming future. Democracy, in a word, is social, that is to say, an ethical conception, and upon its ethical significance is based its significance as governmental. Democracy is a form of government only because it is a form of moral and spiritual association" (John Dewey, *The Collected Works of John Dewey 1882–1953: The Early Works of John Dewey, 1882–1898, Essays, Leibniz's New Essays Concerning the Human Understanding* (Carbondale, IL: Southern Illinois University Press, 1969–90), vol. 1, p. 240; as cited by Richard J. Bernstein, "Dewey's Vision of Radical Democracy," in R. Bernstein, *The Pragmatic Turn* (Cambridge, and Malden, MA: Polity, 2010), p. 73.

This is a conception of democracy which I find very compelling; however, since my concern in this essay is to reveal the incoherence of some contemporary authors who deny that there is a human right to democracy at all, I am not engaging in these broader questions. For another account of democracy in terms of the value of participation and robust citizenship, see also Benjamin Barber, *Strong Democracy* (Berkeley and Los Angeles, CA: University of California Press, 1984).

26 While it is still too early to assess the course of some of these developments, there is little doubt that democratic government is viewed by millions across the world as their legitimate human right. Questions remain, of course, about what form these democracies will take: whether they will respect a bill of human rights, constitutional review and the like or whether they will be more populist in nature, and not grant individuals the full range of liberal freedoms. See Seyla Benhabib, "The Arab Spring. Religion, Revolution and the Public Square," posted by Social Science Research Council Public Sphere Resources at: <http://ow.ly/43jPD>.

27 Charles R. Beitz, *The Idea of Human Rights* (Oxford: Oxford University Press, 2009), pp. 234–5.

28 Beitz, *The Idea of Human Rights*, p. 185.

29 In an argument closely paralleling Beitz's, Jean Cohen also criticizes Joshua Cohen's approach for being "still too demanding," and asks: "Wouldn't suspension of the sovereignty argument when rights to individual dissent, free expression, appeal, and the requirement of public justification of policy are violated amount to a green light to intervene against any regime militarily?" (Jean Cohen, "Rethinking Human Rights, Democracy, and Sovereignty in the Age of Globalization," *Political Theory* 36/4

(2008): 586). This "functional account" (Jean Cohen, p. 582) of human rights considers human rights in terms of their position within international relations and international law and tries to blunt the justification of ever-increasing interventionism. But this is to put the cart before the horse: an adequate conception of human rights cannot be arrived at by asking which minimal list of human rights would prevent interventionism. Some powers will use existing formulations and institutions to their instrumental purposes some or most of the time; normative theory alone cannot prevent such political abuse. None of the human rights declarations cited above create a *general obligation* to intervene in the affairs of other states. As Jean Cohen herself acknowledges, only the Genocide Convention does so (p. 587). That politicians abuse these conventions is not based on the faulty logic of these agreements but rather on power and interests. Why then limit conceptions of human rights to this "functional account" at all, rather than viewing them as instruments of *critique* directed against existing state regimes as well as civil societies?

30 If there is a human right to democracy, who is responsible for enforcing this right? Or does this mean that the world community ought to intervene in non-democratic societies to enforce this right? Most human rights violations do not create obligations to intervene except under exceptional circumstances as specified by the Genocide Convention – genocide, ethnic cleansing, slavery, and mass deportations – and as warranted by self-defense, which is recognized as a right in Article II (7) of the UN Charter, and as authorized by permanent members of the UN Security Council. The human right to democracy is "an aspirational claim," which as the formulators of the UDHR very pertinently say, formulates "a common standard of achievement for all peoples and all nations" (Universal Declaration, Preamble). The force of such aspirational claims is manifest in processes of "democratic iterations" and "jurisgenerative politics" which they set into motion and help sustain. See chapter 7 of this volume.

31 Cohen, "Is There a Human Right to Democracy?," p. 230.

32 I offer democratic iterations as a model to think of the interaction between constitutional provisions and democratic politics. It may be possible to extend democratic iterations to serve as a model for the *pouvoir constituant*, the founding act, as well. In this chapter, I am assuming that democratic iterations are about

236

ordinary as opposed to constitutional politics; however, I am claiming that ordinary politics can embody forms of popular constitutionalism and can lead to constitutional transformation through accretion. There is a lot more that needs to be said about the relationship of a discourse-theoretic analysis of democratic iterations and political liberalism than I can within the scope of this chapter. See Rawls's final reflections in his "Political Liberalism: Reply to Habermas," *The Journal of Philosophy* 92/3 (March 1995): here 172 ff. Thanks to Angelica Bernal for her observations on this problem.

33 I elucidate this distinction further below in chapter 8, "Democratic Exclusions and Democratic Iterations: Dilemmas of Just Membership and Prospects of Cosmopolitan Federalism."

34 This is the chief flaw in Costas Douzinas's powerful recent work on human rights and empire. Repeatedly, Douzinas flattens out the moral dilemmas and political tragedies associated with the defense of human rights, and implicates them in the policies of Empire – meaning primarily, of course, of the American hegemon. See Costas Douzinas, *Human Rights and Empire: The Political Philosophy of Cosmopolitanism* (Oxford and New York: Routledge-Cavendish, 2009 [2007]). Cf. the statement: "Rather than denoting an objective reality, the name chosen and the associated – contested – concept indicate a political decision and a normative preference. *The political judgment of this book is that the differences and distinctions between empire, imperialism and cosmopolitanism are smaller, the continuities greater, than some of their advocates admit*" (my emphasis, p. 147). By contrast, my argument in *this* book is that these differences matter and that such discontinuities are politically significant.

35 Cf. Michael W. Doyle, "The New Interventionism," in Thomas W. Pogge, ed., *Global Justice*, Metaphilosophy Series in Philosophy (Oxford: Blackwell, 2001), pp. 219–41.

36 See J. L. Holzgrefe and Robert O. Keohane, eds, *Humanitarian Intervention: Ethical, Legal, and Political Dilemmas* (Cambridge: Cambridge University Press, 2003); for the view that judges are creating law in this domain, see Allison Marsten Danner, "When Courts Make Law: How the International Criminal Tribunals Recast the Laws of War," *Vanderbilt Law Review* 59/1 (January 2006): 2–63.

37 For a judicious argument which seeks to reconcile cosmopolitan commitments with the "preventive use of force," see Allen Buchanan and Robert O. Keohane, "The Preventive Use of

NOTES AND REFERENCES TO PAGES 90–94

Force: A Cosmopolitan Institutional Perspective," *Ethics and International Affairs* 18/1 (2004): 1–22. I find the suggestion that the Security Council can be sidelined, without the creation of proper institutional alternatives and in the name of a democratic coalition, a bit too vague and cavalier and uncomfortably reminiscent of George Bush's call for a "coalition of the willing" during the lead-up to the Iraq War. See pp. 18 ff.

38 The distinction between NGOs, INGOs, and other aid and development organizations and combat forces is becoming, admittedly, one of the most difficult to maintain in situations of actual armed conflict. It is also a distinction that irregular armed forces disregard, thus putting the lives of many civilian aid workers in jeopardy. Unfortunately, there are far too many cases of such civilians – including many journalists – who have been killed in the course of recent conflicts in Iraq, Pakistan, Afghanistan, Rwanda, the Ivory Coast, and the Congo. For a reflective account of what may be at stake in making these distinctions collapse, see Michael Ignatieff, *The Warrior's Honor: Ethnic War and the Modern Conscience* (New York: Henry Holt, 1997).

39 See Allen Buchanan, "From Nuremberg to Kosovo: The Morality of Illegal International Legal Reform," in *Ethics* 111/4 (July 2001): 673–705.

40 Immanuel Kant [1795], "Perpetual Peace: A Philosophical Sketch," pp. 116–19; also I. Kant, Appendix II, "On the Agreement between Politics and Morality According to the Transcendental Concept of Public Right," pp. 125–30.

CHAPTER 6   TWILIGHT OF SOVEREIGNTY OR THE EMERGENCE OF COSMOPOLITAN NORMS? RETHINKING CITIZENSHIP IN VOLATILE TIMES

1 See *Transformation of Citizenship: Dilemmas of the Nation-State in an Era of Globalization*, The Spinoza Lectures (Amsterdam: Van Gorcum, 2001); Seyla Benhabib, *The Claims of Culture: Equality and Diversity in the Global Era*; *The Rights of Others: Aliens, Citizens and Residents,* the John Seeley Memorial Lectures.

2 In 1957 the Treaty Establishing the European Community, officially referred to as the "Treaty of Rome"/"EC Treaty," was accepted. With the entry into force of the Lisbon Treaty, it has been renamed "Treaty of Lisbon Amending the Treaty on Euro-

pean Union and the Treaty establishing the European Community," the TFEU. See: <http://eur-lex.europa.eu/LexUriServ/LexUriServ.do?uri=OJ:C:2007:306:0001:0010:EN:PDF>; accessed on August 31, 2010.

3   See "The International Human Rights Movement," in Louis Henkin, D. W. Leebron, G. L. Neuman, and D. Orentlicher, eds, *Human Rights* (New York: Foundation Press, 2003), pp. 147 ff.

4   Kees Groenendijk, "Local Voting Rights for Non-Nationals in Europe: What We Know and What We Need to Learn," Publication of the Transatlantic Council on Migration (2008); accessed on 31 August, 2010, at: <http://www.migrationpolicy.org/transatlantic/docs/Groenendijk-FINAL.pdf>.

5   Cf. Aihwa Ong, *Flexible Citizenship: The Cultural Logic of Transnationality* (Durham, NC, and London: Duke University Press, 1999).

6   See Aristide Zolberg and Peter Benda, *Global Migrants. Global Refugees: Problems and Solutions* (New York and Oxford: Berghan Books, 2001).

7   For a more extensive treatment of Arendt's concept see Benhabib, "Kantian Questions, Arendtian Answers," in Seyla Benhabib and Nancy Fraser, eds, *Pragmatism, Critique and Judgment: Festschrift for Richard J. Bernstein* (Cambridge, MA: MIT Press, 2004), pp. 171–97. See also Hauke Brunkhorst, *Hannah Arendt* (Munich: C.H. Beck'sche Verlagsbuchhandlung,1999), pp. 52–84.

8   Giorgio Agamben, *State of Exception*, trans. Kevin Attell (Chicago, IL, and London: University of Chicago Press, 2005); Michael Hardt and Antonio Negri, *Empire* (Cambridge, MA: Harvard University Press, 2001).

9   Etienne Balibar, *We, the People of Europe? Reflections on Transnational Citizenship*, trans. James Swenson (Princeton, NJ, and Oxford: Princeton University Press, 2004); David Held, *Global Covenant: The Social Democratic Alternative to the Washington Consensus* (Cambridge: Polity, 2004).

10 Jean L. Cohen, "Whose Sovereignty? Empire versus International Law," *Ethics and International Affairs* 18/3 (2004): 2.

11 The genesis of cosmopolitan norms goes back to the experiences of two world wars, anti-colonial struggles, the Armenian genocide in the late stages of the Ottoman Empire, and the Holocaust. For an account of the development of international law, see Martti Koskenniemi, *The Gentle Civilizer of Nations: The*

Rise and Fall of International Law 1870–1960 (Cambridge: Cambridge University Press, 2002). See also the accounts of trials against members of the "Union and Progress Party" in the Ottoman Empire, who were responsible for the Armenian genocide, by Taner Akcam, *Armenien und der Völkermord: Die Istanbuler Prozesse und die türkische Nationalbewegung* (Hamburg: Hamburger Edition, 1996); for the Nuremberg trials, cf. Michael Marrus, *The Nuremberg War Crimes Trial 1945–46: A Documentary History* (New York: Bedford/St Martin's, 1997); for Ralph Lemkin's efforts to pass the Genocide Convention, see chapter 2 of this volume. Cf. also Burnkhorst's impassioned defense of "strong human rights," in *Solidarität: Von den Bürgerfreundschaft zur globalen Rechtsgenossenschaft* (Frankfurt: Suhrkamp, 2002).

12 Etienne Balibar, "Prolegomena to Sovereignty," in Balibar, *We, The People of Europe? Reflections on Transnational Citizenship*, p. 152.

13 In a rather deferential but terse review of Anne-Marie Slaughter's, *A New World Order* (Princeton, NJ, and Oxford: Princeton University Press, 2004), Kenneth Anderson distinguishes state sovereignty, democratic sovereignty, sovereign state multilateralism, and multilateralism pooled sovereignty. But he does not explore the implications of distinguishing between state and democratic sovereignty when the latter is understood as popular sovereignty. This is because for him a non-nation-state based conception of sovereignty is unimaginable. See Kenneth Anderson, "Squaring the Circle? Reconciling Sovereignty and Global Governance Through Global Government Networks," *Harvard Law Review* 118 (2005): 1255–1312; here 1261–3. Anderson defines state sovereignty in terms of Lincoln's classic phrase as "a political community, without a political superior." Abraham Lincoln, Message to Congress in Special Session (July 4, 1861), in *The Collected Works of Abraham Lincoln*, ed. Roy P. Basler (1953), pp. 421, 434, as cited by Anderson, ibid., p. 1299. The question is whether "political superiority" is to be understood as *finality of decision-making or as some ultimacy of power*. No state possesses such power in the international domain, and within the domestic realm, such a conception of sovereignty has been repudiated with the rise of cosmopolitan norms; ultimate sovereign power is a non-sensical concept but sovereignty understood as "possessing final authority in decision-making" remains – even if it itself is contested.

14 See David Apter, "Globalization, Marginality, and the Specter of Superfluous Man," in *Journal of Social Affairs* 18/71 (fall, 2001): 73–94.

15 Carl Schmitt, *Der Nomos der Erde im Völkerrecht des Jus Publicum Europaeum*, 4th edn (Berlin: Duncker and Humblot, 1997), p. 99; English trans. Gary L. Ulmen, *The Nomos of the Earth in the International Law of the* Jus Publicum Europaeum, (New York: Telos Press, 2003), pp. 128–9.

16 Stephen D. Krasner, *Sovereignty: Organized Hypocrisy* (Princeton, NJ: Princeton University Press, 1999).

17 For a masterful account, which is also a sustained critique of Schmitt, see Koskenniemi, *The Gentle Civilizer of Nations: The Rise and Fall of International Law 1870–1960*, pp. 98–179. Cf. the statement of the Belgian legal historian Ernest Nys: "A state uses the territories that constitute its private domain as it wishes; it sells them, it rents them out, it attaches such conditions to the concessions it grants as it sees warranted . . . in none of this does it owe an explanation to other States" (from "L'État Indépendent du Congo et les dispositions de l'acte generale," quoted in Koskenniemi, ibid., p. 161).

18 Schmitt's elegy to the *Jus Publicum Europaeum* (the public law of Europe) emphasizes that this system "neutralizes" war by moving away from the medieval notion of "just war." In this transformation, the enemy is no longer viewed as *inimicus* but as *justi hostes* (categories which also return in Schmitt's concept of the "political"). This "neutralized" concept of war is also called "the non-discriminatory concept of war" (*der nicht-diskriminierende Kriegsbegriff*). "All inter-state wars upon European soil, which are carried out through the militarily organized armies of states recognized by European law of nations (Völkerrecht), are just in the sense of the European law of nations of this inter-statal period" (Schmitt, *Der Nomos der Erde*, p. 115 (emphasis in the text); in the English translation, *Nomos of the Earth*, see p. 143). Schmitt here conflates "justice" and "legality," not out of some logical error, but because he rejects all normative standards that go beyond state interests in judging wars.

19 Burke, cited in Arendt, *The Origins of Totalitarianism*, p. 183. See also Hannah Arendt's powerful statement, "The only grandeur of imperialism lies in the nation's losing battle against it," ibid., p. 132.

20 See Janine Brodie, "Introduction: Globalization and Citizenship Beyond the National State," and Satoshi Ikeda, "Imperial

Subjects, National Citizenship, and Corporate Subjects: Cycles of Political Participation/Exclusion in the Modern World System," both in *Citizenship Studies* 8/4 (December 2004): 323–33 and 333–49 respectively.

21 Hania Zlotnik, "Past Trends in International Migration and Their Implications for Future Prospects," in M. A. B. Siddique, ed., *International Migration into the Twenty-First Century: Essays in Honor of Reginald Appleyard* (Boston, MA: Edward Elgar, 2001), p. 227.

22 United Nations, Department of Economic and Social Affairs, *International Migration Report* ST/ESA/SER.A/220, 2002. According to the International Organization for Migration, "There are far more international migrants in the world today than ever previously recorded, and their number has increased rapidly in the last few decades. . . . While the global reach of international migration had already began to extend after 1945, it has expanded sharply only since the 1980s to include all regions of the world today . . . This globalization of international migration involves a wider diversity of ethnic and cultural groups than ever before; there is a growing proportion of women as primary migrants; more or less permanent or settlement migration has increasingly been replaced by temporary and circular migration; and, although the economic crisis may have temporarily slowed the growth of migration outflows, the underlying causes of this globalization of migration, such as demographic, labour market and environmental factors, remain." At: <http://www.iom.int/jahia/Jahia/policy-research/migration-research/world-migration-report-2010/cache/offonce/>; accessed on September 1, 2010.

23 See Benhabib, *The Rights of Others,* pp. 5 ff.

24 See Dieter Grimm, *Souveränität: Herkunft und Zukunft eines Schlüsselbegriffs* (Berlin: Berlin University Press, 2009).

25 Peter Evans, "The Eclipse of the State? Reflections on Stateness in an Era of Globalization," *World Politics* 50/1 (1997): 62–87. The original term is from J. P. Nettl, "The State as a Conceptual Variable," *World Politics* 20 (July 1968): 559–92.

26 Ong, *Flexible Citizenship*, p. 221.

27 Ibid., p. 222.

28 Carolin Emcke, *Echoes of Violence: Letters from a War Reporter* (Princeton, NJ: Princeton University Press, 2007), p. 77 and in general pp.71–97.

29 In Günther Teubner, ed., *Global Law Without a State: Studies in Modern Law and Policy* (Aldershot and Brookfield, Vermont: Dartmouth Publishing Company, 1997), pp. 3–28; here p. 5.

30 Teubner, ibid., p. 8.

31 Ibid., p. 21. For a more optimistic assessment of the human rights obligations of international organizations and what they can do to realize them, see Ernst-Ulrich Petersmann, "Time for a United Nations 'Global Compact' for Integrating Human Rights into the Law of Worldwide Organizations: Lessons from European Integration," *European Journal of International Law* 13/3 (2002): 621–50.

32 Andreas Fischer-Lescano and Günther Teubner discuss this extensively in their article, "Regime-Collisions: The Vain Search for Legal Unity in the Fragmentation of Global Law," trans. by Michelle Everson, in *Michigan Journal of International Law* 25 (summer 2004): 999–1046. Particularly interesting is the conflict between the economic interests of patent holders, such as big pharmaceuticals Merck, Pfizer, Roche, etc., and nation-states. These pharma-companies in 2001 asked the WTO to investigate Brazil for permitting the domestic production of generic drugs via copying patented medicines. Brazil defended itself by pointing out that the AIDS epidemic had taken 150,000 lives since 1981 and that with preventive measures annual infections could be reduced to less than 5,000. This case, entailing a clear human rights claim to health and public protection from epidemic disease, in turn led to a major renegotiation of the terms of TRIPS (Trade Related Intellectual Property Rights) and to further negotiations between WHO and WTO about the preventive and non-commercial use of patented drugs, and led all the way to a resolution of the UN Commission on Human Rights in 2003, reiterated in 2005, protecting the preventive use of generic drugs whenever possible to help combat the spread of disease and epidemics. See Resolution 2003/47 of the United Nations Human Rights Commission (E/CN.4/RES/2003/47), retrievable through: <http://data.unaids.org/Media/Information-No>. At the Doha meetings in 2002, a Declaration on the TRIPS agreement and Public Health was issued, which affirmed the safeguards provided in TRIPS with regards to rights of states to issue measures such as compulsory licensing to cope with health crises in their respective countries. Company representatives in general preferred methods of differential pricing, but conceded that they

must accept the decision of states to deal with their own health problems. Since the DOHA round in 2002, however, trends have apparently gone in the direction of bilateral rather than multi-lateral agreements. See the publication "Intellectual Property Rights," Results of a Stakeholder Dialogue between the World Business Council for Sustainable Development and the Wissen-schaftszentrum Berlin für Sozialforschung (reprint April 2004). Contact: <wbcsd@earthprint.com>. See also Thomas Pogge's pioneering work in this area, *World Poverty and Human Rights: Cosmopolitan Responsibilities and Reforms* (Cambridge: Polity, 2002).

33 William. E. Scheuerman, *Liberal Democracy and the Social Acceleration of Time* (Baltimore, MD, and London: Johns Hopkins University Press, 2004), p. 145.

34 Scheuerman, ibid., p. 169.

35 Saskia Sassen, *Territoriality, Authority and Rights: From Medi-eval to Global Assemblages* (Princeton, NJ: Princeton University Press, 2006).

36 I disagree with Anderson's critique of Slaughter's work that global governance inevitably erodes respect for democracy over time. See: "the system of global governance through global gov-ernment networks, as it grows and develops in ways that Slaugh-ter outlines, *over time* tends to erode the respect for democracy and democratic accountability with which it began and may finally lead to a form of liberal internationalism, a world of de facto federalized global governance" (K. Anderson, "Squaring the Circle? Reconciling Sovereignty and Global Governance," p. 1301). Anderson does not explore the increase in account-ability and transparency that results by giving up the "black box" view of sovereignty; nor how such increase can contribute to the democratic power of the people.

37 Although first translated into English in 2001, the Italian version of *Empire* was written in the period between the Persian Gulf War of 1991 and the Yugoslav Civil War of 1994. Its view of USA power is more benevolent than the subsequent work by Michael Hardt and Antonio Negri, *Multitude: War and Democ-racy in the Age of Empire* (New York: Penguin Press, 2004).

38 The last chapter of Hardt and Negri's *Multitude* is called "May the Force be With You." See pp. 341–8; on carnival, cf. "The various forms of carnival and mimicry that are so common today at globalization protests might be considered another form of weaponry. Simply having millions of people in the streets

for a demonstration is a kind of weapon, as is also, in a rather different way, the pressure of illegal migrations . . . A one-week global biopolitical strike would block any war" (Hardt and Negri, ibid., p. 347).

39 Just as in Michel Foucault's theory of power, the subjects of power are interpellated by it, that is, constituted in part through the network of power rather than preceding it, in Hardt and Negri's analysis too, states and other world institutions disappear as agents and sites of resistance that have prior constitution. I disagree with this theory of power. One can stipulate the existence of very distinct and structured institutions and patterns of resistance to power without presupposing a metaphysical primordiality of either the state or of the subject. The reach of empire is neither as ubiquitous nor as omniscient as Hardt and Negri would like us to think.

40 Hannah Arendt, *On Revolution* (New York: Viking Press, 1963). See also Seyla Benhabib, *The Reluctant Modernism of Hannah Arendt*, pp. 130–72.

41 See David Held, *Global Covenant: The Social Democratic Alternative to the Washington Consensus*, and Andrew Kuper, *Democracy Beyond Borders: Justice and Representation in Global Institutions* (Oxford University Press: Oxford, 2004); Anne-Marie Slaughter, *A New World Order* (Princeton, NJ: Princeton University Press, 2004). There is something all too optimistic and cheery in some of these proposals which downplay the danger of dissociating constitutionalism from democracy and from citizens' will and reason, by transferring it to an expertocracy, even if an expertocracy with as much good-will as the judges and practitioners of international law. While I share this concern with Kenneth Anderson, I think that such concerns can be met within a framework of liberal internationalist governance. Such mechanisms can be democracy-enhancing rather than democracy-diminishing. See n.36 of this chapter, above.

42 Global civil society, as defended here, should not be confused with the appeal to voluntarism and private associations, so characteristic of neo-liberal positions that aim at curtailing state power. I endorse the public provision of public goods in a system of nested interdependencies among public authorities. Global civil society is a space of global civic activism and the counterpart to the model of republican federalism that I develop below. Nancy Fraser is one of the few contemporary social theorists

who focuses on new global social movements; cf. Fraser, *Scales of Justice*, pp. 21–7, 58–67; see also Heather Gautney, "Is Another State Possible?," and Michael Menser, "Disarticulate the State! Maximizing Democracy in 'New' Autonomous Movements in the Americas," both in Heather Gautney, Omar Dahbour, Ashley Dawson, and Neil Smith, eds, *Democracy, States, and the Struggle for Global Justice* (New York and London: Routledge, 2009), pp. 205–35 and 251–73 respectively.

43 Judith Resnik, "Law's Migration: American Exceptionalism, Silent Dialogues, and Federalism's Multiple Ports of Entry," in *The Yale Law Journal* 115 (2006): 1564–1670.

44 Since I have introduced the concept of democratic iterations in *The Rights of Others*, pp. 179 ff., I have been asked to clarify (a) the relationship between practical discourses of justification and democratic iterations, and (b) whether democratic iterations can also be regressive and non-meaning enhancing. Democratic iterations are processes of *legitimation* not of *justification*. They stand in the same relationship to normative discourses of justification as theories of democracy stand to John Rawls's *Theory of Justice*; that is, theories of democracy are concerned with legitimacy as distinguished from theories which consider justice. Second, "jurispathic" democratic iterations, which block the enhancement of meaning and the augmentation of rights claims are possible. See "Reply to My Critics," in *Another Cosmopolitanism*, pp. 158–65, and chapter 8 of this volume.

45 See Jürgen Habermas's early formulation, "Ist der Herzschlag der Revolution zum Stillstand gekommen? Volkssouveränität als Verfahren. Ein normativer Begriff der Öffentlichkeit," in *Die Ideen von 1789 in der deutschen Rezeption*, ed. Forum für Philosophie Bad Homburg (Frankfurt am Main: Suhrkamp, 1989), pp. 7–36.

46 Scheuerman, *Liberal Democracy and the Social Acceleration of Time*, pp. 268–9, fn 52.

47 On the idea of a threshold of justification, see Seyla Benhabib, *The Rights of Others*, pp. 15–21.

48 For the first position, see Andrew Arato and Jean Cohen, "Banishing the Sovereign? Internal and External Sovereignty in Arendt," in Seyla Benhabib, ed., *Politics in Dark Times: Encounters with Hannah Arendt*, pp. 137–72; J. L. Cohen (2004),

"Whose Sovereignty? Empire Versus International Law," *Ethics and International Affairs* 18/3: 1–24; J. L. Cohen (2006), "Sovereign Equality vs. Imperial Right: The Battle over the 'New World Order'," *Constellations* 13/4: 485–505.

For the second position, Carol C. Gould, *Globalizing Democracy and Human Rights* (Cambridge: Cambridge University Press, 2004), pp. 162 ff.; Michael Doyle and Nicholas Sambanis, *Making War and Building Peace: United Nations Peace Operations* (Princeton, NJ: Princeton University Press, 2006).

49 For a cosmopolitan world federalist position, see Eric Cavallero, "Federative Global Democracy," in Ronald Tinnevelt and Helder de Schutter, eds, Special Issue, "Global Democracy and Exclusion," *Metaphilosophy* 40/1 (January 2009): 42–64; Rafaele Marchetti, *Global Democracy. For and Against* (London: Routledge, 2008); for an early and powerful statement of the problem, see Thomas Pogge, "Cosmopolitanism and Sovereignty," in Chris Brown, ed., *Political Restructuring in Europe* (London: Routledge, 1994), pp. 89–122; Cf. also Jürgen Habermas, *The Divided West*, ed. and trans. Ciaran Cronin (Cambridge: Polity, 2006); also Jürgen Habermas, "A Political Constitution for the Pluralist World Society," in *Between Naturalism and Religion*, trans. Ciaran Cronin (Cambridge: Polity, 2006), pp. 312–52; for regionalist visions, see Carol C. Gould, "Envisioning Transnational Democracy: Cross-Border Communities and Regional Human Rights Frameworks," in Heather Gautney, Omar Dahbour, Ashley Dawson, and Neil Smith, eds, *Democracy, States, and the Struggle for Global Justice*, pp. 63–79.

50 The economic crises of member countries of the EU such as Greece, Ireland, Portugal, and possibly Spain and Italy, and the reaction of governing forces in Brussels as well as of the German government to these crises, since the summer of 2010, make one question the project of Europe. While I do not believe that the Euro-zone will collapse, it is clear that the worldwide economic downturn is being used by conservative forces such as Germany's Chancellor, Angela Merkel, and the French President, Nicolas Sarkozy, to cut back the social-welfare state and the rights of wage-earners to social entitlements. It is an open question whether the considerable political achievements of the EU will be powerful enough to generate popular and democratic reassertions of sovereignty to resist this neo-conservative onslaught.

NOTES AND REFERENCES TO PAGES 117-118

CHAPTER 7 CLAIMING RIGHTS ACROSS BORDERS: INTERNATIONAL HUMAN
RIGHTS AND DEMOCRATIC SOVEREIGNTY

1   See Adam Liptak, "U.S. Court, a Longtime Beacon, is Now Guiding Fewer Nations," *New York Times* (September 18, 2008), p. A1, continued on A30. Liptak details how in the last decade citations to decisions of the US Supreme Court have declined, while the influence of the European Court of Human Rights and the Canadian Supreme Court have grown. This evidence is all the more surprising since so many of these courts and their leading constitutional documents – such as the Indian Constitution of 1949, the Canadian Charter of Rights and Freedoms of 1982, the New Zealand Bill of Rights of 1990, and the South African Constitution of 1996 – all drew on American constitutional principles at their inception.

2   See *Roper* v. *Simmons* (2005); and Liptak, p. A30.

3   Cf. *Roper* v. *Simmons*, Justice Scalia dissenting, joined by Chief Justice Roberts and Justice Thomas. The US Congress passed a resolution concerning the citation of foreign law by American Courts. See "Reaffirmation of American Independence Resolution," H.R. Res. 568, 108th Congress (2004).

4   Not only Justice Scalia, but Chief Justice Roberts as well, opposes this liberal-minded problem-solving approach to judicial decision-making that would learn and borrow from other courts. Justice Robert considers the citing of foreign law to be not an innocent exercise in decision-making, but a compromise or dilution of sovereignty. Liptak quotes Justice Roberts from his 2005 confirmation hearings: "If we're relying on a decision from a German judge about what our Constitution means, no president accountable to the people appointed that judge and no senate accountable to the people confirmed that judge. And yet he is playing a role in shaping the law that binds the people in this country" (Liptak, "U.S. Court, a Longtime Beacon, is Now Guiding Fewer Nations," p. A30). By blurring the distinction between "citing an opinion" and "creating a precedent," Justice Roberts raises the specter of the weakening of democratic sovereignty and judicial accountability.

5   This controversy concerns not only the heft and weight of foreign courts in influencing the decisions of Supreme Court justices, but broader issues such as the following. What is the proper epistemology of judicial decision-making? Why should judges not learn from other colleagues who have considered similar prob-

lems in their own jurisdictions? Eric A. Posner and Cass R. Sunstein, in "The Law of Other States," argue, for example, that "The practice of consulting 'foreign precedents' has received a great deal of attention in connection with recent decisions of the Supreme Court of the United States . . . But in some ways, it is quite standard to refer to the decisions of other jurisdictions, and the debate over the references of the Supreme Court should be understood in the context of that standard practice" (Eric A. Posner and Cass R. Sunstein, "The Law of Other States," *Stanford Law Review* 59/131 (2006): 131–80; here 133). After observing that "Consultation of foreign law seems to be the rule, not the exception" (p. 135), the authors set out to provide a framework with reasons why consulting the decisions of other states, domestically or internationally, can enhance the quality of judicial decision-making.

Cf. also Jeremy Waldron, "*The Supreme Court, 2004 Term-Comment: Foreign Law and the Modern* Jus Gentium," *Harvard Law Review* 119/1 (2005): 129–47; Mark Tushnet, "When is Knowing Less Better than Knowing More? Unpacking the Controversy over the Supreme Court Reference to Non-U.S. Law," *Minnesota Law Review* 90/5 (2006): 1275–1302.

6   Among the literature discussing "world constitutionalization," see Bardo Fassbender, "The United Nations Charter as Constitution of the International Community," *Columbia Journal of Transnational Law* 3 (1998): 529–619; " 'We the Peoples of the United Nations': Constituent Power and Constitutional Form," in M. Loughlin and N. Walker, eds, *The Paradox of Constitutionalism* (2007), pp. 269–90; Arnim von Bogdandy, "Constitutionalism in International Law," *Harvard International Law Journal* 47/1 (2006): 223–42; Brun-Otto Bryde, "Konstitutionalisierung des Völkerrechts und Internationalisierung des Verfassungsbegriffs," in *Der Staat* 1 (2003): 61–75; Hauke Brunkhorst, "Globalizing Democracy without a State: Weak Public, Strong Public, Global Constitutionalism," in *Millennium: Journal of International Studies* 31/3 (2002): 675–90; Hauke Brunkhorst, "Die Globale Rechtsrevolution. Von der Evolution der Verfassungsrevolution zur Revolution der Verfassungsevolution?," in Ralph Christensen and Bodo Pieroth, eds, *Rechtstheorie in rechtspraktischer Absicht* (Berlin: FS Müller, 2008), pp. 9–34; and the helpful overview of this literature, Hauke Brunkhorst, "There Will be Blood: Konstitutionalisierung Ohne Demokratie?," in H. Brunkhorst, ed., *Demokratie in*

der Weltgesellschaft, Special issue, *Soziale Welt, Nomos* (2009): 99–123. For historical antecedents, cf. Hans Kelsen, *Das Problem der Souveränität und die Theorie des Völkerrechts: Beitrag zu einer reinen Rechtslehre*, 2nd edn (Vienna: Scientia Allen [1928] 1960); Alfred Verdross, *Die Verfassung der Völkerrechtsgemeinschaft* (Vienna, 1926).

There are parallel discussions concerning constitutionalization in the EU, in the WTO, and the IMF, and so on. See, Alec Stone Sweet, "Constitutionalism, Legal Pluralism, and International Regimes," *Indiana Journal of Global Legal Studies* 16/2 (2009): 621 ff. This essay gives a lucid overview of the various sorts of systems and institutions that the term "constitutionalization" is being applied to. From the standpoint of Stone's own theory, however, my position would belong among those naive normativists who establish connections between constitutions, the social legitimacy of a legal system, and the community's collective identity.

7   For a thoughtful case against "universalist harmonization schemes," arguing that "normative conflict among multiple, overlapping legal systems is unavoidable and might even be desirable, both as a source of alternative ideas and as a site for discourse among multiple community affiliations," see Paul Berman, "Global Legal Pluralism," *Southern California Law Review* 80 (2008): 1155–1237.

8   Cf. also Robert O. Keohane, Stephen Macedo, and Andrew Moravcsik, "Democracy-Enhancing Multilateralism," in *International Organization* 63 (winter 2009): 1–31, for a kindred argument.

9   In her influential work, Beth Simmons has provided empirical case studies to analyze the impact of states' ratification of various human rights treaties on domestic adherence to human rights norms. Simmons observes that "the more interesting cases, however, are those in which governments ratify an international human rights agreement, yet make no move to implement or comply with it. Why should a ratified treaty make a difference in such cases?" See Beth Simmons, "Civil Rights in International Law: Compliance with Aspects of the 'International Bill of Rights'," *Indiana Journal of Global Legal Studies* 16/2 (summer 2009): 437–81; here 443. One reason may be that, since treaties constitute law in some jurisdictions, they could strengthen civil rights litigation. The more interesting cases are when ratified treaties enable citizens' mobilization. Simmons focuses on "non-

democracies" to argue that "ratification injects a new model of rights into domestic discourse, potentially altering expectations of domestic groups and encouraging them to imagine themselves as entitled to forms of official respect" (ibid., p. 445). Furthermore, "Treaties create additional political resources for pro-rights coalitions under these circumstances. They resonate well with an embryonic rule of law culture and gather support from groups that not only believe in the specific rights at stake, but also believe they must take a stand on rule–governed political behavior in general" (ibid., p. 447). Simmons then presents an analysis of the impact of the ICCPR on civil liberties and religious freedoms. "These results suggest," she writes, " a modest but important conclusion: international treaty commitments quite likely have made a positive contribution to civil rights practices in many countries around the world" (ibid., p. 480). Simmons's research strengthens evidence for what I call the "jurisgenerative" effect of cosmopolitan norms, yet nowhere in this article are "non-democracies," identified in contradistinction to "strong democracies" and "strong autocracies." The research is largely quantitative and ahistorical, and does not permit us to understand the political and social context of struggles very well. The case of Women Living Under Muslim Laws, which I discuss below, provides evidence for Simmons's conclusion since most of these women are citizens of "non-democracies"; yet their alliance with Canadian women suggests more transnational activism, which cannot easily be fitted into Simmons's categories. See pp. 132–5 of this volume. Nevertheless, Simmons's work shows that "jurisgenerativity" is not a theoretical abstraction alone.

10   Harold Koh, "International Law as Part of Our Law," *American Journal of International Law* 98/1 (2004): 43–57; here 52. Cf. also Harold Koh, "Transnational Legal Process," in *Nebraska Law Review* 75: 181–208, and Harold Koh, "Transnational Public Law Litigation," in *Yale Law Journal* 100: 2347–2402. See also Judith Resnik, Joshua Civin, and Joseph Frueh, "Ratifying Kyoto at the Local Level: Sovereigntisme, Federalism, and Translocal Organizations of Government Actors (TPGAs), *Arizona Law Review* 50/3 (fall 2008): 709–86; and Paul Schiff Berman, "Global Legal Pluralism," *Southern California Law Review* 80 (2008): here 1165.

11   For a particularly shrill argument in defense of the nation-state, which considers the European Union to be nothing but a revival

of the dreams of European domination once entertained by Hitler's Third Reich, see Jeremy A. Rabkin, *Law without Nations? Why Constitutional Government Requires Sovereign States* (Princeton, NJ: Princeton University Press, 2005).

12 One of the most biting criticisms of American policies and American exceptionalism, often repeated in recent years, was Carl Schmitt's: "With the growing power of the United States its peculiar kind of vacillation would also become visible, a vacillation back and forth between a clear *isolation* behind a line of separation that was drawn over and against Europe on the one hand and a universalist-humanitarian *intervention* which would encompass the earth on the other" (my translation and emphasis in the text). This is the beginning of Schmitt's caustic commentary on the destructive role of the United States upon the *Jus Publicum Europaeum*. See Carl Schmitt, *Der Nomos der Erde im Völkerrecht des jus publicum Europaeum* (Berlin: Duncker and Humblot [1950] 1997), p. 200; English trans Gary Ulmen, *The Nomos of the Earth in the International Law of Jus Publicum Europaeum* (New York: Telos Publishers Ltd, 2006).

In the period before and after George Bush's Iraq War, Schmitt's work has found receptive audiences. Gary Ulmen, "The Military Significance of September 11th," *Telos* 121 (fall 2001): 174–84; Giorgio Agamben, *State of Exception*, trans. Kevin Attell Chicago, IL: London: University of Chicago Press, 2005); Chantal Mouffe, "Carl Schmitt's Warning on the Dangers of a Unipolar World," in Louiza Odysseos and Fabio Petito, eds, *The International Political Thought of Carl Schmitt: Terror, Liberal War, and the Crisis of Global Order* (London and New York: Routledge, 2007), pp. 147–53; Susan Buck-Morss, "Sovereign Right and the Global Left," *Cultural Critique* 69 (spring 2008): 145–71.

For a lively historical account of American government's vacillations and trepidations during the Armenian Genocide in the Ottoman Empire in 1915 and subsequently Woodrow Wilson's foreign policy gyrations, see Samantha Power, *"A Problem from Hell": American Foreign Policy in the Age of Genocide* (New York: Basic Books, 2002), and Gary J. Bass, *Freedom's Battle: The Origins of Humanitarian Intervention* (New York: Alfred A. Knopf, 2008). Bass engages directly with the ambivalence of humanitarian interventionism as an aspect of imperialist politics, but believes that one can distinguish between imperial and humanitarian interventions. Cf. Bass, pp. 367–75, in particular.

13 Cf. the following statement by John Bolton: "While the term 'sovereignty' has acquired many, often inconsistent, definitions, Americans have historically understood it to mean our collective right to govern ourselves within our constitutional framework." And "'Sharing' sovereignty with someone or something else is thus not abstract for Americans. Doing so by definition will diminish the sovereign power of the American people over their government and their own lives, the very purpose for which the Constitution was written" ("The Coming War on Sovereignty," *Commentary* 127/3 (March 2009), accessed through commentarymagazine.com, on March 25, 2009: <http://www.commentarymagazine.com/the-coming-war-on-sovereignty>). Bolton served briefly and controversially as the United States Permanent Representative to the United Nations in 2005–6.

14 Thomas Nagel, "The Problem of Global Justice," *Philosophy and Public Affairs* 33 (2005): 113–47; Quentin Skinner, *Liberty Before Liberalism* (Cambridge: Cambridge University Press, 2008 [1998]); Michael Walzer, *Spheres of Justice: A Defense of Pluralism and Equality* (New York: Basic Books, 1983); Michael J. Sandel, *Democracy's Discontent: America in Search of a Public Philosophy* (Cambridge, MA: The Belknap Press of Harvard University Press, 1996). Cf. Sandel's statement: "If the global character of the economic suggests the need for transnational forms of governance, however, it remains to be seen whether such political units can inspire the identification and allegiance – the moral and civic culture – on which democratic authority ultimately depends" (Sandel, p. 399).

15 Nagel also argues that, for membership in a political society, "the engagement of the will that is essential to life inside a society . . . and the dual role each member plays both as one of the society's subjects and as one in whose name its authority is exercised," is paramount. "One might say that we are all participants in the general will . . . [A] sovereign state is not just a cooperative enterprise for mutual advantage" (Nagel, "The Problem of Global Justice," *Philosophy and Public Affairs* 33/2: 128). This aspect of Nagel's argument is quite compatible with the argument presented in section 5 of this article about democratic iterations. In each case, the *political* interpretation of rights through the practices and decisions of a self-governing community and the role of citizens as authors and subjects to

the law is emphasized. Where my analysis differs from Nagel's is that I see international human rights norms as enabling and not hindering democratic iterations, whereas Nagel either construes them too narrowly or sees the authority of international law, in general, as deriving from mere contractual obligations among states.

16 Nagel, ibid., p. 120.

17 Joshua Cohen and Charles Sabel, "Extra Republicam Nulla Justitia?," *Philosophy and Public Affairs* 34 (2006): 157–75; Thomas Pogge, *World Poverty and Human Rights: Cosmopolitan Responsibilities and Reforms* (Cambridge: Polity, 2003; reissued 2004); Thomas Pogge, ed., *Freedom from Poverty as a Human Right* (Oxford: Oxford University Press, 2007); see also Seyla Benhabib, *The Rights of Others*, concerning Rawls's inadequate sociological understanding of the political economy of the world society, pp. 97–105.

18 Exceptions are Jürgen Habermas, "The Postnational Constellation and the Future of Democracy," in *The Postnational Constellation: Political Essays*, ed. and trans. Max Pensky (Cambridge: Polity, 2001), pp. 58–112; Jürgen Habermas, *The Divided West*, trans. Ciaran Cronin (Cambridge: Polity, 2006); Jürgen Habermas, *Time of Transitions*, trans. Ciaran Cronin and Max Pensky (Cambridge, MA: MIT Press, 2006); for discussions of Habermas's recent writings on these matters, see Peter Niesen and Benjamin Herborth, eds, *Anarchie der kommunikativen Freiheit: Jürgen Habermas und die Theorie der internationalen Politik* (Frankfurt: Suhrkamp, 2007); William E. Scheuerman, "Global Governance without Global Government? Habermas on Postnational Democracy," *Political Theory* 36/1 (2008): 133–51. The pioneering work in this field was that of Daniele Archibugi and David Held, eds, *Cosmopolitan Democracy* (Cambridge: Polity, 1995); David Held, *Democracy and the Global Order* (Cambridge: Polity, 1995); Joshua Cohen and Charles F. Sabel, "Global Democracy," *International Law and Politics* 37 (2005): 763–97; and Daniele Archibugi, *The Global Commonwealth of Citizens: Toward Cosmopolitan Democracy* (Princeton, NJ, and Oxford: Princeton University Press, 2008).

19 For the first position, see Günther Teubner, "Global Bukovina," in G. Teubner, ed., *Global Law Without a State*, pp. 3–28; and, for the second, Anne-Marie Slaughter, *A New World Order*, both discussed in chapter 6 of this volume.

20 Cf. Michael Hardt and Antonio Negri, *Empire*. A more interesting version of the empire thesis has been recently provided by
James Tully, who names such cosmopolitan rights discourse "the
Trojan horse" of a neo-imperial order extending throughout the
globe. "The two cosmopolitan rights," writes James Tully,
harking back to the development of cosmopolitan discourse in
the eighteenth century, namely, "of the trading company to trade
and the voluntary organizations to convert – also fit together in
the same way as with the nation-state. The participatory right
to converse with and try to convert the natives complements the
primary right of commerce . . . From the perspective of non-
Western civilizations and of diverse citizenship, the two cosmopolitan rights appear as the Trojan horse of western imperialism"
(James Tully, "On Global Citizenship and Imperialism Today:
Two Ways of Thinking about Global Citizenship," Lecture presented at the Political Theory Workshop, Yale University, ISPS,
May 1, 2008). Tully develops a concept of "diverse citizenship"
in this essay, which he believes can serve as a counter-hegemonic
challenge to the modern-statist conception of citizenship. I would
argue that cosmopolitan norms, in the sense in which I develop
in this chapter, are also enabling conditions of diverse citizenship.
For a balanced assessment of the relationship between human
rights and the global economy that shies from facile causal gen-
eralizations, see David Kinley's statement: "The phenomenon of
human rights and the global economy are two of the most
prominent and influential features of international relations. Like
star actors sharing the same scene, they jostle for attention, try
to pull rank and sometimes undermine each other, all the while
knowing – if they are wise – that their best prospects for individual success lie with ensuring that the other succeeds too"
(*Civilizing Globalization: Human Rights and the Global
Economy* (Cambridge: Cambridge University Press, 2009), p. 1).
Written before the world economic downturn beginning in September 2008, this book may be a bit more sanguine than is due
about the prospects of the global economy. But the general thesis
still stands.

21 Jean L. Cohen, "A Global State of Emergency or the Further
Constitutionalization of International Law: A Pluralist
Approach," *Constellations: An International Journal of Critical
and Democratic Theory* 15/4 (fall 2008): 456–84; Kim Lane
Scheppele, "International State of Emergency: Challenges to
Constitutionalism After September 11," Yale Legal Theory

Workshop, September 21, 2006. According to this analysis, it is the creation of *an international emergency situation* primarily through the actions of the UN Security Council that must be heeded: "the seemingly arbitrary redefinition of domestic rights violations as a threat to international peace and security, and the selective imposition of debilitating sanctions, military invasions, and authoritarian occupation administrations by the SC or by states acting unilaterally ('coalition of the willing'), framed as 'enforcement' of the values of the international community, gave some of us pause. This discursive framework opened a Pandora's box, the import of which is becoming clear only now, in the third post 9/11 phase of the transformation of public international law" (Jean Cohen, "A Global State of Emergency or the Further Constitutionalization of International Law: A Pluralist Approach," p. 456). The member-states of the UN can neither oppose these measures, nor can they amend them, since the amendment rules place the UN Security Council out of their reach by endowing its members with special veto rights.

But there is now significant judicial opposition to the authority of the Security Council. In the much discussed cases of *Kadi* (C-402/05P) and *Al Barakaat* (C-415/05P), the judgment of the European Court of Justice of September 3, 2008, reversed the judgment of the European Court of First Instance. Through this decision, the ECJ annulled the relevant EC measures that implemented the Security Council's Chapter VII resolution, blacklisting certain individuals as supporters of terrorism and freezing their assets. This case was all the more fascinating since, in earlier instances, the European Court of Human Rights had complied with the UN Security Council measures. Cf. *Behrami and Saramati* v. *France, Norway and Germany*; judgment of the European Court of Human Rights of May 2, 2007 (Appl 71412/01, 71412/01 and 78166/01). The European Court of the First Instance followed this precedent and upheld the European Council decisions regarding the freezing of the assets of Mr Kadi and Al Barakaat. Cf. Court of First Instance Case T- 315/01, *Kadi* v. *Council and Commission* (2005), and Court of First Instance Case T-306/02, *Yusuf and al Barakaat International Foundation* v. *Council and Commission* (2005). For a provocative discussion which views this case as a paradigmatic "conflict of norms" in the pluralist global legal order, see Grainne de Burca, "The European Court of Justice and the International

Legal Order After Kadi," Fordham Legal Studies Research Paper No. 1321313; *Harvard International Law Journal* 1/51 (winter 2010): 1–50.

22 Mahmood Mamdani, "The New Humanitarian Order," *The Nation* 287/9 (September 29, 2008): 18, and Mahmood Mamdani, *Saviors and Survivors: Darfur, Politics, and the War on Terror* (New York: Pantheon Books, 2009). For a recent contribution along the same lines by an author who hardly shares Mamdani's politics, see Eric A. Posner, *The Perils of Global Legalism* (Chicago, IL: University of Chicago Press, 2009).

23 Mahmood Mamdani, "The New Humanitarian Order," p. 18.

24 Karl Marx, "The *Grundrisse*," in Robert C. Tucker, ed., The *Marx-Engels Reader*, 2nd edn (New York: W.W. Norton , 1978), pp. 238–44.

25 Upon the initiative of the then UN General Secretary, Kofi Annan, a Special Report of the International Commission on Intervention and State Sovereignty was issued in 2001. Called "The Responsibility to Protect," the report maintains: "The idea that sovereign states have a responsibility to protect their own citizens from avoidable catastrophe, but that when they are unwilling or unable to do so, that responsibility must be borne by the broader community of states. We hope very much that the report will break new ground in a way that helps generate a new international consensus on these issues." Of course, the sensitive question is who and how the process of states' being "unwilling or unable to do so" will be interpreted. The Report has not been adopted by the General Assembly and does not have the status of international law. Cf. <http://www.iciss.ca/pdf/ Commission-Report.pdf>, accessed on June 22, 2009.

26 Seth Mydans, "Myanmar Faces Pressure to Allow Major Aid Effort," *New York Times* (May 8, 2008); <http://www.nytimes. com/2008/05/08/world/asia/08iht-08myanmar.12682654. html>; and Robert Kaplan, "Aid at the Point of a Gun," *New York Times* (May 14, 2008), Op-Ed: *<www.nytimes. com/2008/05/14/opinion/ 14kaplan.html>*.

27 Jean Cohen's concerns are motivated by an internal critique of the extra-legal powers that the UN Security Council is usurping for itself and not by a rejection of the "constitutionalization of public law," which she characterizes "as a feasible, albeit diffi- cult to obtain, utopia" (Cohen, "Constitutionalization of Inter- national Law," p. 467).

NOTES AND REFERENCES TO PAGES 123–124

28 Nagel, "The Problem of Global Justice," p. 114; see also Haber-mas's comments on Nagel's article, in "The Constitutionaliza-tion of International Law and the Legitimacy Problems of a Constitution for a World Society," in *Constellations: An Inter-national Journal of Critical and Democratic Theory* 15/4 (December 2008): 444–55; on human rights, see pp. 445 and 447, in particular. I should add that under internationally valid human rights Nagel only includes "negative rights like bodily inviolability, freedom of expression and freedom of religion" (Nagel, "The Problem of Global Justice," p. 152). See also ch.5, n.3, above.

29 Habermas, "The Constitutionalization of International Law," ibid., pp. 448–9.

30 Ibid., p. 449.

31 For a powerful elucidation of the transformation of interna-tional law in the post-World War II period, and the emergence of the individual as subject of international law through deci-sions of the Permanent Court of International Justice and the Charter of the United Nations, see Hersch Lauterpacht, *Inter-national Law and Human Rights*, with an Introduction by Isodore Silver, The Garland Library of War and Peace (New York: Garland Publishing, Inc., 1973). Lauterpacht writes: "Moreover, irrespective of the question of enforcement, there ought to be no doubt that the provisions of the Charter in the matter of fundamental human rights impose upon the Members of the United Nations a *legal* duty to respect them" (p. 34).

32 Debates about the status of the Universal Declaration of Human Rights – whether it is binding law, and, if so, how it is to be enforced; whether it is a mere declaration with moral-hortatory intent alone – have accompanied it from the start. In "The Strange Triumph of Human Rights, 1933–1950," the historian Mark Mazower gives a very good account of why the superpow-ers, and in particular the United States and Great Britain, asserted "domestic jurisdiction," and made sure that "the human rights provisions of the UN Charter would not be automatically appli-cable at home." They eventually agreed to the UDHR only because "it was a declaration," and not "a covenant" (Mark Mazower, "The Strange Triumph of Human Rights," *The His-torical Journal* 47/2 (2004): 379–98; here pp. 393 and 395). Internationalist jurists such as Hersch Lauterpacht and Hans Kelsen, however, were dismayed very early on that neither the Universal Declaration nor the rights clauses within the UN

Charter made provisions for a court with the authority to adjudicate on rights' violations, nor allowed the right of petition. See Hersch Lauterpacht, *International Law and Human Rights*, pp. 286 ff.; Hans Kelsen, "The Preamble of the Charter – a Critical Analysis," *Journal of Politics* 8 (1946): 134–59.

Yet, taken together, the institution of the UN Charter, the UDHR and the Genocide Convention of 1948, had the cumulative effect of opening the floodgates to petitions from around the world, complaining about human rights violations, race discrimination, and the like. The most well-known of these petitions was presented by W. E. B. du Bois on behalf of the NAACP, detailing the history of racial discrimination in the USA. The "father" of the Genocide Convention, Ralph Lemkin, was dismayed at this and claimed that it was a Russian ploy to diplomatically embarrass the US. See chapter 3 above. The jurisgenerative effect of these declarations, charters, and covenants far exceeds their legal intentions, unleashing a moral surge toward their legalization in various domestic jurisdictions. Even a cautious observer, such as Mark Mazower, concedes this point and argues that analyzing these documents, compendia, and so on, is not neutral; they continue the hope that "moral aspirations might come themselves to be regarded as the source of law" (Mazower, ibid., p. 397).

33 Universal Declaration on Human Rights, G.A. res. 217A (III) (December 10, 1948); hereinafter, "UDHR".

34 Convention relating to the Status of Refugees, G.A. res. 429 (V) (entered into force April 22, 1954).

35 International Covenant on Civil and Political Rights, G.A. res. 2200A (XXI), 21 U.N. GAOR Supp. (No. 16) at 52, U.N. Doc. A/6316 (1966), 999 U.N.T.S. 171 (entered into force March 23, 1976).

36 International Covenant on Economic, Social and Cultural Rights, G.A. res. 2200A (XXI), 21 U.N.GAOR Supp (No. 16) at 49, U.N. Doc. A/6316 (1966), 993 U.N.T.S. 3 (entered into force January 3, 1976).

37 The Convention to Eliminate All Forms of Discrimination Against Women, United Nations, General Assembly Resolution 34/180, December 18, 1979 (entered into force, September 3, 1981), available at: <http://www.un.org/womenwatch/ daw/ cedaw/econvention.htm> (hereinafter, "CEDAW"). These provisions are, of course, augmented by many others, such as the International Convention on the Elimination of All Forms of

Racial Discrimination, by General Assembly resolution 2106 (XX) of 21 December, 1965 (entered into force 4 January, 1969, in accordance with Article 19), available at: <http://www2. ohchr.org/english/law/cerd.htm>; Convention of the Rights of the Child, G.A. res. 44/25, November 20, 1989 (entered into force, September 2, 1990). See also, Declaration on the Human Rights of Individuals Who are not Nationals of the Country in which They Live, G.A. res. 40/144, annex, 40 U.N. GAOR Supp. (No. 53) at 252, U.N. Doc. A/40/53 (1985) (providing such "aliens" with rights to leave, liberty of movement within a country, as well as to have their spouses and minor children of legal aliens be admitted to join and stay with them, and to protect them from expulsion by requiring opportunities for hearings and for decision-making not predicated on discrimination based on "race, colour, religion, culture, descent or national or ethnic origin"); Convention on the Reduction of Statelessness, 989 U.N.T.S. 175, (December 13, 1975) (requiring that nations grant nationality rights, under certain conditions, to "persons born in its territory who would otherwise be stateless"); Migration for Employment (Revised) (ILO No. 97), 120 U.N.T.S. 70 (January 22, 1952) (providing that members of the ILO make work policy and migration policies known and treat fairly "migrants for employment"); Declaration on Territorial Asylum, G.A. res. 2312 (XXII), 22 U.N. GAOR Supp. (No. 16) at 81, U.N. Doc. A/6716 (1967).

38 I define *moral cosmopolitanism* as a position that espouses a universalistic morality that considers each individual as being worthy of equal moral concern and respect. *Cultural cosmopolitanism* emphasizes that all cultures learn and borrow from one another and that they form a dizzying multiplicity, variety, and incongruity. *Legal cosmopolitanism* is distinct from both positions. While sharing with moral cosmopolitanism the view that each person deserves equal moral respect and concern, on the question as to whether universalistic obligations always trump particularistic ones owed to kin and clan, the legal cosmopolitan is agnostic. For these definitions and further elaboration, see Seyla Benhabib, "The Legitimacy of Human Rights," *Daedalus: Journal of the American Academy of Arts and Sciences* 137/3 (summer 2008): 94–104; here, 97.

39 See Robert Cover, "Foreword: Nomos and Narrative," The Supreme Court 1982 Term, *Harvard Law Review* 97/4 (1983/84): 4–68.

40 Robert Cover, "Foreword: *Nomos* and Narrative," p. 18.

41 This, of course, is the crucial insight of H. L. A. Hart's work; cf. *The Concept of Law*, Clarendon Law Series (Oxford: Oxford University Press [1961]; this edn 1997), pp. 79–100.

42 Let me clarify that my reliance on Cover's concept of jurisgenerativity does not mean that I minimize or disregard the "legal origins of legitimacy"; jurisgenerativity is not a process of *law-making but one of law-interpreting*, or, properly speaking, it is about the interplay of legal and non-legal sources of normativity. I do not share Cover's claim that "Interpretation always takes place in the shadow of coercion . . . *Courts, at least the courts of the state, are characteristically 'jurispathic'*" (Cover, "Nomos and Narrative," p. 40 (emphasis mine)). While the state and the courts undoubtedly seek to control "the circulation of meaning," the courts' relationship to processes of norm interpretation and meaning-generation can be more creative and fluid than suggested here. For Cover, "redemptive constitutionalism" (33) originates with "*nomoi* communities" and social movements, but rarely with formal institutions. What I am trying to develop is a more complex understanding of legal process, social movements, and transnational actors than Cover offered us.

43 Jacques Derrida, "The Force of Law: The 'Mystical Foundation of Authority,'" in *Cardozo Law Review* 11/919 (1989–90): 920–1046, bilingual text, trans. Mary Quaintance.

44 For a more empirical perspective, see Margaret E. Kick and Kathryn Sikkink, *Activists Beyond Border* (Ithaca, NY: Cornell University Press, 1998); Thomas Risse, Steven Rapp, and Katryn Sikkink, *The Power of Human Rights: International Norms and Domestic Change* (Cambridge: Cambridge University Press, 1999); Beth Simmons, *Mobilizing for Human Rights: International Law in Domestic Politics* (Cambridge: Cambridge University Press, 2009).

45 See the classical essay by Ronald Dworkin, "Taking Rights Seriously" (1970), in *Taking Rights Seriously*, pp. 184ff. But it is important to add Habermas's caveat here as well: "Hence we must not understand basic rights or *Grundrechte*, which take the shape of constitutional norms, as mere imitations of moral rights, and we must not take political autonomy to be a mere copy of moral autonomy. Rather, norms of action *branch out* into moral and legal rules" (Jürgen Habermas, *Between Facts and Norms: Contributions to a Discourse Theory of Law and*

Democracy, trans. William Regh (Cambridge: Polity, 1996), p. 107).

46 In *A Theory of Justice,* Rawls invokes H. L. A. Hart's discussion in *The Concept of Law* to introduce this distinction. See John Rawls, *A Theory of Justice* (Cambridge, MA: Harvard University Press, 1971), here p. 5, and H. L. A. Hart, *The Concept of Law* (Oxford: Clarendon Press, 1975 [1961]), pp. 155–9. My usage of these terms is more kindred to Dworkin's as cited in n.47 of this chapter, below. Many thanks to the late Ed Baker for clarifying some of the intertextual issues involved here.

47 Dworkin, "Constitutional Cases," in *Taking Rights Seriously,* pp. 131–49; here pp. 134 ff.

48 Since I consider individuals as "generalized" and as "concrete" others, taking into account their embodiment, the protection of the bodily integrity of persons, and their immunity from sexual harassment and assault is an important human right. It is not only heterosexual women who are subject to sexual violence; many gay men and lesbians are too; however, because of their capacity to become pregnant, forced and arbitrary violence against women affects their personhood and capacities for communicative freedom differently from gay men. The important point is to keep in view the different kinds of violence that one can be subject to as a result of sexual difference and to incorporate this into our understanding of human rights. Many governments, including the USA and Canada, now recognize and grant as legitimate, requests for asylum for women escaping Female Genital Mutilation.

49 As has been discussed in chapter 4, there are differences between discourse theorists such as myself and Rainer Forst who justify human rights philosophically on the basis of the presuppositions of "speech-immanent" commitments, and Rawlsians such as Joshua Cohen and Kenneth Baynes who prefer to see human rights as elements of a "political conception" of global justice and reason. See Rainer Forst, "The Basic Right to Justification: Toward a Constructivist Conception of Human Rights," *Constellations* 6/1 (1999): 35–60; R. Forst, "The Justification of Human Rights and the Basic Right to Justification: A Reflexive Approach," *Ethics* 120/4 (2010): 711–40. For a helpful overview of these positions and clarifications of the philosophical stakes, see Kenneth Baynes, "Discourse Ethics and the Political Conception of Human Rights," *Ethics and Global Politics* (2009): DOI: 10.3402/egp.v2il.1938.

50   Seyla Benhabib, *The Claims of Culture: Equality and Diversity in the Global Era*, pp. 154–68.
51   Title IX, Education Amendments of 1972, 20 U.S.C. §§ 1681–8 (1972); at: <http://www.justice.gov/crt/cor/coord/titleixstat.php>; accessed on December 1, 2010.
52   I owe this formulation to Habermas's thesis of the co-originality of public and private autonomy. See J. Habermas, *Between Facts and Norms*, pp. 84–104. The final sentence refers, of course, to Kant's famous formula that "Thoughts without concepts are empty, intuitions without concepts are blind." See Immanuel Kant, *Critique of Pure Reason*, unabridged edn., trans. Norman Kemp Smith (New York: St Martin's Press, 1965), p. 93. Although I am indebted to Habermas's general discussions of the relationship between public and private autonomy and his analysis of the discursive legitimation of law, I do not follow his "discourse-theoretic deduction of basic rights." Habermas claims that "One begins by applying the discourse principle to the general rights to liberties – a right constitutive for the legal form as such – and ends by legally institutionalizing the conditions for a discursive exercise of political autonomy" (ibid., p. 121), "This 'deduction' – if we can call it such – yields a classification of basic rights into five groups: rights concerning individual liberties; rights concerning the status of membership in a voluntary association; rights to the legal protection of the individual; basic rights in which citizens exercise political autonomy and basic rights to the provision of living conditions (social, technological, and ecologically safeguarded . . ." (ibid., pp. 122–3). I don't quite see how one can get at this classification of rights from the introduction of the "discourse principle" together with the "legal form" to yield the idea of democracy. We seem to have already presupposed what democracy means and what democratic citizenship entails by way of basic rights. In addition to the circularity of the process of deduction (which Habermas admits, ibid., p. 122), there is also the problem that this reconstruction of the "logical genesis of rights" takes the teeth out of the experience of social struggles in history. It is simply not the case that democracy, as a historical institution, always and necessarily presupposes the classification of rights postulated here; nor is it the case that every legal system, which we may be ready to consider legitimate, would need to be subject to this kind classification. I think that Habermas is seeking to minimize the conceptual as well as historical indeterminacy of the experience of democracy,

263

by trying to harmonize the liberal conception of individual rights with that of the republican understanding of citizens' rights. The "co-originality" of public and private autonomy must not be interpreted as if it were a guaranteed historical necessity but rather as a critique of the individualistic, natural right construction of rights, which places the holder of rights "outside" the polity. But beyond this valid point, one should not minimize the potential conflict between the claims of private and public autonomy. See my review of Habermas's *Between Facts and Norms*, in the *American Political Science Review* 91/3 (1997): 725-6.

53   Cf. Jacques Derrida, "Signature Event Context," in *Limited, Inc.* (Evanston, IL: Northwestern University Press, 1988), pp. 1-24.

54   Jürgen Habermas, *Between Facts and Norms*, p. 110.

55   Habermas, ibid., p. 123.

56   Robert Post, "Theorizing Disagreement: Re-conceiving the Relationship Between Law and Politics, *California Law Review* 98/4 (2010): 1319-50. See also the concept of "democratic constitutionalism," developed by Robert Post and Reva B. Siegel, "Roe Rage: Democratic Constitutionalism and Backlash," *Harvard Civil Rights and Civil Liberties Review* 42 (2007): 373-434.

57   Post, "Theorizing Disagreement," p. 1347.

58   I am much indebted to the following formulation by David Owen who redescribes such processes of contextualization in terms of "the inseparability of justification and application, namely, that while the rule/norm can't be reduced to, or exhaustively specified by, any range of particular cases, you don't know what the rule/norm is independently of its exercise in a range of particular cases. So assenting to a law requires incorporating in the practical reasoning process attention to 'standard' cases but then the justification of the norm is always raised anew by new cases" (personal communication to the author during our stay in June-July 2010 at the Forschungskolleg Humanwissenschaften, Bad-Homburg).

59   Sally Engle Merry, *Human Rights and Gender Violence: Translating International Law into Local Justice* (Chicago, IL: University of Chicago Press, 2006), cf. chapter 5, "Legal Transplants and Cultural Translation: Making Human Rights in the Vernacular," pp. 134.

60   It is common to state practice to place "RUDs" – Reservations, Understandings, and Declarations – on various treaties to blunt contradictions that may exist between existing state practices

and treaty provisions and expectations. But see n.9 of this chapter, above, for the impact of treaty ratification on domestic actors and institutions.

61 Harold Koh, "Why Do Nations Obey International Law?," Review Essay, *The Yale Law Journal* 106/8 (June 1997): 2599–2659; here 2626–7.

62 "This Constitution, and the Laws of the United States which shall be made in Pursuance thereof; and all Treaties made, or which shall be made, under the Authority of the United States, shall be the supreme Law of the Land; and the Judges in every State shall be bound thereby, any Thing in the Constitution or Laws of any State to the Contrary notwithstanding" (Article VI, United States Constitution on "Debts, Supremacy, Oaths").

63 That critique has been made more generally about many forms of international law. See Martti Koskenniemi, *The Gentle Civilizer of Nations: The Rise and Fall of International Law 1870–1960* (Cambridge: Cambridge University Press, 2001).

64 See Judith Resnik, "Law's Migration: American Exceptionalism, Silent Dialogues, and Federalism's Multiple Ports of Entry," *The Yale Law Journal* 15/7 (2006): 1564–1670; Judith Resnik, "Law as Affiliation: 'Foreign' Law, Democratic Federalism, and the Sovereigntism of the Nation-State," *International Journal of Constitutional Law* 6/1 (2008): 33–66; Judith Resnik, "Categorical Federalism: Jurisdiction, Gender, and the Globe," *Yale Law Journal* 111 (2001): 619–80. Lauterpacht also claimed that "duly ratified treaties are a self-executing part of municipal law"; and "that the Constitution of the US, gives Congress the right to define and punish, *inter alia*, 'offenses against the law of nations'," in Article 1, Section 8, Clause 10, Lauterpacht, *International Law and Human Rights*, pp. 28 and 39 respectively. See Lauterpacht's discussion of the *Oyama* v. *California* (1948), 332 U.S., 633, according to which the concurring opinion of four justice of the Supreme Court relied upon "the provisions of the [UN] Charter in the matter of human rights . . . as a source of legal obligations" (Lauterpacht, ibid., p. 151, fn. 12).

65 See, for example, the case of Saudi Arabia, which, despite ratifying CEDAW and the Convention on the Rights of the Child, has made general reservations to the effect that where there is a conflict between a Convention Article and Islamic law principles, Islamic law shall have precedence. Nevertheless, international standards have started impacting the legal judgments of Saudi judges. Zainah Almihdar, "Human Rights of Women and

Children under the Islamic Law of Personal Status and its Application in Saudi Arabia," in *Muslim World Journal of Human Rights* 5/1 (2008); the Berkeley Electronic Press, pp. 1–15, at: <http://www.bepress.com/mwjhr/>.

66 See Gerald Neuman, "Human Rights and Constitutional Rights: Harmony and Dissonance," *Stanford Law Review* 55/5 (May 2003): 1863–1901.

67 Valentine Moghadam, "Global Feminism, Citizenship, and the State," in Seyla Benhabib and Judith Resnik, eds, *Migrations and Mobilities: Citizenship, Borders, and Gender* (New York: New York University Press, 2009), pp. 255–76.

68 See Judith Resnik, "Procedure as Contract," *Notre Dame Law Review* 80 (2005): 593.

69 Audrey Macklin, "Particularized Citizenship: Encultured Women and the Public Sphere," in Seyla Benhabib and Judith Resnik, eds, *Migrations and Mobilities*, pp. 276–304.

70 Ibid., p. 286.

71 On decent hierarchical peoples, see John Rawls, *The Law of Peoples*, pp. 62–79.

CHAPTER 8 DEMOCRATIC EXCLUSIONS AND DEMOCRATIC ITERATIONS: DILEMMAS OF JUST MEMBERSHIP AND PROSPECTS OF COSMOPOLITAN FEDERALISM

1 For one of the earliest statements, see Michael Walzer, *Spheres of Justice: A Defense of Pluralism and Equality* (New York: Basic Books, 1983); among early influential statements are: Rainer Bauböck, *Transnational Citizenship: Membership and Rights in International Migration* (Cheltenhaim: Edward Elgar, 1994), and Joe Carens, "Aliens and Citizens: The Case for Open Borders," in Ronald Beiner, ed., *Theorizing Citizenship* (Albany, NY: SUNY Press, 1995), pp. 229–55; cf. also Philip Cole, *Philosophies of Exclusion: Liberal Political Theory and Immigration* (Edinburgh: Edinburgh University Press, 2000).

2 Angelia Means, "*The Rights of Others*," in *European Journal of Political Theory* 6/4 (October 2007): 406–23. This issue of the journal will be abbreviated as *EJPT* in this chapter. All page references are to this issue.

3 Rainer Bauböck, "*The Rights of Others* and the Boundaries of Democracy," in *EJPT*, pp. 398–406; here p. 400.

4 See also Jeremy Bendik-Keymer's comments on *The Rights of Others*, "Why Can't Democracies be Universal? How Do

Democracies Resolve Disagreement Over Citizenship?," *Social Philosophy Today* 22 (2006): 233–8, delivered during the Annual Meeting of the North American Society for Social Philosophy and published as a symposium in *Social Philosophy Today* with my Reply, "Democratic Boundaries and Economic Citizenship. Enhancing the 'Rights of Others'," pp. 249–60.

5 David Jacobson, *Rights Across Borders: Immigration and the Decline of Citizenship* (Baltimore and London: Johns Hopkins University Press, 1997). Angelia Means writes of "political liberalism's principle of closure," by which she means the work of John Rawls. But as Rawls's many statements in *The Law of Peoples* make clear, his position is situated somewhat ambivalently between the communitarian and civic republican ones. At various times, he uses both sets of arguments – the ones about cultural community as well as the ones about the nature of citizenship – to justify closure (John Rawls, *The Law of Peoples*, p. 39, note).

6 Thomas Hobbes, *Leviathan* (1651), ed. with Introduction and Notes by Edwin Curly (Indianapolis, IN: Hackett Publishing, 1994), ch. xvi.

7 Means's question has two parts: first, *how much* immigration and, second, *what kind* of immigration? I deal with some of the issues of the cultural integration of Muslim migrants to Europe in chapter 9.

8 See Stephen Holmes, "Precommitment and the Paradox of Democracy," in Jon Elster and Rune Slagsted, eds, *Constitutionalism and Democracy* (Cambridge: Cambridge University Press, 1988), pp. 195–240; see also Jon Elster, *Ulysses Unbound: Studies in Rationality, Precommitment, and Constraints* (Cambridge: Cambridge University Press, 2000). There are different ways of characterizing the problem of closure. The best-known statements are: Frederick G. Whelan, "Prologue: Democratic Theory and the Boundary Problem," in J. R. Pennock and J. W. Chapman, eds, *Nomos XXV: Liberal Democracy* (New York: New York University Press, 1983), pp. 13–47; Robert Dahl, *Democracy and its Critics* (New Haven, CT: Yale University Press, 1989), pp. 119–31. Robert E. Goodin prefers to call it "constituting the demos," which is close to my terminology. But as I will explicate below, our arguments point in quite different directions. See Robert E. Goodin, "Enfranchising All Affected Interests, and its Alternatives," *Philosophy and Public Affairs* 35/1 (2007): 40–68.

9   Nancy Fraser writes: "Thus, instead of throwing up our hands in the face of a logical paradox, we should try to envision ways to finesse it, by imagining institutional arrangements for resolving such arguments democratically" (*Reframing Justice, Spinoza Lectures* (Van Gorcum: University of Amsterdam, 2005), p. 33). Certainly, my concept of democratic iterations envisages precisely such discursive processes of critically examining and adjusting what Fraser calls "the frame of justice claims." However, since justifying the "who" involved in discussing justice claims will confront us anew with each *new* frame of justice, there will always be some who are included and others who are excluded. This paradox will not go away even if the "how" of the discussions, the procedures for inclusion and exclusion are altered, and rendered more reflexive, as Fraser wishes them to be. While I agree with Fraser that such a process of reflexive adjustment of the frame of justice is necessary, I have also clarified above that there can be no conclusive solutions to questions of inclusions and exclusion but only ever more contested processes of adjustment through what Fraser calls "good enough deliberation." See Nancy Fraser, "Two Dogmas of Egalitarianism," in *Scales of Justice: Reimagining Political Space in a Globalizing World* (New York: Columbia University Press, 2009) p. 45.

10 Arizona Senate Bill 1070 (SB1070), enacted April 23, 2010, at: <http://www.azleg.gov/legtext/49leg/2r/bills/sb1070s.pdf>.

11 As reported by Randal C. Archibold, "Judge Blocks Arizona's Immigration Law," *New York Times* (July 28, 2010): <http://www.nytimes.com/2010/07/29/us/29arizona.html>.

12 I will introduce some qualifications in the final section of this chapter about the concept of "all affected interests," and make more precise how I understand it. The difficulties of this term were not that clear to me at the time of the original publication of this article in 2007, though, as I explain below, I had misgivings about Habermas's use of "the all affected principle" in his formulation of "universalizability" as early as 1992. See n.46 below.

13 See the moving account of immigrant activism in Corey Robin's review of *The Rights of Others*. "The point was brought home to me one Saturday night eight years ago," writes Robin, "when I was organizing in Los Angeles around several items on the ballot . . . Walking door to door with a Spanish-speaking hotel worker from Guatemala, I listened to her explain to

her neighbors the ins an outs of American electoral law, the powers of local versus state governments and the US Constitution. The irony was not lost on me. Not only do immigrants deepen democracy; they sometimes understand its substance and procedures better than its native proponents do" (Corey Robin, "Strangers in the Land," *The Nation* (April 10, 2006), p. 31).

14 Alexander Aleinikoff, "Comments on the *Rights of Others*," *EJPT*, pp. 424–31.

15 The clearest formulation of the nature of the hermeneutic circle is still Hans-Georg Gadamer, Garrett Barden, and John Cumming, eds, *Truth and Method* (New York: The Seabury Press, 1975). Originally published as *Wahrheit und Methode* (Tübingen: J.C.B. Mohr, 1960).

16 The question may seem silly to the point of irrelevance. But it is not. The moral point of view obliges us to consider every other as a human being – as a generalized and a concrete other – and not as an enemy. All anti-war and peace movements have as their premise that what unites us as human beings is far more important and far deeper than what divides us as members of nations. This is not a blanket defense of pacifism; if we treat the "other" as a conversation partner rather than as an enemy, we may be able to activate our political imagination and move beyond resorting to state violence. Collective and peaceful movements of peoples such as those of Gandhi in India and Solidarnoŝć in Poland have brought down empires. The task of political philosophy is to deepen our commitments to such normative principles while extending our imagination; we are not the messengers of states and of their myopic vision of the political. See Jonathan Schell, *The Unconquerable World: Power, Nonviolence and the Will of the People* (New York: Henry Holt and Company, 2003).

17 See again the rigorous objections by Corey Robin, in "Strangers in the Land," p. 32. See my discussion of this issue, in *The Rights of Others*, p. 142, fn. 3.

18 I agree with Rainer Bauböck – one of the few scholars in the literature who distinguishes between immigration as a freedom right and matters of redistributive justice – when he writes: "Would open borders lead to an international redistribution of wealth that benefits the globally worst off, or would such a policy instead merely enhance inequalities within each society and leave immobile populations in developing countries even

worse off? . . . Would liberal welfare states be undermined by an open door policy or could they be sustained through effective internal controls of employment standards?" (Rainer Bauböck, "Global Justice, Freedom of Movement and Democratic Citizenship," *Archives Européennes de Sociologie* L/1 (2009): 1–31; here 4).

19 See Joel P. Trachtman, *The International Law of Economic Migrations: Toward the Fourth Freedom* (Michigan, MI: W. E. Upjohn Institute for Employment Research, 2009).

20 To some, this language requirement may seem like a nationalist stipulation which asks the immigrant to deny her original language. What I am defending is not mono-lingualism but pluri-lingualism. I envisage migrants being competent in the language of their host country as well as their own and exercising both freely. The equal right to membership imposes an obligation on the host country to offer subsidized and free language classes to all who wish to naturalize. This is not linguistic nationalism but a plea for polyglotism, coupled with a social realism in recognizing that not mastering the language of the host country marginalizes the newcomer and diminishes his/her chance of successful employment and integration. Of course, in many regions such as the Quebec province in Canada and Cataluna in Spain, there is more than one officially recognized language. Immigrants then should be able to demonstrate competence in one or the other official languages and should not be forced to choose between *one or the other* (as is the case, for example, with migrants from Francophone countries to Quebec, who are forbidden to naturalize via showing English language competence). There are also other cases when the nature of immigration into a particular country might reveal the necessity for multi-lingualism in that country and for acknowledging the presence of more than one official language. This is the current status of Spanish in the USA, which, for all practical purposes, in vast regions of the land, has become the (quasi-) official language.

21 On the absence of international regulations on citizenship norms, see Peter Spiro, *Beyond Citizenship: American Identity after Globalization* (Oxford: Oxford University Press, 2008), and on harmonization attempts within the EU, see Marc Moje Howard, *The Politics of Citizenship in Europe* (Cambridge: Cambridge University Press, 2009).

22 Corey Robin, "Strangers in the Land," *The Nation* 282/14 (April 10, 2006): 28–33. Robin writes, "It's ironic that a regime

implementing Benhabib's criteria of 'marketable skills' could prove more restrictive than the United States that allowed my grandfather into this country a century ago" (p. 32). This is a misunderstanding as I explain in the text.

23 Saskia Sassen, *The Mobility of Labor and Capital: A Study in International Investment and Labor Flow* (Cambridge: Cambridge University Press, 1988); Saskia Sassen, *Losing Control? Sovereignty in an Age of Globalization* (New York: Columbia University Press, 1996).

24 See my article, "Israel's Stalemate," at <www.resetdoc.org> for further discussions of Israel's citizenship and naturalization policies.

25 See Thomas Pogge, *World Poverty and Human Rights: Cosmopolitan Responsibilities and Reforms* (Cambridge: Polity, 2002), on the "global resource dividend."

26 This objection was first raised by Bonnie Honig in her response to my Tanner Lectures held at the University of California in Berkeley in March 2004. See Bonnie Honig, "New Facts, Old Norms. Response to Benhabib's 'Reclaiming Universalism'" (on file with the author). This response was revised and reprinted as "Another Cosmopolitanism? Law and Politics in the New Europe," in Seyla Benhabib, *Another Cosmopolitanism*, pp.102–27.

27 For an earlier statement of my position, see Seyla Benhabib, "Deliberative Rationality and Models of Democratic Legitimacy," *Constellations: A Journal of Critical and Democratic Theory* 1/1 (April 1994): 25–53; revised and expanded version: Seyla Benhabib, "Toward A Deliberative Model of Democratic Legitimacy," in Benhabib, ed., *Democracy and Difference: Contesting the Boundaries of the Political* (Princeton, NJ: Princeton University Press, 1996), pp. 67–94. Nancy Fraser asks whether democratic iterations may not be "populist," perhaps idealizing or romanticizing the deliberative capacities of the *demos*, in "Abnormal Justice," *Scales of Justice: Reimagining Political Space in a Globalizing World* (New York: Columbia University Press, 2009), p. 189, fn. 34. Insofar as democratic iterations need to fulfill conditions of practical discourses to be called democratic at all, and since democracy in my view is not identified with simple majority rule, the charge of populism is unfounded.

28 Cf. Seyla Benhabib, *Situating the Self: Gender, Community and Postmodernism*, pp. 23–67.

271

29 See Ian Shapiro, *Democratic Justice* (New Haven, CT: Yale University Press, 1999).
30 Robert Cover, "*Nomos* and Narrative," *Harvard Law Review* 97/1 (1983): 4–68; Frank Michelman, "Law's Republic," *Yale Law Journal* 97/8 (1988): 1493–1537. Aleinikoff and Sassen both point to the affinity between the concept of "democratic iterations" and Harold Koh's "transnational processes." See pp. 131ff, for my discussion of Koh.
31 As I have discussed above (ch. 7, n.39). Robert Cover sees formal institutions such as the courts as being principal sources of such "jurispathy" (Cover, "Nomos and Narrative," p. 40). For Cover, "redemptive constitutionalism" (ibid., p. 33) originates with "nomoi communities" and social movements but rarely with formal institutions. The politics of human rights in the last three decades across the globe belies this. In chapter 5 of *The Rights of Others*, I have attempted to develop the more complex interplay between courts, social movements, and the public sphere. See *The Rights of Others*, 182–209, and chapter 9 of this volume, "The Return of Political Theology. The Scarf Affair in Comparative Constitutional Perspective in France, Germany, and Turkey."
32 Thomas Franck, *Fairness in International Law and Institutions* (Oxford: Clarendon Press, 1995), p. 24.
33 Saskia Sassen, "Response," *EJPT*, pp. 431–45; here p. 435.
34 Sassen, "Response," p. 436.
35 In the context of discussing the EU's evolving jurisprudence in matters of immigration, Sassen cites some new literature on the transfer of coordination of immigration policy from the third pillar of the EU (subject to member-states' authority and the method of open coordination) to the first pillar (governed by EU community law). With the enactment of the Amsterdam Treaty as binding as of May 1, 2004, immigration legislation by individual member-states was subject to the unanimous decision of the ministers of the European Council. The sovereignty of member-states had indeed been reduced but not eliminated; and it was up to each individual state to decide how many migrants, refugees, and asylum seekers it was willing to admit within its borders. Furthermore, with the European Commission's Directive 109, which came into force in February 2004, the concept of "civic citizenship" was enacted for members of third-country nationals. According to this directive, third-country nationals can acquire the status of "long-term residency" after five years

in their host countries, and it was recommended that they be entitled to a "bundle of rights and duties" commensurate with those of citizens and across national borders.

Some of these developments took place after the publication of *The Rights of Others*, but the criticisms I voiced of the then prevailing EU policy pointed clearly toward the necessity of a "civic citizenship" status for third-country nationals, and I am delighted that official EU policy is now more consonant with these normative considerations. See pp. 150–2.

The "Treaty of Lisbon Amending the Treaty on European Union and the Treaty establishing the European Community," the TFEU (see: <http://eur-lex.europa.eu/LexUriServ/LexUriServ.do?uri=OJ:C:2007:306:0001:0010:EN:PDF>; accessed on August 31, 2010) introduced further modifications into the EU's immigration, asylum, and third-country nationals' policy. The most important change is that it transformed the "three pillar model" of previous legal frameworks into one "tree model." Since the implementation of the Treaty of Lisbon, all regulations regarding migration, asylum, and integration are decided via a "co-decision" between the European Parliament and the Council. Within the Council, specific acts of common policy regarding the integrated management of external borders, common policy on visas and short-stay residence permits, and conditions under which nationals of third countries have the freedom to travel within the Union for short periods (Article 77) can be adopted via a qualified majority rule. Article 78 states that the Union shall develop a common policy on asylum, and a uniform status of asylum, valid throughout the Union. Article 79 entitles the Union to develop a common immigration policy, but this Article does not affect "the right of member states to determine the volumes of admission of third-country nationals coming to their territory in order to seek work, whether employed or self-employed."

36 See Giorgio Agamben, *Homo Sacer: Sovereign Power and Bare Life*, trans. Daniel Heller-Roazen (Minneapolis, MN: University of Minnesota Press, 1998); Giorgio Agamben, *State of Exception*, trans. Kevin Attell (Chicago, IL, and London: University of Chicago Press, 2005).

37 See Robert F. Goodin, "Enfranchising All Affected Interests, and its Alternatives," *Philosophy and Public Affairs* 35/1: 40–68; A. Abizadeh, "Democratic Theory and Border Coercion: No Right to Unilaterally Control Your Own Borders," *Political Theory* 36/1 (February 2008): 37–65; David Miller, "Why Immigration

Controls are not Coercive: A Reply to Arash,"*Political Theory* 38/1 (2010): 111–20; David Miller, "Democracy's Domain," *Philosophy and Public Affairs* 37/3 (2009): 201–28. The following discussion has been added after the original publication information acknowledged in this chapter above, p. 138.

38 Frederick G. Whelan, "Democratic Theory and the Boundary Problem," p. 22. Note that Whelan does not address the second aspect of the paradox that I also deal with throughout this book – namely, that of "democratic pre-commitments." This involves the *demos* accepting as constraints on its decisions a series of substantive and procedural commitments that together protect human rights which are then reiterated by members of the *demos*, certainly not in processes of slavish imitation but creative reappropriation.

39 Robert Dahl, *Democracy and its Critics* (New Haven, CT: Yale University Press, 1989), pp. 119–31; Robert Dahl, *After the Revolution* (New Haven, CT: Yale University Press, 1970), pp. 59–63.

40 Goodin, "Enfranchising All Affected Interests," p. 51; quoting Dahl, *After the Revolution*, p. 64.

41 Goodin, "Enfranchising all Affected Interests," p. 64.

42 Ibid., p. 68.

43 Nancy Fraser, "Two Dogmas of Egalitarianism," in *Scales of Justice*, p. 40. Fraser herself gives up the "all affected principle" because of all these difficulties and replaces it by the "all subjected principle." I will consider her arguments further in this chapter.

44 I agree with Rainer Bauböck's observation: "My conclusion is that the 'all affected interests' principle substantiates ethical duties for democratic legislators to take externally affected interests into account, to seek agreements with the representatives of externally affected polities and to transfer some decisions on global problems to international institutions, but it cannot provide a criterion for determining claims to citizenship and political participation" (Bauböck, "Global Justice, Freedom of Movement and Democratic Citizenship," p. 18).

45 In Ian Shapiro's version, "the all affected principle" is not a membership rule at all but a decision procedure which entails consequences quite opposed to those drawn by Robert Goodin. Shapiro writes: "everyone affected by the operation of a particular domain of civil society should be presumed to have a say in its governance. This presumption follows from the root democratic idea that the people appropriately rule over themselves."

But, for Shapiro, this does not mean that "every say should be of equal weight," or that there may not be good reasons often for "outsiders to a domain (who may be subject to its external effects)" to have less of a say than insiders concerning governance and it may even lead us to "disenfranchise some participants in some circumstances" (Ian Shapiro, "Elements of Democratic Justice," in *Democracy's Place* (Ithaca, NY, and London: Cornell University Press, 1996), p. 232). Shapiro does not specify what those reasons may be or how they would be applied; this is because, for him, "the all affected principle" is a decision rule rather than a membership criterion or a strong democratic legitimacy procedure.

46 In one of the earlier formulations of the principle of universalizability in discourse ethics, Habermas wrote: "Unless all affected can *freely* accept the consequence and side effects that the general observance of a norm can be expected to have for the satisfaction of the interests of each individual ..." that norm could not be considered valid (J. Habermas, "Discourse Ethics: Notes on a Program of Philosophical Justification," in *Moral Consciousness and Communicative Action* (Cambridge, MA: MIT Press, 1990), pp. 43–116, here p. 93). This formula is obviously subject to the same kinds of criticisms about the indeterminacy of interests, the butterfly effect, and so on, as that of Goodin's. I, therefore, rejected it very early on and insisted that the principle of practical discourse, D, "Only those norms can claim to be valid that meet (or could meet) with the approval of all concerned in their capacity as participants in a practical discourse," would suffice. For a detailed discussion of this problems, see Seyla Benhabib, "In the Shadow of Aristotle and Hegel. Communicative Ethics and Current Controversies in Practical Philosophy," in Benhabib, *Situating the Self: Gender, Community and Postmodernism in Contemporary Ethics*, pp. 34–8.

47 I believe this is the crucial insight behind Nancy Fraser's eventual rejection of "the all affected principle" and her preference instead for the "all subjected principle." According to the latter, all those who are subject to a given governance structure have moral standing as subjects in relation to it. On this view, what turns a collection of people into fellow subjects of "justice is neither shared citizenship nor nationality; nor common possession of abstract personhood; nor the sheer fact of causal interdependence – but rather their joint subjection to a structure of governance that sets the ground rules that govern their interaction"

(Fraser, "Abnormal Justice," in *Scales of Justice*, p. 65). Governance structures, in turn, are understood as comprising non-
state agencies such as the WTO and the IMF, which set ground
rules for the world economy, as well as other non-state forms
and trans-state forms of governmentality. The difficult question
remains whether a "structure of subjection" is understood in
terms of formally established institutional organizations alone
or whether non-institutionalized but significant patterns of
power relations also constitute "structures of subjection," and
how we can distinguish between the one and the other. My
distinction between "state" versus "popular" sovereignty follows
a similar line of reasoning. Cf. Fraser, "Abnormal Justice" and
"Reframing Justice in a Globalizing World," in *Scales of Justice*,
pp. 12–29.

48   I owe this insight to David Owen, "The Duty of Justification:
On the Form and Normative Role of the All Affected Interests
Principle," Fellow at the Institute for Advanced Studies in the
Humanities, Bad Homburg, and presented at Rainer Forst's Col-
loquium at J. W. Goethe University in May 2010; on file with
the author.

49   Abizadeh, "Democratic Theory and Border Coercion," p. 38.

50   Ibid., p. 41.

51   Ibid., p. 45.

52   Ibid., p. 59.

53   Ibid., p. 40.

54   Ibid., p. 48.

55   Fraser, "Two Dogmas of Egalitarianism," in *Scales of Justice*,
p. 45. I am not exploring here what Fraser calls "participatory
parity" more closely, but assuming a rough equivalence between
conditions of reciprocity and equality presupposed in practical
discourses and her concept of parity. Winnicott introduces his
idea of the "good enough mother" in Donald Winnicott, "Transitional Objects and Transitional Phenomena" [1953], *International Journal of Psycho-Analysis* 34 (1953): 89–97.

CHAPTER 9   THE RETURN OF POLITICAL THEOLOGY: THE SCARF AFFAIR
IN COMPARATIVE CONSTITUTIONAL PERSPECTIVE
IN FRANCE, GERMANY AND TURKEY

1   There is, of course, a great deal of essentializing and geopolitical
mystification in all of this. Islam is taken as if it were a homo-

geneous whole, without any sense of its historicity, any in-depth appreciation of the complexity of its evolution, or any deep knowledge of differences between Sunnism, Shi'ism, Alevism, Sufism, and so on, let alone any appreciation of the distinctions between Indonesian and Indian Islam; Turkish versus Iranian Islam. These geo-political shorthands are another version of the "West" and "the rest" thinking, with Islam now coming to stand in for the "rest" at large. Not only is the geopolitics of this debate based on ignorance, but the very instability of the terms of the opposition – Islamism, political Islam, Islamic fundamentalism, Jihadism, and so on – reveal that we are trading in metaphors and muddled prejudices and fear rather than reasoned analysis. I will use the term "political Islam," following Olivier Roy, to refer to a very diverse, contradictory set of theologico-political movements, riven by their own rivalries and antagonisms. See Olivier Roy, *Secularism Confronts Islam* (New York: Columbia University Press, 2007); cf. also, for recent accounts, Ian Buruma, *Murder in Amsterdam: The Death of Theo van Gogh and the Limits of Tolerance* (New York: Penguin, 2006); Jytte Klausen, *The Cartoons that Shook the World* (New Haven, CT: Yale University Press, 2009).

2 Max Weber, "Wissenschaft als Beruf" (1919), translated as "Science as a Vocation," in *From Max Weber: Essays in Sociology*, trans. and ed. H. H. Gerth and C. Wright Mills (New York: Oxford University Press, 1946).

3 Hans Blumenberg, *The Legitimacy of the Modern Age*, trans. Robert M. Wallace (Cambridge, MA: MIT Press, 1983); Karl Löwith, *Meaning in History: The Theological Implications of the Philosophy of History* (Chicago, IL: University of Chicago Press, 1949).

4 Seyla Benhabib, *The Claims of Culture: Equality and Difference in the Global Era*, pp. 5 ff.

5 For an unusually lucid account of the types of dilemmas that such issues pose for jurisprudence in liberal constitutional democracies, see Dieter Grimm, "Conflicts Between General Laws and Religious Norms," in *Cardozo Law Review* 30/6 (June 2009): 2369–82.

6 Jürgen Habermas, "Notes on a Postsecular Society," at: <http://www.signandsight.com/features/1714.html>; accessed June 20, 2008. Also delivered at the RESET Istanbul Conference on June 3, 2008.

7 Carl Schmitt, *Political Theology: Four Chapters on the Concept of Sovereignty,* trans. with an Introduction by George Schwab (Chicago, IL, and London: University of Chicago Press, 1985), based on the revised edition of 1934. All references in the text are to the English translation.

8 Carl Schmitt, *The Concept of the Political,* trans. and with an Introduction by George Schwab, expanded edn (Chicago, IL: University of Chicago Press, 2007); Carl Schmitt, *Crisis of Parliamentary Democracy,* trans and with an Introduction by Ellen Kennedy (Cambridge, MA: MIT Press, 1988).

9 Otto Kirchheimer, "Remarks on Carl Schmitt's Legality and Legitimacy," in William Scheuerman, ed., *The Rule of Law under Siege: Selected Essays of Franz L. Neumann and Otto Kirchheimer* (Berkeley, CA: University of California Press, 1996), pp. 64–98. On the influence of Carl Schmitt on Walter Benjamin who wanted to dedicate his doctoral dissertation on German baroque drama to Schmitt, see Richard Wolin, "Between Proust and *Zohar.* Walter Benjamin's *Arcades* Project," in *The Frankfurt School Revisited and Other Essays on Politics and Society* (London and New York: Routledge, 2006), pp. 21–45; on Hans Morgenthau and Carl Schmitt, see Martti Koskenniemi, *The Gentle Civilizer of Nations: The Rise and Fall of International Law 1870–1960,* pp. 413–40, and William Scheuerman, "Carl Schmitt and Hans Morgenthau: Realism and Beyond," in Michael C. Williams, ed., *Realism Reconsidered: The Legacy of Hans. J. Morgenthau in International Relations* (Oxford: Oxford University Press, 2007), pp. 62–92; on Leo Strauss and Carl Schmitt, see Leo Strauss, "Notes on Carl Schmitt, The Concept of the Political," in Schmitt, *The Concept of the Political,* trans. G. Schwab, pp. 81–109, and Heinrich Meier, *Carl Schmitt, Leo Strauss und "Der Begriff des Politischen"* (Stuttgart: J. B. Metzler Verlag, 1998); Chantal Mouffe, *The Challenge of Carl Schmitt* (London: Verso, 1999), and Chantal Mouffe and Ernesto Laclau, *Hegemony and Social Strategy: Towards a Radical Democratic Politics* (London: Verso, 1986; 2nd edn 2001).

10 Giorgio Agamben, *State of Exception,* trans. Kevin Attell (Chicago, IL: University of Chicago Press, 2005).

11 Ibid., pp. 23–35.

12 Hent de Vries, "Introduction. Before, Around, and Beyond the Theologico-Political," in Hent de Vries and Lawrence E. Sullivan, eds, *Political Theologies: Public Religions in a Post-Secular World* (New York: Fordham University Press, 2006), p. 3.

13 Hans Jonas, *Braucht der Mensch Religion? Über Erfahrungen der Selbsttranszendenz* (Freiburg im Breisgau: Herder, 2004), pp. 124–5; quoted in de Vries, "Introduction," p. 4.

14 "Universal Declaration of Human Rights," at: <http://www.un.org/en/documents/udhr/>.

Cf. Article 18 of the International Covenant on Civil and Political Rights, which was adopted and opened for signature, ratification, and accession by General Assembly resolution 2200A (XXI) of 16 December 1966, and entered into force 23 March, 1976. Cf. <http://www1.umn.edu/humanrts/instree/b3ccpr.htm>; accessed November 13, 2009.

The European Convention on Human Rights, Article 9, "provides a right to freedom of thought, conscience and religion. This includes the freedom to change a religion or belief, and to manifest a religion or belief in worship, teaching, practice, and observance, subject to certain restrictions that are 'in accordance with law' and 'necessary in a democratic society.'" Cf.: <http://www.hri.org/docs/ECHR50.html#C.Art9>; accessed November 13, 2009.

15 Earlier versions of this discussion have appeared in Seyla Benhabib, *The Claims of Culture: Equality and Diversity in the Global Era*, chapter 5, and Seyla Benhabib, *The Rights of Others: Aliens, Citizens and Residents*, chapter 5. Since this case is the most widely known in the literature, I will briefly update it in the light of recent publications. The pioneering work remains Nilufer Gole, *The Forbidden Modern: Civilization and Veiling* (Ann Arbor, MI: University of Michigan Press, 1996).

16 A note of terminological clarification first: the practice of veiling among Muslim women is a complex institution that exhibits great variety across many Muslim countries. The terms *chaddor, hijab, niqab, foulard* refer to distinct items of clothing which are worn by Muslim women coming from different Muslim communities: for example, the *chandor* is essentially Iranian and refers to the long black robe and headscarf worn in a rectangular manner around the face; the *niqab* is a veil that covers the eyes and the mouth and only leaves the nose exposed; it may or may not be worn in conjunction with the *chandor*. Most Muslim women from Turkey are likely to wear either long overcoats and a *foulard* (a head scarf) or a *çarşaf* (a black garment which most resembles the *chandor*). These items of clothing have a symbolic function within the Muslim community itself: women coming from different countries signal to one another their ethnic and

national origins through their clothing, as well as signifying their distance or proximity to tradition in doing so. Seen from the outside, this complex semiotic of dress codes gets reduced to one or two items of clothing, which then assume the function of symbols in complex negotiations among Muslim religious and cultural identities and Western cultures.

17 Françoise Gaspard and Farhad Khosrokhavar, *Le Foulard et la République* (Paris: Découverte, 1995); references in the text are to this edition; for some girls' perspectives, see *Alma et Lilly Lévy: Des Filles comme les Autres*, interviews by Véronique Giraud and Yves Sintomer (Paris: La Découverte, 2004).

18 Gaspard and Khosrokhavar, *Le Foulard et la République*, p. 11.

19 Gaspard and Khosrokhavar, ibid., pp. 44–5; my translation.

20 Nilufer Gole, *The Forbidden Modern: Civilization and Veiling* (Ann Arbor, MI: University of Michigan Press, 1996).

21 Nusrat Choudhury, "From the Stasi Commission to the European Court of Human Rights: L'Affaire du Foulard and the Challenge of Protecting the Rights of Muslim Girls," *Columbia Journal of Gender and Law* 16/199 (2007): here 205.

22 Joan Wallach Scott, *The Politics of the Veil* (Princeton, NJ: Princeton University Press, 2007); see Christian Joppke, *Veil: Mirror of Identity* (Cambridge: Polity, 2009), p. 52. All references in the text are to this edition.

23 In August 2004, two French journalists were kidnapped in Iraq. The Islamist terrorist group threatened to kill them if the French government introduced the law prohibiting the Islamist scarf in French schools. This led to massive demonstrations in Paris in which Muslim groups also protested against the kidnapping of the journalists and sharply rejected the involvement of outside groups in France's internal affairs, such as the passing of the law banning the wearing of headscarves in schools. Cf., for further information, European Social Survey, accessible through: <http://www.europeansocialsurvey.org/index.php?view=details&id=48 09%3Afrench-journalists-kidnapped&option=com_eventlist &Itemid=326>.

24 On the Belgian ban on the *burqa*, passed in April 2010, see: <http://news.bbc.co.uk/2/hi/europe/8652861.stm?utm_source= twitterfeed&utm_medium=twitter>; in January 2010, CNN reported that French lawmakers had moved toward a "partial ban" on the *burqa*. "The ban on the 'voile integrale' – which literally means 'total veil' – would apply in public places like hospitals and schools, and on public transport, a French parlia-

mentary commission announced . . . It would also apply to anyone who attempts to receive public services, but it would not apply to people wearing the burqa on the street, the commission said." At: <http://articles.cnn.com/201-01-26/world/france.burqa.ban_1_veil-public-places-french-people?_s=PM:WORLD>.

25 I have discussed this case previously, too, in Benhabib, *The Rights of Others*, pp. 198–202.

26 The German legislators responded to the mandate of the court rather speedily and, after Baden-Württemberg, Bavaria also passed a bill banning the wearing of headscarves in schools. Christian and Jewish symbols were not included in this ban. Civil rights organizations and groups representing Muslims living in Germany (estimated at 3.2 million) have criticized the proposed ban.

27 Quoted by Joppke, *Veil: Mirror of Identity*, p. 53.

28 C. Emcke points out that, in an earlier decision concerning the presence of crucifixes in the classroom, what the German Supreme Court declared to be unconstitutional was not the existence of religious symbols in public spaces or public schools, but rather the *obligation* to display the crucifix regularly. "In this sense," she concludes, "there are no constitutional grounds against religious symbols as such" (Carolin Emcke, *Kollektive Identitäten. Sozialphilosophische Grundlagen* (Frankfurt and New York: Campus Verlag, 2000), p. 284).

29 As the sociologist Faruk Birtek points out, the parliamentary vote to reverse the ban on the headscarf, *strictu sensu*, contradicted Supplement 17 to the Legislation known as "YÖK Kanunu" – that is, the Law of the Council of Higher Education. In order for the wearing of the headscarf to become fully legal this clause needed to be rescinded and this was never the case. See interview with Faruk Birtek, in TARAF by Nese Duzel: <http://www.taraf.com.tr/Detay.asp?yazar=7&yz=21>; accessed June 29, 2008.

30 The Justice and Development Party in 2010, in turn, challenged Turkey's Constitutional Court by initiating a reform of the 1982 Constitution, which itself was put into effect as a result of a military coup. Although the constitutional reform package is ambivalent, containing many aspects that enhance civil liberties, such as privacy laws, undoubtedly it was an attempt by the politicians to increase their influence on the composition of the court and to limit the terms served by the judges. In September

2010, the Constitutional Reform proposals were accepted by 51 percent of Turkish voters. For general discussions preceding the vote, see Serap Yazici, "Turkey's Constitutional Amendments: Between the Satus Quo and limited Democratic Reforms," *Insight Turkey* 12/2 (2010): 1–11; Andrew Arato, "The Constitutional Reform Proposal of the Turkish Government: The Return of Majority Imposition," *Constellations: An International Journal of Critical and Democratic Theory* 17/2 (June 2010): 345–51.

31   Rifat Bali, *Cumhuriyet Yillarinda Turkiye Yahudileri: Bir Turklestirme Seruveni. 1923–1945 [Turkish Jews in the Epoch of the Republic: An Adventure in Turkification. 1923–1945]* (Istanbul, 1999).

32   For a thoughtful analysis of the intertwining of democratization, the rise of Islam and the continuing threats to women's rights in Turkey, originating with the patriarchal attitudes and policies of members of the AKP, see Yesim Arat, "Religion, Politics and Gender Equality in Turkey: Implications of a Democratic Paradox?," in *Third World Quarterly* 31/6 (2010): 869–84.

33   The discussion prompted by the remarks of the Archbishop of Canterbury on *Shari'a* courts continues across many countries, including failed attempts to introduce Islamic Arbitration Boards in Canada with the jurisdiction to decide in matters of family law. Cf. BBC News, February 7, 2008, "Sharia Law in UK is 'Unavoidable.'" At: <http://news.bbc.co.uk/2/hi/uk_news/7232661.stm>; accessed November 13, 2009; for a lucid discussion of the Canadian case, see Audrey Macklin, "Particularized Citizenship: Encultured Women and the Public Sphere" in Seyla Benhabib and Judith Resnik, eds, *Migrations and Mobilities: Citizenship, Borders and Gender*, pp. 276–304.

34   On the relationship between normative validity and democratic legitimacy, see Benhabib, *Another Cosmopolitanism*, pp. 45 ff., and chapter 8 of this volume, "Democratic Exclusions and Democratic Iterations."

35   Taking place in the shadow of worsening world-economic crises, in particular, and continuing military confrontations with the Taliban in Afghanistan, as well as domestic political pressures, public opinion both in the USA and in Europe is traversing a jurispathic process of projecting onto the other the sources of its own helplessness and malaise. Just as the increasing criminalization and militarization of immigration along the US–Mexico border will not solve economic problems in the United States,

nor will the banning of minarets resolve the growing sense of anxiety about identity in countries such as Switzerland, which heavily rely on migrant labor for their well-being.

36 Jürgen Habermas, "Notes on a Post-secular Society," at: <http://www.signandsight.com/features/1714.html>; accessed June 20, 2008. Also delivered at the Istanbul Conference on June 3, 2008.

CHAPTER 10 UTOPIA AND DYSTOPIA IN OUR TIMES

1 Ernst Bloch, *Natural Law and Human Dignity* [1961], trans. Dennis J. Schmidt (Cambridge, MA: MIT Press, 1986), p. xxix.

2 For further discussion, see Seyla Benhabib, *Critique, Norm and Utopia: A Study of the Foundations of Critical Theory* (New York: Columbia University Press, 1986); published in German as *Kritik, Norm und Utopie: Zur normativen Grundlagen der Kritik* (Frankfurt: Fischer Verlag, 1992).

3 Jürgen Habermas, "Labor and Interaction: Remarks on Hegel's Jena *Philosophy of Mind*," in *Theory and Practice*, trans. John Viertel (Boston, MA: Beacon Press, 1973), pp. 142–69. At the level of the "experience of consciousness" in Hegel's *Phenomenology of Spirit*, these distinctions between activities of work, production, and artistic creation, on the one hand, and the experiences of moral learning and struggle for recognition, on the other, are observed and retained; it is only at the level of the experience of *das Wir*, the philosophical observer who recollects all these experiences into a single unitary narrative, that the distinction between labor and interaction gets lost. See also Axel Honneth, *The Struggle for Recognition: The Moral Grammar of Social Conflicts*, trans. J. Anderson (Cambridge: Polity, 1995); Honneth's critique of the confusions of these two dimensions in the work of the Critical Theory of the Frankfurt School is analyzed in "Horkheimer's Original Idea: The Sociological Deficit of Critical Theory," in *The Critique of Power: Reflective Stages in a Critical Social Theory*, trans. Kenneth Baynes (Cambridge, MA: MIT Press, 1997), pp. 5–31.

4 Cf. Nancy Fraser, *Justice Interruptus: Critical Reflections on the "Postsocialist" Condition* (New York: Routledge, 1997); Nancy Fraser and Axel Honneth, *Redistribution or Recognition: A Political-Philosophical Exchange* (London: Verso, 2003).

5 Ernst Bloch, *The Spirit of Utopia* [1923], trans. Anthony A. Nassar (Stanford, CA: Stanford University Press, 2000), p. 240.
6 For a good overview of conflicts around this kind of politics within the Marxist tradition, see Dick Howard and Karl E. Klare, *The Unknown Dimension: European Marxism since Lenin* (New York: Basic Books, 1972).
7 See Mark Lilla's polemical and dismissive treatment of Bloch as a "godless theologian," in *The Stillborn God: Religion, Politics and the Modern West* (New York: Vintage Books, 2007), pp. 285–92; here p. 288.
8 Ernst Bloch, "Naturrecht und menschliche Würde. Rundfunkvortrag 1961," in *Bloch-Almanach. 5. Folge* (Baden-Baden, hrsg. Von Ernst-Bloch-Archiv , 1985), pp. 165–79; here p. 173. Translation my own.
9 See the very instructive treatment by Hans-Ernst Schiller, "Kant in der Philosophie Ernst Blochs," in *Bloch-Almanach. 5. Folge* (Baden-Baden: hrsg. Von Ernst-Bloch-Archiv, 1985), pp. 45–93.
10 See Ernst Bloch, *The Principle of Hope* [1959], vol. 1, trans. Neville Plaice, Stephen Plaice, and Paul Knight (Cambridge, MA: MIT Press, 1986).
11 See Benhabib, *Critique, Norm and Utopia*, p. 351.
12 Seyla Benhabib, "The Generalized and Concrete Other: The Kohlberg-Gilligan Controversy and Moral Theory," in *Situating the Self: Gender, Community and Postmodernism in Contemporary Ethics*, pp.148–78.
13 Immanuel Kant [1795], "Perpetual Peace: A Philosophical Sketch," trans. H. B. Nisbet, in *Kant: Political Writings*, ed. Hans Reiss, pp. 93–130.

INDEX